D1119255

Tricks
of the
eBay®
Masters
Second Edition

Michael Miller

800 East 96th Street, Indianapolis,
Indiana 46240 USA

Tricks of the eBay® Masters, 2nd Edition

Copyright © 2006 by Que Publishing

International Standard Book Number: 0-7897-3543-1

Library of Congress Catalog Card Number: 2006920304

Printed in the United States of America

Fourth Printing: June 2006

08   07   06   7   6   5   4

Trademarks

All terms mentioned in this book that are known to be trademarks or service marks have been appropriately capitalized. Que Publishing cannot attest to the accuracy of this information. Use of a term in this book should not be regarded as affecting the validity of any trademark or service mark.

Warning and Disclaimer

Every effort has been made to make this book as complete and as accurate as possible, but no warranty or fitness is implied. The information provided is on an "as is" basis. The author and the publisher shall have neither liability nor responsibility to any person or entity with respect to any loss or damages arising from the information contained in this book.

Bulk Sales

Que Publishing offers excellent discounts on this book when ordered in quantity for bulk purchases or special sales. For more information, please contact

U.S. Corporate and Government Sales
1-800-382-3419
corpsales@pearsontechgroup.com

For sales outside the United States, please contact

International Sales
international@pearsoned.com

Associate Publisher
Greg Wiegand

Acquisitions Editor
Michelle Newcomb

Development Editor
Laura Norman

Managing Editor
Charlotte Clapp

Project Editor
Tonya Simpson

Indexer
Aaron Black

Proofreader
Kathy Bidwell

Technical Editors
Jenna Lloyd
Michele Brantner

Publishing Coordinator
Sharry Lee Gregory

Interior Designer
Anne Jones

Cover Designer
Anne Jones

Page Layout
Nonie Ratcliff

Contents at a Glance

Table of Contents

About the Author

Michael Miller is a top eBay seller and a successful and prolific author. He has a reputation for practical, real-world advice and an unerring empathy for the needs of his readers.

Mr. Miller has written more than 75 nonfiction books since 1989, for Que and other major publishers. His books for Que include *Easy eBay, Absolute Beginner's Guide to eBay, Making a Living with Your eBay Business,* and *Absolute Beginner's Guide to Computer Basics.* He is known for his casual, easy-to-read writing style and his ability to explain a wide variety of complex topics to an everyday audience.

You can email Mr. Miller directly at ebay-tricks@molehillgroup.com. His website is located at www.molehillgroup.com, and his eBay user ID is trapperjohn2000.

Dedication

To my sister Melanie and brother Mark, for no particular reason.

Acknowledgments

Thanks to the usual suspects at Que, including but not limited to Greg Wiegand, Michelle Newcomb, Laura Norman, and Tonya Simpson, and thanks as well to the book's technical editors, Jenna Lloyd and Michele Brantner. I'd also like to give my special thanks to the hundreds of eBay users who contributed their tricks to this book. Your advice is well received, and I truly appreciate your help and participation. I hope to meet up with you all again, soon!

We Want to Hear from You!

As the reader of this book, *you* are our most important critic and commentator. We value your opinion and want to know what we're doing right, what we could do better, what areas you'd like to see us publish in, and any other words of wisdom you're willing to pass our way.

As an associate publisher for Que Publishing, I welcome your comments. You can email or write me directly to let me know what you did or didn't like about this book—as well as what we can do to make our books better.

Please note that I cannot help you with technical problems related to the topic of this book. We do have a User Services group, however, where I will forward specific technical questions related to the book.

When you write, please be sure to include this book's title and author as well as your name, email address, and phone number. I will carefully review your comments and share them with the author and editors who worked on the book.

      Email: feedback@quepublishing.com

      Mail: Greg Wiegand
              Associate Publisher
              Que Publishing
              800 East 96th Street
              Indianapolis, IN 46240 USA

For more information about this book or another Que title, visit our website at www.quepublishing.com. Type the ISBN (excluding hyphens) or the title of a book in the Search field to find the page you're looking for.

Introduction

- **Who Are the eBay Masters?**
- **Where Can You Find the eBay Masters?**
- **How the Tricks Are Organized**
- **What's New in the Second Edition**
- **Tricks Credits**
- **One Last Word About the eBay Masters**
- **Let Me Know What You Think**

This is the most unusual book I've ever written. And I've written a lot, somewhere north of 75 books in the past 17 years or so—including a half-dozen other books on eBay and online shopping. But this one takes the cake; it's unlike anything else I've ever done.

What makes *Tricks of the eBay Masters* such an unusual book—and why should you care?

The book you hold in your hands is unusual in that while I wrote the words, most of the ideas inside came from other people—from close to 200 other people, to be precise. These people just happen to be eBay buyers and sellers, successful ones, who were willing to share some of the secrets of their success. Those secrets are the "tricks" in this book, tips and advice you can use to become more successful at your eBay transactions.

And that's where this book is different from any other eBay book on the market, and what makes it especially valuable to you. Yeah, I can tell you everything *I* know about eBay, but that's just one person's opinion—based on one person's experience. How much better to learn from the experience of 200 people, all of them Masters at eBay buying and selling. These are tricks learned from hard experience, and they're presented here in one place, the better for you to benefit.

Of course, the nature of these 600 tricks means that this isn't a traditional how-to or tutorial book. In fact, it kind of jumps around in spots, depending on what tricks the eBay Masters submitted. So if you're expecting a beginner's-level introduction to eBay, I recommend you look elsewhere. (A good book of this ilk is my own *Absolute Beginner's Guide to eBay*, no doubt available at the same place you purchased this book.)

Where *Tricks of the eBay Masters* excels is imparting very specific bits of wisdom and information, about particular types of eBay activities. Want to learn the best day of the week to list an item? Or how to avoid waiting in line at the post office? Or how to pack a china plate? Or promote your eBay Store? Or find closeout items to sell? All those tricks—and 595 more—are here, courtesy of the eBay Masters. You might not find all the tricks here useful or applicable, but I know you'll find a lot of them so, and that's why you're reading this book, isn't it?

Who Are the eBay Masters?

Okay, so this book includes a ton of advice from eBay's most successful buyers and sellers. But who are these people? Who are the eBay Masters?

Here's the neat thing. eBay's most successful members are just regular folks, like you and me. They've learned all they know by doing; their tricks come from experience. When they do something right, they remember it. When they do something wrong, they remember that, too, and learn from it. Just normal folks, with a penchant for success—and a willingness to share their wisdom with others.

Don't believe me? Then read about some of the eBay Masters who contributed tricks to this book, in their own words:

april0403

Member since 1998, Feedback: Turquoise star

I retired after 35 years working in a major electronics firm in Dallas. I had bought a few items on eBay. I registered on eBay as a buyer in 1998, I believe. I had a friend who signed on as a seller, and figured I could try it as a hobby, something to keep me off the streets and out of pool halls, LOL. I had a designer handbag that was about fifteen years old, and always wanted to sell it... so I did, and there was no looking back after that. My oldest daughter got interested in selling, I coached her a bit, and now we have a lot of fun with this. She's actually done more business than me with eBay. I love it here.

bobbibopstuff

stores.ebay.com/BobbiBopStuff

www.bobbibopstuff.com

PowerSeller

Member since 1998, Feedback: Red star

I'm John, 57, and semi-retired, LOL. Sandi, my wife of 35 years, will be semi-retired in a couple of months, and then we can devote more time to our four grandchildren and traveling with our financial counseling ministry. In the meantime, we are testing the eBay waters and have been pleased and amused with our efforts. This is a great business to learn and supplement our time and income. We are trying our hand at many categories, and are learning which ones to leave to others and which ones we can find room and business in.

clact

stores.ebay.com/Once-Upon-A-Bid

PowerSeller

Member since 2002, Feedback: Red star

My wife and I have been selling since late January 2003, and made PowerSeller in just three months. It is a lot of work, of course. I'm an accountant (CPA) in my day job.

dfrazier18

stores.ebay.com/Fraziers-Finds

Member since 2000, Feedback: Red star

I'm Debra. I began on eBay back in October 2000. My now 15-year-old son was a big-time LEGO fan and I bought dozens and dozens of retired sets (some never made available in the U.S.) from many different sellers in Germany, Belgium, the Netherlands, Denmark, France, Italy, and the U.K. And I paid cash (USD and DM) for all of them. I started selling in September 2002, to fund all the LEGO I was buying—first selling Clinique Gift With Purchase samples, and eventually expanding into "home decor" items. Candle accessories are my specialty. I opened my eBay Store September 2003, with the intention of closing it down in January. But like so many others, I became addicted.

going1nceamc

stores.ebay.com/GOing1nceAMC

www.going1nce.com

PowerSeller

Member since 1999, Feedback: Red star

GOing1nceAMC is me, Sally, with my partner, Kyle. A few years back, I launched my eBay career when my friend, Wayne, called upon my computer/web-savvy and graphic designer skills to help run his eBay auctions. I bought a Coke can bank to learn a bit about eBay, and then started listing coins for Wayne's company. Today I manage both Wayne's eBay business and my own, with the help of an assistant on each. I have learned a lot in my short, brilliant career on eBay. I am also a registered eBay Trading Assistant.

hortonsbks

stores.ebay.com/Hortonsbks

PowerSeller

Member since 2000, Feedback: Red star

I am not a volume seller, usually averaging about 40-50 books at a time. My sell-through rate is fairly low. I'm never going to make a fortune hawking my used books, but it's what I know best, so I'll stick with it.

ilene

stores.ebay.com/Ilenes-Discount-Collectibles

PowerSeller

Member since 1997, Feedback: Green star

I am somewhat unusual for an eBay PowerSeller. I work full-time at a professional job which includes commuting between two cities. I maintain Gold PowerSeller status about 50% of the year, but I spend very little time doing it. I have a partner who puts up half the cash and does the pictures and the packing. I do all the buying, selling, and dealing with buyers. I have been doing this for about seven years and I have lots of ways of simplifying everything. Time is my biggest problem.

jimrick1

Member since 2001, Feedback: Turquoise star

A friend and I have been serious music listeners and LP collectors for many years. Vintage stereo equipment has become another passion for us these last few years. We are having a lot of fun buying locally and selling on eBay. We get to hear "new to us" equipment in our homes regularly—we each keep what works best for us, and sell the rest.

makeabuckstore

stores.ebay.com/Make-A-Buck-Store-LLC

www.makeabuckstore.com

PowerSeller

Member since 1999, Feedback: Green star

Our names are Kay and Dean. We joined eBay in 1999 but had absolutely no intentions of turning this venue into a full-time venture. When Kay's company downsized their IT staff, she tried to make a few bucks by selling items on eBay. Talk about tons of mistakes on those first few sales—we sure could have used one of your books back then! What started out with one meager sale from home has swelled into a thriving clicks & mortar business with five full-time employees. Our business is now an eBay drop-off center with over 900 consignment customers (and growing). We churn out 400–500 auctions a week and are Titanium PowerSellers.

raeosenbaugh

stores.ebay.com/OLD-BOOKS-NEW-BOOKS

Member since 2001, Feedback: Red star

I am Rae from central Nebraska. I started on eBay when I was diagnosed with breast cancer in late 2001. I spent much of my time at home and started selling some of my own books. I enjoy buying interesting items, so my sales help pay for all the special things I bought. My "hobby" has mushroomed since then and as I have regained my strength I go to sales and thrift stores to find unique items to resell to feed my habit. My brush with breast cancer has given me a different outlook on life—and that of my family. We have always been close, but now more than ever.

slfcollectibles2

stores.ebay.com/A-Collectible-Diecast-N-More-Store

stores.ebay.com/A-Gift-for-Her

PowerSeller

Member since 2001, Feedback: Red star

My name is Shana and I began selling on eBay January 1, 2004. I first started selling my fiancé's Hot Wheels collection. We did this to make some quick money so that I could "open a business" on eBay. Well, it worked! I started selling SpecCast *diecast models toward the end of February, and have now branched out to sell Liberty Classics, as well. I am proud of the fact that I earned Bronze PowerSeller status mid-April with only 157 feedback at the time, and then three weeks later earned Silver. It will take a bit longer to reach the Gold level, but I will get there! After all, who wouldn't want over $10,000 a month in sales?*

As you can see, the eBay Masters represent a wide range of buyers and sellers. Some are relatively small, some run their own eBay stores, some have even achieved PowerSeller status. But even with all their differences, they share one thing in common—they love buying and selling on eBay, and they're good at it!

Where Can You Find the eBay Masters?

The eBay Masters spend a lot of time on eBay, as you might suspect. Not only do they have a lot of auctions running at any given time, they're also a vital part of the eBay community.

What is this eBay community, you ask? Well, eBay has a vibrant set of discussion forums (located at pages.ebay.com/community/boards/), where the most interested— and most interesting—buyers and sellers hang out and discuss the issues of the day. These discussion forums are where I found most of the eBay Masters, all of whom gladly offered to contribute their words of wisdom for this book.

And here's the interesting thing. The eBay community is actually a number of different small communities. The folks you meet on the Auction Listings board are different folks those you meet on the Packaging & Shipping board, who are different from the folks you meet on the Collectibles board. Since each board is organized around a particular topic or type of merchandise, members tend to pick one or two forums and make their contributions there. The result is that the Clothing, Shoes, & Accessories board has a completely different personality than the Booksellers board, and you'll meet different users on each board. The common factor is that they're all friendly, and they're all incredibly helpful. Spend some time on the boards with the eBay Masters, and don't be shy about asking questions—or offering your own unique contribution.

How the Tricks Are Organized

This book contains 600 individual tricks, organized by topic into 20 chapters. The 20 chapters themselves are divided into three main parts, as follows:

- **Part I, "Tricks That Any eBay Member Can Use,"** presents some solid advice for all eBay members, specifically focusing on choosing a user ID, avoiding scams, and dealing with eBay's feedback system.

- **Part II, "Tricks for More Successful Bidding,"** presents a bevy of tricks that can help you win more auctions, pay less for what you win, and bid— and buy—more safely.

- **Part III, "Tricks for More Successful Selling,"** is the heart of the book, with hundreds of tricks that can make your life as a seller that much easier. You'll learn how to create more attractive auction listings, how to automate the auction process, how to get higher bids, how to pack and ship more effectively, and even how to run your own eBay Store or Trading Assistant business. Best of all, this section ends with a completely new chapter for this second edition, "How to Become an eBay PowerSeller," which contains advice about PowerSellers by PowerSellers—eBay's most successful sellers!

From Trick #1 ("Register Without Providing Financial Information") to Trick #600 ("PowerSellers Never Stop Learning") you'll find a lot of terrific advice, as offered by the eBay Masters. Sometimes the advice is contradictory (even the most experienced users don't agree on everything!), and some of it is extremely specific, but that's okay. Read all the tricks, and use the ones that make sense to you.

What's New in the Second Edition

Those of you who already own the first edition of this book will find a lot that's new—although all the new stuff isn't in one place. What I did was keep about 480 of the best tricks from the first edition (updating them as necessary), and then add 120 or so new tricks from the eBay Masters. The new tricks are fairly evenly scattered throughout the book; they're identified by a "new" icon, like the one here.

I've also rearranged things a bit, to try to provide more tricks for high-volume sellers and sellers who are trying to run their own eBay businesses. This resulted in two new chapters for this edition: Chapter 17, "Turning Your eBay Sales into a Real Business," and Chapter 20, "How to Become an eBay PowerSeller." Lots of new tricks in those chapters, of course.

Tricks Credits

Each trick in this book is attributed to a specific eBay Master. While the description— and any elaboration—of the trick is mine, the basic idea of the trick comes from the eBay user credited. The information beside the trick identifies the eBay Master by his or her eBay user ID, and includes their eBay Store address (if they have a store, that is), how long they've been an eBay member, and their feedback "star" rating. If they're a PowerSeller, that's noted, too.

When a trick is too general to be attributed to any specific member, or if it's one I've thought of on my own, I've credited that trick to me. My credit looks like this:

> **trapperjohn2000**
>
> stores.ebay.com/Molehill-Group-Store
>
> Member since 1998, Feedback: Purple star

To translate, my user ID (**trapperjohn2000**) is on the first line; the URL for my eBay Store is stores.ebay.com/Molehill-Group-Store; I've been an eBay member since 1998; and my feedback rating is at the purple star level.

By the way, if you don't know how the feedback star ratings work, here's a quick guide:

Star Color	Feedback Rating
Yellow	10–49 points
Blue	50–99 points
Turquoise	100–499 points
Purple	500–999 points
Red	1,000–4,999 points
Green	5,000–9,999 points

In many cases I've found it useful and interesting to present specific advice in the words of the Masters themselves. So when you see a quote, like this, you know you're getting a great tip, right from the horse's mouth:

> *This is a direct quote from an eBay Master. Notice how it's set apart from the regular text?*

One Last Word About the eBay Masters

Close to 200 eBay Masters contributed their wisdom to this book. They did so freely, without any thought of compensation. For this, I am extremely grateful. So do me a favor. When you see an eBay auction from one of these terrific users, buy something. You know they're good folks, and you'll have a great transaction!

Let Me Know What You Think

I always love to hear from readers. If you want to contact me, feel free to email me at ebay-tricks@molehillgroup.com. I can't promise that I'll answer every message, but I will promise that I'll read each one!

If you want to learn more about me and any new books I have cooking, check out my Molehill Group website at www.molehillgroup.com. Who knows—you might find some other books there that you'd like to read.

Part I:

Tricks That Any eBay Member Can Use

How to Get Smarter About Buying and Selling on eBay

We'll start things off with a variety of tricks that can be used by any eBay member—buyer or seller. These tricks will help you get started as a new eBay user, and get you up to speed on a variety of important operations.

Signing Up and Choosing an ID

One of the most important parts of signing up for eBay is choosing your user ID. This is the name that everyone will know you by, whether you're buying or selling—and can be a critical marketing tool if you're a seller. Or not. Read on to find out what the eBay Masters recommend when you're signing up and choosing a user ID.

Trick #1: **Register Without Providing Financial Information**

> **sluggo404**
>
> Member since 2004, Feedback: Blue star

When you sign up to sell on eBay, you have to provide a bit more information than when you're signing up just to buy. Chief among this extra information that eBay wants are your credit card and bank account numbers. For most people this isn't an issue, but some people might be reluctant to provide this personal financial information to eBay.

There are any number of reasons for not wanting to give eBay this information, not the least of which is simple distrust of giving out this information to anyone. (When it comes to warding off identity theft, a little paranoia is sometimes a good thing.) Heck, you might not even have a credit card.

In any case, just because you don't want to divulge your financial information doesn't mean that you're forever barred from selling on eBay. eBay has a special ID Verify program that lets you register to sell without having to provide all this info. For a $5.00 fee you can sign up to sell without providing a credit card, although you do have to answer some other personal questions (and provide your driver's license number). It's not nearly as onerous as the normal seller's registration.

Learn more here: pages.ebay.com/help/policies/identity-idverify.html.

Trick #2: **It's Okay to Change Your ID**

> **going1nceamc**
>
> stores.ebay.com/GOing1nceAMC
>
> www.going1nce.com
>
> PowerSeller
>
> Member since 1999, Feedback: Red star

If for whatever reason, you don't like your user ID, you can always change it. Member **going1nceamc** reports no harm from making such a change:

I've changed my IDs a couple times. I've noticed no adverse effects from changing this ID or my other one over a period of time.

Trick #3: **Use Two Different IDs**

> **lady-frog-vintage-jewelry**
>
> stores.ebay.com/SOMETHING-TO-RIBBIT-ABOUT
>
> Member since 2000, Feedback: Red star

You're not limited to a single ID. eBay lets you create multiple IDs, which you can use in a number of ways. You can use one ID for buying and another for selling, or use a separate ID for eBay's discussion boards, or use different IDs for selling different types of products.

For example, seller **lady-frog-vintage-jewelry** has one ID for her main business, selling jewelry, and a second ID (**oregon-duck-fan-a1**) for selling other types of items. Member **dixiedollie** uses one ID for selling and another for posting on discussion boards; that way, if any person takes issue with her comments, they can't ruin her auctions or leave unwarranted negative feedback.

Of course, any feedback you accumulate under one ID doesn't show up on the other one, so if you're trying to build feedback fast, you probably want to stick with a single ID. Still, many members think that it's a good idea to keep your buying and selling activity separate with separate buying/selling IDs. As member **jav_pheonix** says, if you don't keep separate IDs, your buyers will know an awful lot about you…your name and address and phone number, plus your buying history, etc. And if you get a wacko seller they can ruin your selling account with bad feedback. So for maximum privacy, establish separate buying and selling IDs.

Note, however, that to establish a second ID, you need to supply eBay with a second email address. That is, you need separate email addresses for each eBay ID you create. (Of course, it's no big deal to get a free email account from Hotmail or Yahoo! Mail to use for that second ID.)

Learning More About eBay

Once you join up and choose your eBay ID, you can start buying and selling immediately. But a more informed user makes better deals, so it's a good idea to learn as much as you can about how eBay works. Here are some tricks to help you get smarter about buying and selling on eBay.

Trick #4: **Use the Site Map**

> **mississippi*mercantile**
>
> Member since 2003, Feedback: Turquoise star

If you have a question about how eBay works, the answer is probably located somewhere on the eBay site. Unfortunately, finding that particular page isn't always easy; eBay does a good job of effectively hiding some of the best parts of their site.

That said, you can find just about any part of the eBay site from the Site Map page, shown in Figure 1.1. Just click the Site Map link at the top of any eBay page.

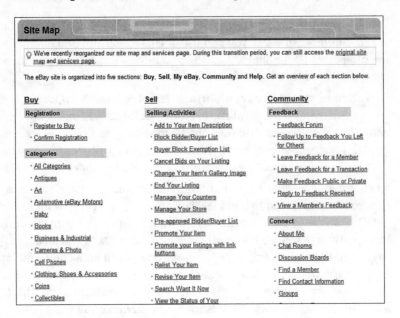

FIGURE 1.1

Find any page on the eBay site from the Site Map page.

Trick #5: **Use eBay's Live Help**

bobal

www.bulls2.com/indexb/bobstips2.html

Member since 1998, Feedback: Turquoise star

Even more help is available from eBay's staff. While you can't call them up and talk by phone, you can contact eBay staff live, in real time, by using the Live Help system. Just click the Live Help link near the top of eBay's home page. When the intro window appears, enter your user ID, select a topic, and click the Send button. The main chat window now appears, as shown in Figure 1.2; wait for an agent to come online, enter your question into the lower window, and wait for a reply.

FIGURE 1.2

Enter your question into the chat window, and await a live response, in real time.

Trick #6: **eBay's Help Doesn't Have *All* the Answers**

berties_house_of_horrors

stores.ebay.com/Berties-Emporium

PowerSeller

Member since 1999, Feedback: Red star

The eBay site has an okay help system, and even better Live Help, as just discussed. But don't expect eBay to be helpful about *everything*—especially when it comes to saving you money on the eBay site. Remember, eBay is in business to make money for itself. So expect to see lots of prodding within the eBay help system (and throughout the site) to purchase various listing upgrades. As **berties_house_of_ horrors** cautions:

> *eBay help is there to help eBay, not you! eBay will never tell you how to save on insertion fees, decrease closing fees, and so on. What they will do is tell you about all the listing upgrades that they promise can help you sell your item. But remember—most of these upgrades will put money in eBay's pockets, not yours!*

Trick #7: **Learn from Your Sellers**

berties_house_of_horrors

stores.ebay.com/Berties-Emporium

PowerSeller

Member since 1999, Feedback: Red star

The more transactions you make, the smarter you get. You can learn something from every bid you make—even the losing ones. And when you win an auction, pay particular attention to how the seller transacts business. Note the emails you receive, the way payments are handled, how long it takes to receive your purchase, and how the item is packed and shipped.

Personally, I've learned a lot about packing and shipping from other eBay sellers. When I'm thinking about selling a particular type of item, I'll purchase something similar from an experienced eBay seller, and then note how that seller packed the item—what type of packing material was used, what kind of box it was packed in, and so forth. It's a quick education in how other eBayers do things right!

Trick #8: **Let eBay Notify You of News and Happenings**

trapperjohn2000

stores.ebay.com/Molehill-Group-Store

Member since 1998, Feedback: Purple star

eBay is constantly changing. There's something new practically every day, and it's tough to keep track of all the changes. Fortunately, eBay keeps you up-to-date on all the latest goings on via official announcements. There are three ways to access these almost-daily updates:

- In the My Messages section of the My eBay My Summary page, as shown in Figure 1.3.
- At the eBay General Announcements board (www2.ebay.com/aw/marketing.shtml).
- Via email. Signing up is harder than it needs to be, but here's how it works. Click the Community link at the top of any eBay page, and when the next page appears, click the Groups link in the Connect section. When the Group

Center page appears, go to the News & Events section and click the Announcements link. When the next page appears, click the eBay Announcements link, and when the next page appears, click the Join Group link at the bottom of the page.

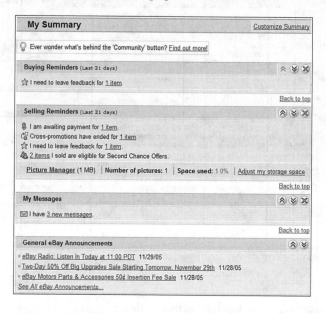

FIGURE 1.3

Check My eBay for the latest eBay announcements.

Trick #9: **Get the Latest Auction News at AuctionBytes**

sluggo404

Member since 2004, Feedback: Blue star

Just reading the official announcements won't tell you all there is to know. For that you need a dispassionate third-party source, such as AuctionBytes (www. auctionbytes.com). As you can see in Figure 1.4, AuctionBytes not only features the latest eBay news, but also a ton of tips and other information about eBay and other online auction sites. You can also subscribe to the free *Update* and *NewsFlash* online newsletters to have current news delivered directly to your email inbox.

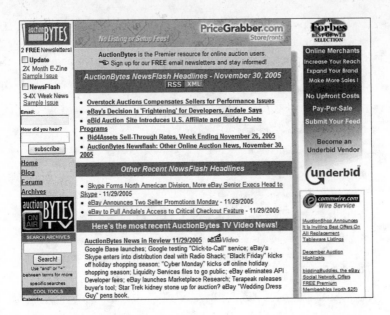

FIGURE 1.4

Get the latest news about eBay at AuctionBytes.

Trick #10: Subscribe to an eBay Newsletter

trapperjohn2000

stores.ebay.com/Molehill-Group-Store

Member since 1998, Feedback: Purple star

In the previous trick you learned not only about the AuctionBytes websites, but also about AuctionBytes' email newsletters. Well, these aren't the only newsletters to which you can subscribe. There are several other informative newsletters you can use to learn more about how eBay works, and to improve your auction success.

Some of the most popular of these online auction newsletters include the Auction Guild's *TAGnotes* (www.auctionguild.com) and Auction KnowHow's *Auction Gold* (www.auctionknowhow.com/AG/). eBay also has its own official newsletter, *The Chatter* (shown in Figure 1.5). You can read it online at pages.ebay.com/community/chatter.

FIGURE 1.5

eBay's official online newsletter, *The Chatter*.

Trick #11: **Frequent the eBay Discussion Boards**

> **rosachs**
>
> stores.ebay.com/My-Discount-Shoe-Store
>
> home.midsouth.rr.com/rosachs/RKS/
>
> PowerSeller
>
> Member since 1997, Feedback: Red star

Here's a trick that many members offered. You can get *tons* of help from other eBay users, via eBay's community discussion boards. Just click the Community link at the top of any eBay page (or go directly to hub.ebay.com/community) and then click the Discussion Boards link to see all the boards available. As you can see in Figure 1.6, there are boards for individual product categories, as well as more general boards for buying, selling, and creating auction listings. The users who frequent these boards are extraordinarily helpful and can answer just about any question you pose. (In fact, it's through these discussion boards that I found most of the contributors for this book!)

Know, however, that as helpful as the board members are, they probably can't answer all the questions you might have. In particular, don't expect these users to reveal their personal buying/selling secrets, merchandise suppliers, or other proprietary information. So be realistic about the help you can get—and make sure you thank those who answer your questions!

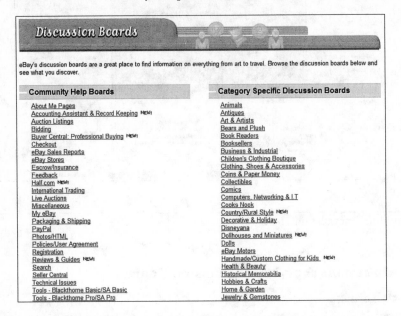

FIGURE 1.6

Visit one of eBay's community discussion boards to mingle with fellow eBayers.

eBay member **rosachs** relates one particularly informative situation:

> *When I got my contract to start selling shoes, I hadn't sold a single shoe in my four years selling to that date. Not a clue how to do it. Total blank. But I knew there were others who sold shoes. So I used the resources available—the eBay Clothing, Shoes & Accessories discussion forum. I posted a few general inquiries, questions where the answers are so obvious now but totally elusive then, and got dozens of responses from the very sellers who would become my competitors in time. Some I didn't agree with; others sounded interesting. But in about a week's time I had collected years' worth of experience from these people!*

While all the boards are useful, I particularly recommend the Auction Listings and Seller Central boards. And don't forgot those category-specific boards, which are good for answering questions about buying and selling specific types of products. They're all good!

Trick #12: **Search the Boards Before You Post**

going1nceamc

stores.ebay.com/GOing1nceAMC

www.going1nce.com

PowerSeller

Member since 1999, Feedback: Red star

There's no point in reinventing the wheel. Chances are someone else has been through your current situation, and already posted about it on one of eBay's discussion boards—which means you don't have to ask the question again. Instead, do a search on that board for the topic at hand. This will return all recent and relevant discussions about that topic, including the original post and all replies. In fact, if your problem is particularly common, it's likely been discussed over and over, so there will be plenty of information already available.

In addition, know that the "anchored" posts (the ones locked at the top of the forum message list) typically contain answers to questions that get asked over and over. Read these posts first, and you're likely to find a lot of useful information.

Trick #13: **Subscribe to Other Online Auction Groups**

trapperjohn2000

stores.ebay.com/Molehill-Group-Store

Member since 1998, Feedback: Purple star

eBay's official community forums aren't the only online communities devoted to the topic of online auctions. There are a number of well-populated Yahoo! groups, which you can either read in your web browser or have messages delivered to you via email. The nice thing about these unofficial groups is that you don't have the eBay content police reading over your shoulder, so pretty much anything goes, with no censorship.

My favorite of these Yahoo! groups are ebaygroup (groups.yahoo.com/group/ebaygroup/) and eBay-Sellers (groups.yahoo.com/group/eBay-Sellers/). Check 'em out!

Trick #14: **Learn the Lingo**

> **lludwig**
>
> stores.ebay.com/LLudwig-Books
>
> PowerSeller
>
> Member since 1998, Feedback: Green star

Whether you're participating in an official eBay forum or an unofficial Yahoo! group, these discussion boards have a particular language all their own. Take your time and look around a little before you make your first post; this will also give you a little time to learn that particular board's lingo. One that took me a while to catch on to was the abbreviation "OP," which I had always thought meant "out of print." Not so on the boards, where "OP" means "original poster"—the person who started a particular discussion thread. And if you see someone talking about a PITA, know that this acronym stands for "pain in the a**"—of which there are apparently more than a few !

Trick #15: **Attend eBay University**

New Trick

> **abc-books**
>
> stores.ebay.com/ABC-Books-by-Ann
>
> www.abcbooksbyann.com
>
> PowerSeller
>
> Member since 1999, Feedback: Red star

Another way to get educated about eBay is to attend eBay University. No, this isn't a real-life ivy-covered campus, but rather a series of online and local classes put on by the eBay staff. eBay University Online offers classes on both buying and selling; the classes cost $19.95 apiece, and are also available on self-paced CD-ROMs. The live classes travel across the country, at about 2–3 locations every month. The live classes especially are terrific experiences, both in terms of getting smarter about eBay and in being able to meet and network with other eBay buyers and sellers. Learn more at pages.ebay.com/university/.

Trick #16: **Go to eBay Live**

New Trick

> **smallseeds**
>
> stores.ebay.com/Small-Seeds
>
> PowerSeller
>
> Member since 2000, Feedback: Purple star

If you're *really* serious about eBay buying and selling, take the time out of your hectic schedule to attend eBay Live, eBay's yearly conference and trade show. eBay Live is a great way to find out more about eBay's various products and services, as well as those offered by third-party suppliers. It's also a terrific place to meet other eBay buyers and sellers (especially PowerSellers), as well as eBay staff. It's the best place to network with other eBayers, and to get all your questions answered. It's also a lot of fun!

Here's what **smallseeds** has to say about the eBay Live experience:

> *A lot of eBay executives, developers, and employees attend—you can get a lot of help and answers to your questions that you can't find on the discussion boards or even from the help lines of eBay and PayPal. The executives and employees can even direct you to other sellers or eBayers that can help you out. Other interesting networking can be accomplished with developers, PowerSellers, and vendors—all of whom attend the show.*

In 2005, eBay Live was in San Jose, home of eBay's corporate offices. I was there, signing copies of the first edition of this book, and got to meet lots of readers and network with all manner of eBayers. In 2006, eBay Live is in Las Vegas.

Trick #17: **Find a Mentor**

New Trick

> **rosachs**
>
> stores.ebay.com/My-Discount-Shoe-Store
>
> home.midsouth.rr.com/rosachs/RKS/
>
> PowerSeller
>
> Member since 1997, Feedback: Red star

As you've no doubt noted, some of the best advice comes from other eBay users—like the eBay Masters who've contributed to this book! To that end, it helps to partner up with another, more experienced user, who can act as a mentor to you when you're first starting out. Mentors don't have to be specifically aware that they're mentoring you; they may just be people you meet in one of the eBay forums or other chat or message areas who have similar items for sale but more experience selling. While these casual mentors are not going to give away all their secrets, you're likely to find that they'll be happy to share basic information to help you get started.

Creating Your Own About Me Page

You can remain relatively anonymous on the eBay system, or you can choose to tell everyone a little bit about yourself, via an About Me page. As you can see in Figure 1.7, an About Me page can contain a mix of personal information, auction listings, feedback listings, and links to your favorite pages on the Web. You can create your own About Me page by going to the eBay Site Map and clicking the About Me link in the Community section, or just going directly to pages.ebay.com/community/aboutme.html. Follow the onscreen instructions from there.

FIGURE 1.7

The author's About Me page.

Trick #18: **Use Your About Me Page to Offset a Low Feedback Rating**

> **selectro_cute**
>
> Member since 2000, Feedback: Turquoise star

When you're first starting out on eBay, you haven't yet established your reputation, as recorded by your feedback rating. (Learn more about feedback in Chapter 2, "How to Deal with Feedback.") In this situation, you can use your About Me page to tell potential buyers and sellers a little about yourself, which can help offset any dubious opinions they may have of your low feedback rating. Make sure that your About Me page is as professional-looking as possible, so that you leave a good impression. The more reliable you look, the more comfortable other eBayers will be in dealing with you.

Trick #19: **Make Your About Me Page About You**

lora_and_steve

stores.ebay.com/Our-Hutch/

www.ourhutch.com/examples/

Member since 1999, Feedback: Red star

It's important that your About Me page actually be about you—that is, that it reflect your personal likes and dislikes. You can do this not only via the information you include, but also in your choice of design, colors, and graphics. As member **lora_and_steve** notes, this is particularly important if you're a seller:

> *A page that reflects you, your feelings, your ideas, your attitude, will create a positive comfort level in potential buyers who will feel they are getting to know the real you, not just some imaginary Internet company or business. I think this is very important for conducting eBay business.*

Of course, you need to do this while remembering the real purpose of the About Me page—to provide potential buyers/sellers with information that will help their buying/selling decisions. This is particularly important when you're a seller; you can use your About Me page to build a rapport with buyers, and help them get comfortable with buying from you. To this end, be as personal (and as personable) as you want, but try to avoid volatile topics (such as politics and religion) that might turn off some potential buyers.

Trick #20: **Use Your Own HTML**

lesley_feeney

stores.ebay.com/Lesleys-Auction-Template-Designs

www.zoicks.com/ebaylinks.htm

PowerSeller

Member since 2000, Feedback: Purple star

You can choose from one of eBay's predesigned About Me templates, or you can use HTML to create a more customized page. To use your own HTML, select the Enter Your Own HTML Code option on the About Me: Choose Your Editing Option page. When the Edit Your HTML page appears, as shown in Figure 1.8, enter your HTML code into the editing window. (To start completely fresh, delete any existing code first—or you can simply use HTML to supplement the current page.)

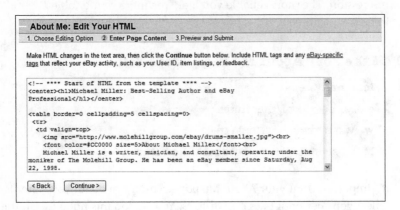

FIGURE 1.8

Enter your own HTML code into the editing window.

I won't go into all the available HTML codes here. To learn more about HTML, go to Chapter 9, "How to Enhance Your Product Listings with HTML."

Trick #21: **Use eBay Tags for Specific Information**

> **lesley_feeney**
>
> stores.ebay.com/Lesleys-Auction-Template-Designs
>
> www.zoicks.com/ebaylinks.htm
>
> PowerSeller
>
> Member since 2000, Feedback: Purple star

eBay offers a number of special HTML tags you can include in your About Me page to display your specific account and auction information. When you use these tags, your current information is automatically inserted into your page and kept constantly updated.

Table 1.1 shows all the eBay-specific tags you can use in your About Me page.

Table 1.1   **eBay HTML Tags**

Tag	Usage
<eBayFeedback>	Displays your user feedback. You can add the following parameters, within the brackets, to further format your feedback table:
	SIZE="*n*" (specifies how many items you want to display)
	COLOR="*color*" (displays the lower feedback line in color)
	ALTERNATECOLOR="*color*" (displays the upper feedback line in color)
	BORDER="*n*" (adds a border of *n* width around the listings)
	CAPTION="*text*" (displays a customized caption above the feedback list)
	TABLEWIDTH="*n*" (specifies the width of the feedback table, as a percentage of the available width)
	CELLPADDING="*n*" (adds spacing between the feedback comments)
<eBayItemList>	Displays the items you currently have for sale. You can add the following parameters, within the brackets, to further format your item list:
	BIDS (displays the items you are currently bidding on)
	SORT="*n*" (sorts your items by a specific method; replace *n* with 8 to sort by date newest first, with 2 to sort by date oldest first, with 3 to sort by end date of auction newest first, or 4 to sort by price in ascending order)
	CATEGORY="*n*" (lists items in the specified category; replace *n* with the category number)
	SINCE="*n*" (specifies the number of days ended auctions stay in your list)
	BORDER="*n*" (adds a border of *n* width around the listings)
	CAPTION="*text*" (puts a customized caption at the top of your items table)
	TABLEWIDTH="*n*" (specifies the width of the item table, as a percentage of the available width)
	CELLPADDING="*n*" (adds spacing between the items)
<eBayMemberSince>	Displays the date of your eBay registration
<eBayTime>	Displays the current eBay system time
<eBayUserID>	Displays your user ID. You can add the following parameters, within the brackets, to further format your ID:
	BOLD (displays your user ID in bold)
	NOLINK (displays your user ID without a link to your Member Profile page)
	NOFEEDBACK (displays your user ID without your feedback rating)
	EMAIL (also displays your email address)
	NOMASK (hides the "shades" new user icon)

Avoiding Scams and Spams

Now, don't get all freaked out about this, but there are a lot of scam artists out there, and they're all intent on parting you from your money. These crooks existed long before the Internet came into existence, but they've learned to adapt their thieving ways to the new online medium. They also know a good thing when they see it, so many of these scammers have focused intently on eBay's massive user base for potential victims.

Some scammers focus on eBay buyers; I discuss these frauds in Chapter 4, "How to Be a Smarter—and Safer—Buyer." Other scammers target eBay sellers; I discuss these frauds in Chapter 15, "How to Deal with Customer Problems—and Problem Customers." But there are also a class of scams that target *all* eBay users, and you need to know about them.

Trick #22: **Beware Fake Emails**

> **mikeology**
> Member since 2002, Feedback: Purple star

Probably the biggest eBay-related scam is the fake email—commonly called a *spoof* or *phishing* scheme. This scam comes in the form of an official-looking email message, purportedly from eBay or PayPal. These fake emails, like the one in Figure 1.9, typically seek to inform you about some problem with your account, and request that you update your personal information to avoid having your account canceled. When you click on the link in the message, you go to a web page that *looks like* the eBay or PayPal site, and you're provided with a form to fill out; said form usually asks for your name, address, user name, password, and credit card information.

The problem, of course, is that this web page isn't an official eBay or PayPal page, appearances to the contrary. The page actually resides on the scammer's website, and as soon as you enter your information, it's now in the scammer's hands. Enter your user ID and password and the scammer can hijack your eBay account. Enter your PayPal information and the scammer can appropriate all the funds in your PayPal account. Enter your credit card information, and the scammer gets to go on a shopping spree—at your expense.

I recently got hoodwinked by a slightly more devious phishing scheme. I received an email message that looked like an official eBay email, notifying me that I had a question from a buyer regarding one of my auctions. Not thinking twice, I clicked the link in the message and was taken to what looked like the normal eBay sign-in screen. I entered my user ID and password, and then saw a page that looked like the "answer a question" screen, except that the question didn't have anything to do with any of my current auctions. A quick check revealed that this was a phony site, and I'd just given my password to the phisher. I promptly logged onto the *real* eBay site and changed my password, so no harm was done. But it does show that some of these phishing schemes are sophisticated enough to fool even a seasoned user, such as myself.

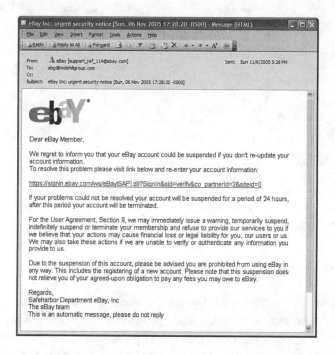

FIGURE 1.9

A typical spoof email—it's not really from eBay.

How do you tell a fake email from a real one? It used to be simple, because eBay never asks for your personal information via email. But when the messages look identical to official eBay messages, and lead you to a real-looking site to enter your ID and password, it's a little trickier.

The best advice is simple: Never enter any information on a page that you get to by clicking a link in an email message. If you need to change your eBay or PayPal information, go directly to the official site (either www.ebay.com or www.paypal. com); do *not* click to the site from a link in an email message.

Even better, go to the My Summary page in My eBay. Scroll to the My Messages section, and you can click through to all the official messages and announcements sent to you by eBay, as shown in Figure 1.10. If the suspicious message isn't listed here, you know it's a fake. (And, to be extra safe, you can simply read your messages directly from the My Messages page.)

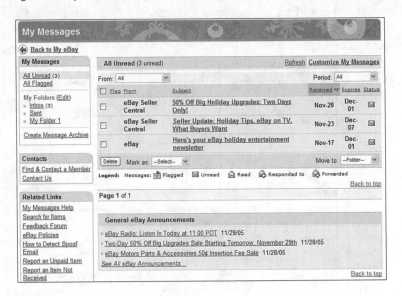

FIGURE 1.10

Reading your official eBay messages on the My Messages page.

And here's something else. You should report any scam emails to eBay. When you receive one of these fake messages, just click the Forward button and send it off to spoof@ebay.com. Whatever you do, don't click on any of the email links, and definitely do not submit any personal information. Remember—it's a fake!

Trick #23: **Minimize eBay-Related Spam**

trapperjohn2000

stores.ebay.com/Molehill-Group-Store

Member since 1998, Feedback: Purple star

Many users find that when they sign up for eBay their daily spam starts increasing in volume. This can happen if you're not careful when choosing your user ID. If you choose an ID that matches your regular email name, it's easy for spammers to put two and two together and add your address to their spam list.

Here's an example. Let's say your email address is bobby-example@hotmail.com. When you register at eBay you choose the user ID **bobby-example**. That's when the trouble starts. A spammer will scour eBay for user names and start adding common domain names to each ID, hoping to find a new email address. In this example, they find the user ID **bobby-example**, add hotmail.com to the end, and thus uncover your bobby-example@hotmail.com address—and you start getting more spam.

The solution is easy—create a user ID that doesn't match your email address. This may be as simple as adding a "01" or "02" to your name, or you can do something more creative. In any case, avoid eBay ID and email matching—unless you really want more spam every day.

General Advice

Finally, we'll end this chapter with a few general tricks that didn't fit anywhere else in the book. (They may not fit, but that doesn't make them any less useful!)

Trick #24: **Use the eBay Toolbar**

> **selling4-u**
>
> stores.ebay.com/Selling-4-U-Consignment-Store
>
> www.selling4-u.com
>
> PowerSeller
>
> Member since 2002, Feedback: Purple star

Many frequent eBay operations can be accessed directly by the eBay Toolbar, an add-on toolbar that attaches to the Internet Explorer web browser. With the eBay Toolbar installed (and a live Internet connection) you're a button click away from doing pricing research, checking on your auction bidders, and going directly to your My eBay. (The eBay Toolbar also includes an Account Guard function that warns you if you accidentally navigate a spoofed eBay site.)

You can download the eBay Toolbar for free at pages.ebay.com/ebay_toolbar/. (Figure 1.11 shows the eBay Toolbar attached to Internet Explorer.)

FIGURE 1.11

Get quick access to eBay operations with the eBay Toolbar.

You can add custom buttons to the toolbar for a variety of operations, as member **selling4-u** notes:

> I also add bookmarks to the FedEx, USPS, and UPS tracking pages to make it easy to check up on my packages.

If you're a heavy eBay user, the eBay Toolbar is an indispensable tool!

Trick #25: **Contact Other Members**

betty*blackbent

stores.ebay.com/betty-blackbents-world-of-stuff

PowerSeller

Member since 2002, Feedback: Red star

Most users don't know that they can send emails to any other user on the eBay system. Of course, it's easy to email the seller in one of your auctions; just click the Contact Seller link on the auction listing page.

eBay also lets you send an email to anybody with a user ID. All you have to do is locate the member (use the Search page, accessible from the Search link at the top of any page, or the buyer/seller links on any auction listing page) and click their feedback number to get to their Member Profile page. From there, click the Contact Member button to display the Contact Member page, shown in Figure 1.12; enter your message into the editing box and click the Send Message button to make your contact.

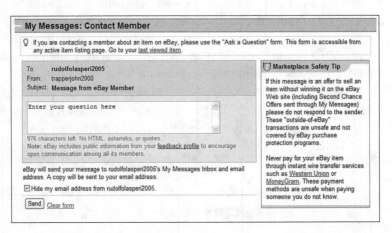

FIGURE 1.12

Send an email to any eBay member.

Trick #26: **Help Your Kids Buy and Sell**

> **eberlyy**
> Member since 2003, Feedback: Turquoise star

eBay requires you to be 18 years of age to buy or sell on its site. But that doesn't stop younger buyers and sellers from taking part in the fun. The thing to remember is that all transactions have to be completed by an adult, and that adult will be held responsible. So if you have kids, you can do their trading for them.

eBay member **eberlyy** reports that she's helped her 10-year-old son buy and sell several items on eBay. Here's how they handled the bidding and buying:

> *He found what he wanted and gave instructions as to how much he was willing to pay. I then conducted and finished the transaction, with my son over my shoulder stating his direction. I could then step in by not following his direction if he got caught up in the moment, so to speak. He paid me full funds, but I used my PayPal account to pay the seller. So I, an adult, worked with the seller or buyer making the contracts binding.*

It's kind of bidding by proxy—with you as your child's proxy. (Not to be confused with eBay's proxy bidding system, of course.) It's a great way to get your kids involved in the whole process—while still making sure everything is on the up and up, legally.

Trick #27: **Get a High-Speed Connection**

> **bej-collectibles**
> Member since 2003, Feedback: Purple star

Technology is your friend—especially high-speed Internet technology. While there's nothing stopping you from accessing eBay with a traditional dial-up connection, it's a more pleasant experience when you connect at broadband speeds. Most eBay auction listings include at least one picture, and pictures load quite a bit faster with a cable modem or DSL connection. Plus, those crucial last-second bids zip through a lot smoother when you're not waiting on your slow phone line to connect.

How to Deal with Feedback

eBay's feedback system is how users get graded on their performance. A buyer generates good feedback by paying promptly; a seller generates good feedback by offering quality merchandise and shipping soon after being paid.

You can use feedback to help you decide which eBay users to deal with, or not. That's because the higher one's feedback rating, the more trustworthy that user is—in most cases. For that reason, experienced eBay users zealously guard their feedback status, and strive for as close to a perfect score (that is, the fewest negatives) possible.

Read on to learn some of the feedback tricks used by the eBay Masters.

Using Feedback as a Buying Tool

When you're dealing with strangers (which you are, when you buy and sell on eBay), it helps to know what others think of that person. If other users have found that buyer or seller difficult to work with, you might want to avoid dealing with that person. If other users have found that buyer or seller a joy to work with, then you should feel comfortable dealing with that person, too.

You'll find a user's feedback score next to their user ID. Click the user's name to view their Member Profile page, like the one in Figure 2.1. The section at the top summarizes the key data, including the user's feedback score and percentage. The rest of the page lists individual feedback comments.

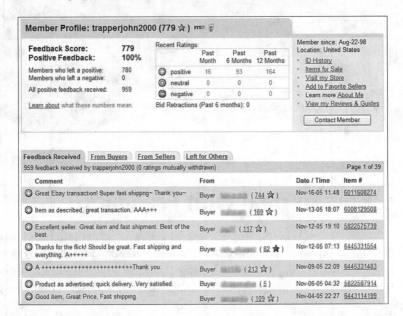

FIGURE 2.1

A typical Member Profile page, complete with feedback score, percentage, and comments.

Learn how to read the information on the Member Profile page, then read through the following tricks to find out how to use eBay's feedback to guide your buying and selling decisions.

Trick #28: **Avoid Sellers with Negative Feedback Scores**

> **quiltworks**
>
> Member since 1999, Feedback: Turquoise star

It goes without saying that a user with a negative feedback score is probably a bad risk. (A negative score means that the user has received more negative than positive remarks—and is, overall, unsatisfactory.) Many users take an extra step and say they won't deal with users who have a zero feedback score.

Here's why.

A user with zero feedback is, most likely, a brand new user. (It's also possible they're an experienced user whose negatives have cancelled out their positives—which is also not a good deal.) New users aren't automatically risky (especially if they're new buyers), but a zero-feedback seller could be a scammer in disguise. It's relatively easy for a scammer to set up a new ID, list some fake merchandise, take your money, and disappear. You're safer buying from a seller with at least a little bit of history—say, a feedback score of 10 or more.

Trick #29: **Don't Automatically Dismiss Low-Feedback Users**

trapperjohn2000

stores.ebay.com/Molehill-Group-Store

Member since 1998, Feedback: Purple star

I know this contradicts the previous trick, but it goes to show how eBay strategy differs from user to user. Just because a user has low feedback doesn't make them a bad buyer or seller. In fact, some low-feedback users exhibit the "Hertz effect"—they try harder to get a higher feedback rating.

So if you run into a low-feedback seller with an item you really want, take that extra step and email them before you bid. It might be worth your while!

Trick #30: **Set an Acceptable Feedback Percentage**

betty*blackbent

stores.ebay.com/betty-blackbents-world-of-stuff

PowerSeller

Member since 2002, Feedback: Red star

The raw feedback rating doesn't tell the whole story. A user could have a rating of 2000 but still have a number of bad transactions. For that reason, it pays to look at the feedback percentage as well as the feedback number. This will give you an idea of what percent of the time the user gets the job done.

As far as how low a feedback percentage is acceptable, here's some advice from user **betty*blackbent**:

Everyone has their own threshold of what's acceptable. For someone with a high-feedback number, I'll accept users with feedback of 98% or higher. On the other hand, 90% is pretty abysmal; even 95% is lower than I'm comfortable with. Think of it this way...to have a 90% rating, one transaction in ten was bad.

But don't be too inflexible in your judgment. A user with one negative feedback in 50 transactions is going to fall below that 98% rule, and anybody can have one bad transaction. A low-feedback percentage against a large number of transactions is perhaps a bit more worrisome.

So determine an acceptable feedback percentage, and don't deal with any users who fall below that level.

Trick #31: **Look Beyond the Feedback Numbers**

betty*blackbent

stores.ebay.com/betty-blackbents-world-of-stuff

PowerSeller

Member since 2002, Feedback: Red star

You can learn even more about a particular user by taking the time to read the individual feedback comments left by their trading partners. Read the positive comments to see if they're tempered in any way. Read the negatives to see what they're for, and if (and how) the user responded. For example, if a user gets negatives for slow shipping, that may not be a big deal if you're not in a hurry.

It also helps to check out the feedback of those users leaving negative comments. Some users have a history of handing out negatives, and you might need to discount their remarks. In short, look for the story behind the numbers to get a better picture about a user's true performance.

Trick #32: **Isolate the Negative Comments with Toolhaus.org**

ghsproducts

stores.ebay.com/GHSProducts

Member since 1998, Feedback: Purple star

Let's face it; what you're really interested in is a user's negative feedback. If something went wrong with a transaction, you want to read all the details. Sometimes the other user is just a grouch, sometimes the complaint is justified; you can get a good idea from reading the individual comments.

However, scrolling through pages and pages of feedback ratings just to find the negative comments is a bit of a hassle, particularly if the user has a large number of transactions under his or her belt. A better solution is to use a third-party tool that isolates and displays only the negative feedback comments, such as Toolhaus.org (www.toolhaus.org), shown in Figure 2.2. Just enter a user's eBay ID, then click the Received By or Left By buttons to view all negative comments either received or left by that user. It's a darned sight faster than doing it by hand in eBay!

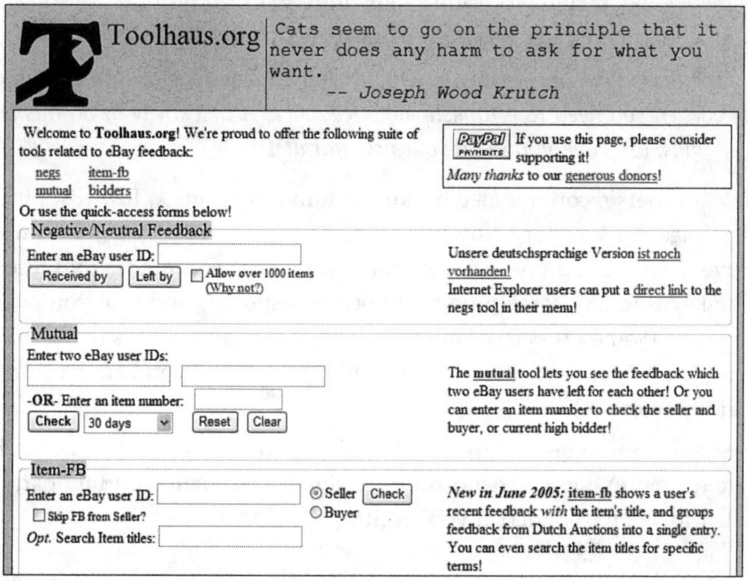

FIGURE 2.2

Checking for negative feedback comments at Toolhaus.org.

Building Up Your Own Feedback

As you can tell from the previous tricks, if you're a new eBayer, many established users won't want to deal with you. This situation changes, of course, as you participate in more auctions and build up your own feedback score. Here are some tips on how to do that.

Trick #33: **Establish Fast Feedback Before You Sell**

bushellcollectibles

stores.ebay.com/Bushells-Collectibles

Member since 1999, Feedback: Red star

Anybody can sell on eBay; you don't have to be an established member, all you have to do is sign up. Of course, that doesn't mean that anyone will want to buy from you. A lot of experienced buyers tend to shy away from complete newbies; they figure dealing with a first-timer is often more trouble than it's worth.

With that in mind, many eBay Masters recommend that you establish a bit of a feedback rating before you offer your first item for sale. How do you earn feedback before you sell your first item? By *buying*, of course. Make some quick buys to earn some feedback; then you won't look quite so green around the ears as you actually are. As eBay member **bushellcollectibles** points out:

> For those who are wondering why they are having a hard time selling as a new eBayer, you need to establish some feedback. A quick way to do this is buy some things, use PayPal, and hit your first star at 10.

Several users recommended making a handful of quick, low-cost purchases to establish a feedback history. Buy It Now items are particularly good for this, as you don't have to wait out a seven-day auction to make the purchase and receive feedback. The key is to buy something that doesn't cost a lot, and that you probably needed anyway. (Some users recommend buying "instant" items, such as e-book, website templates, or recipes delivered via email—anything you can get shipped *immediately* via the Internet.)

Just remember—because not every seller leaves feedback, you might have to buy two (or more) items to get a single feedback comment! (And it's okay to ask the seller to leave feedback, if you want.)

Trick #34: **Build Your Reputation by Writing Reviews and Guides**

New Trick

trapperjohn2000

stores.ebay.com/Molehill-Group-Store

Member since 1998, Feedback: Purple star

eBay's new Reviews & Guides feature is a great way for you to enhance your reputation on eBay without having to conduct hundreds of auctions to build your feedback. Anyone can write a review or Guide; the more you write, the higher your Reviews & Guides ranking becomes. (High-ranking review and Guide writers get an icon beside their user ID.)

Writing a review is easy. Go to the main Reviews & Guides page (reviews.ebay.com) and search for the particular product you want to review. Click on the link for that product's review page, then click the **Write a Review** link. When the Write a

Review page appears, as shown in Figure 2.3, enter a title for your review, and then write the review itself. The title can be up to 55 characters in length; the review can be up to 3,500 characters. Click the Submit Review button when you're done.

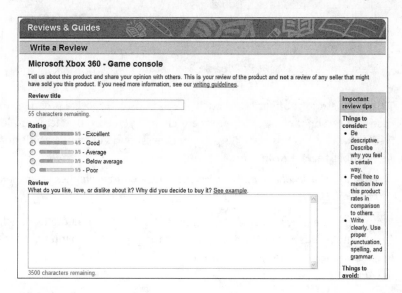

FIGURE 2.3
Writing your own product review.

The process for writing a Guide is similar, although here it really helps if you're an expert or experienced collector—that is, if you know enough to write a useful Guide. Again, you start at the main Reviews & Guides page, but this time you click the **Write a Guide** link. When the Write a Guide page appears, enter the Guide's title, then start writing the Guide. Make sure you format the Guide so that it's readable, then enter up to five "tags" that other members can use to search for your Guide.

Leaving Feedback

The issue of precisely when to leave feedback for a buyer or seller is surprisingly controversial, especially among high-volume sellers. Some sellers say to leave feedback right after payment is received, others say to hold off and wait until after the buyer has left his or her feedback. There are good arguments for both sides, and I'll present them all and leave you to decide for yourself.

Trick #35: **Leave Feedback as Soon as You're Paid**

terrisbooks

stores.ebay.com/Terris-Books

www.terrisbeads.com

PowerSeller

Member since 2002, Feedback: Red star

This is the straightforward approach. As soon as you receive payment (and, in the case of a personal check, that payment clears), you ship the item and leave positive feedback. It's good business, it's quick business, and your buyers will appreciate it. As member **terrisbooks** says,

> *Leaving good feedback makes everyone happy and encourages future sales from first-time buyers, too!*

Many other members offered their approval of the "immediate feedback" approach. For example, **bushellcollectibles** makes the point that if you wait for the buyer to leave feedback they might be waiting for you—"and then neither of you will leave it!"

So if you follow the advice of these eBay Masters, you'll make it a practice to leave feedback as soon as you're paid—and not keep the buyer waiting.

Trick #36: **Don't Leave Feedback Until the Buyer Leaves Feedback**

stephen2

PowerSeller

Member since 1998, Feedback: Red star

Not all sellers agree with the "immediate feedback" strategy. These sellers wait until the buyer has received the merchandise and left feedback of their own, and *then* leave their feedback. Why? Read the reasoned argument from member **stephen2**:

> *As a full-time seller, I can say this from experience. It is not a good decision to leave feedback after payment. Why? It's much easier for a person with the slightest problem to leave a neutral/negative instead of contacting you to fix the problem.*

See the problem? If you have a finicky buyer, he might use the feedback system as a public complaint department, instead of contacting you to resolve any issues. By this time, if you followed the "immediate feedback" strategy, you would have already left that buyer positive feedback, and thus be up the proverbial stream without a proverbial paddle.

If, on the other hand, you haven't left feedback yet, the buyer has to think twice about leaving you a negative. If they leave you a negative, you can leave them a negative—and nobody wants negative feedback. In this instance, troublesome buyers are more apt to contact you if they have a problem, rather than hastily leaving negative feedback. They won't risk your retaliatory negative.

In addition, you can use your feedback as leverage if the customer has what you feel is an unjustified complaint about the auction. If the buyer threatens to leave negative feedback against you, just tell him that your feedback will mirror the feedback that he leaves. With the threat of negative feedback hanging out there, the buyer might be more willing to come to a compromise on the auction. At the very least, it means that the buyer will have to contact you first if he has a problem, rather than just leaving negative feedback without any contact.

One big problem with this strategy, of course, is that *someone* has to go first. If it's not you, it's the buyer—and what if he takes the same "I'll leave my feedback last" approach? In addition, not leaving immediate feedback will turn a lot of buyers off. It sends off a vibe that you don't trust your customers—which, while it may be true, isn't always good for business.

The bottom line is you have to make up your own mind on this issue. I tend to side with the "immediate feedback" approach but understand the second option, especially if a seller has been burned by bad feedback in the past. (And if you employ the "delayed feedback" approach, state so in your item listing and end-of-auction emails—"Feedback left after successful receipt of merchandise," or something similar.)

Trick #37: **Leave Feedback Once a Month**

> **lady_gotrocks!**
> stores.ebay.com/The-Carat-Farm
> PowerSeller
> Member since 2002, Feedback: Red star

Then there's the approach that ignores the entire "leave it first or leave it last" issue, in favor of a more operational approach. When you do a lot of buying and selling on eBay, it may simply be more convenient to save up your feedback comments and leave a bunch all at once. Pick a convenient time of the month, and leave all your feedbacks for the past 30 days at one time. This could take up quite a bit of time, but you only have to do it once a month—on your schedule.

Trick #38: **Be Factual**

> **trapperjohn2000**
>
> stores.ebay.com/Molehill-Group-Store
>
> Member since 1998, Feedback: Purple star

When you're leaving feedback, it's important that you take the emotion out of your comments. Even if you've had a bad experience, it pays to be professional. State the facts, and nothing but the facts. That way, when other users read your comments, they'll be sure to take you seriously—and not think that you're some ticked-off whack-job.

Trick #39: **Leave Tracking Information in Your Feedback**

> **trapperjohn2000**
>
> stores.ebay.com/Molehill-Group-Store
>
> Member since 1998, Feedback: Purple star

Here's a trick that I think is pretty neat. Instead (or perhaps in addition to) leaving the standard "great buyer!" type of comment, try inserting tracking information into your feedback comments. It's a good way of transmitting vital information, plus it protects from any unscrupulous buyers who might claim they never received an item. By making the tracking information public, it tells anyone involved that it's been shipped.

Handling Negative Feedback

Not all feedback is positive. No one likes to receive negative feedback, and many eBay users will go out of their way to avoid risking any negatives. But even the best buyer or seller can't totally avoid negative feedback, so here are some tricks on how to deal with less-than-positive comments.

Trick #40: **Don't Risk Retaliatory Negatives**

> **ilene**
>
> stores.ebay.com/Ilenes-Discount-Collectibles
>
> PowerSeller
>
> Member since 1997, Feedback: Green star

Some easily-provoked eBayers will respond to negative feedback by leaving a negative in return—even if they were actually in the wrong. This is the dreaded "retaliatory negative," and it's a risk whenever you leave a negative comment about another user.

The only way to avoid a retaliatory negative is to never leave any negative feedback of your own. Since eBay is loathe to remove feedback comments—even unjustified ones—I can understand this approach. Of course, it sort of abrogates your responsibility of warning other users about the bad seeds, but it does protect your feedback reputation.

So what do you do if you have a bad transaction? If it's a deadbeat bidder, you can still file a non-paying bidder claim, even if you don't leave any feedback. Other members recommend leaving negative feedback only in the case of non-paying bidders, although you still risk a retaliatory negative.

Trick #41: **Don't Be Afraid of Negative Feedback**

> **satnrose**
>
> PowerSeller
>
> Member since 1998, Feedback: Green star

The fear of retaliatory negatives isn't shared by all eBayers. Some view the occasional negative as a necessary cost of doing business and refuse to be bullied by members who try to hold feedback hostage. As **satnrose** bravely says,

> *If you never get a neg, you're a pushover.*

One negative feedback among a hundred positives won't hurt your reputation. Smart users will read *all* your feedback comments and judge your reputation from the whole.

Trick #42: **Leave Negative Comments in Positive Feedback**

> **ilene**
>
> stores.ebay.com/Ilenes-Discount-Collectibles
>
> PowerSeller
>
> Member since 1997, Feedback: Green star

There's a way to sneak negative comments into otherwise-positive feedback, thus diminishing your risk for a retaliatory negative while still informing your fellow users of a bad transaction. All you have to do is leave positive feedback, but use the feedback comments to write what you really feel about the transaction. Since many users only look at their feedback numbers, this sometimes gets you in under the radar. And, besides, what justification would someone have to leave you a retaliatory negative if, in fact, you left them a positive?

Trick #43: **Respond to Negative Comments**

trapperjohn2000
stores.ebay.com/Molehill-Group-Store
Member since 1998, Feedback: Purple star

If you receive what you feel is an unjustified negative comment, you don't have to put up with it in silence. eBay lets you respond to any feedback comment left about you, positive or negative. All you have to do is go to your Member Profile page, scroll down to the bottom, and click the Reply to Feedback Received link. This takes you to a list of all the feedback comments you've received; click the Reply link next to the comment you want to comment on, and click through to the Reply to Feedback Received page. Enter your reply, then click the Leave Reply button; your comments will now be inserted below the original feedback comments. Remember, this won't remove the original negative comment, but it will let you tell your side of the story to anyone reading your feedback comments.

Trick #44: **Ask eBay to Remove Unjustified Negatives**

trapperjohn2000
stores.ebay.com/Molehill-Group-Store
Member since 1998, Feedback: Purple star

While eBay doesn't make a practice of removing negative comments, sometimes a comment is so off the wall they'll get rid of it for you. It has to be an unusual situation, however, typically when the comments have nothing to do with the auction at hand. Just go to pages.ebay.com/help/policies/feedback-abuse-withdrawal.html, read the restrictions, then scroll down to the bottom and click the link that says Report Listing Violations or Problems with Another eBay Member. Fill in the blanks to inform eBay about the situation; then sit back and see what happens.

Part II:

Tricks for More Successful Bidding

3

How to Find What You Want to Buy

With millions of items for sale every day, the eBay marketplace is a shopper's paradise—and a shopper's nightmare. That's because with so many items for sale, it's increasingly difficult to find that exact item you're looking for. It's like searching for a needle in a haystack; you know it's there, but you have no idea where to look.

One of the first tricks to becoming a successful bidder is learning where to look. That's what this chapter is all about—helping you master eBay's various search functions.

By the way, this chapter is unique in that most of the tricks don't come from other users, they come from me. That's because I am, in all modesty, somewhat of a search guru, so you might as well get your tricks from the horse's mouth, so to speak. I guarantee that if you use the tricks in this chapter, you'll stand a much better chance of finding the merchandise you want to buy!

Using eBay's Search Feature

eBay offers two ways of finding merchandise for sale. You can browse through the product categories, or you can search for specific items. Guess which method provides the best results?

Trick #45: **Search, Don't Browse**

> **trapperjohn2000**
>
> stores.ebay.com/Molehill-Group-Store
>
> Member since 1998, Feedback: Purple star

Here's something all eBay Masters realize, sooner or later. Searching for an item is quicker than browsing for it. Searching is pretty much a one-click operation; browsing requires you to click through subcategory after subcategory after subcategory, and even then you still end up with dozens of pages of merchandise to sift through. So if you know what you're looking for, don't go through the time-consuming hassle of clicking and loading and clicking and loading to access a particular item category—use the search function instead.

Trick #46: **Use the Search Page, Not the Search Box**

> **trapperjohn2000**
>
> stores.ebay.com/Molehill-Group-Store
>
> Member since 1998, Feedback: Purple star

Most users do their searching directly from eBay's home page, using the search box at the top of the page. That's okay for many searches (especially if you use some of the search operators I discuss later in this chapter), but I prefer to use the more powerful Search page.

You access the Search page, shown in Figure 3.1, by clicking the Advanced Search link under the search box. This page, unlike the simple search box, lets you search by several criteria: You can search by listing title, by specific words in the listing, by item number, by location, by seller, or by bidder. You can even choose to search *completed* auctions—which is a great way to get a handle on final selling prices for various types of items. And you can expand the number of search options available by clicking the Advanced Search link at the bottom of the basic Search page; these options let you create even more powerful searches.

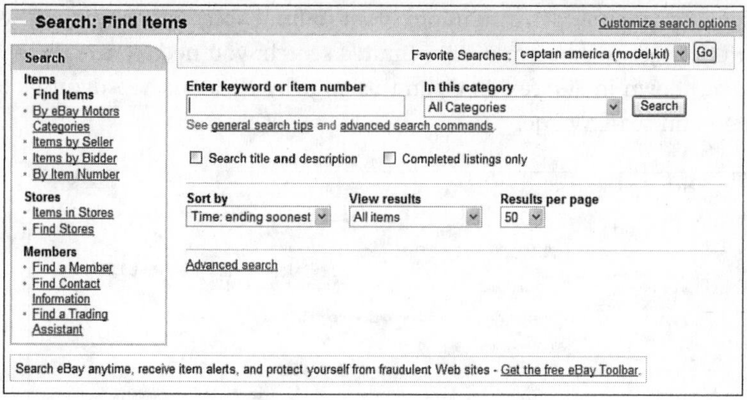

FIGURE 3.1
Perform more precise searches from eBay's Search page.

Trick #47: **Search the Full Description**

> **abc-books**
>
> stores.ebay.com/ABC-Books-by-Ann
>
> www.abcbooksbyann.com
>
> PowerSeller
>
> Member since 1999, Feedback: Red star

When you use the Search page, you have lots of options available that you don't have from the home-page search box. One of my favorite options lets you search the complete auction description. eBay's default search only looks in the listing titles; when you expand your search to include the full item description, you can find a lot more items that match your query.

All you have to do is go to the Search page, enter your query, and select the Search Title and Description option. Click the Search button and you'll see many more results than you would otherwise.

Trick #48: **Search by Price Range**

> **trapperjohn2000**
>
> stores.ebay.com/Molehill-Group-Store
>
> Member since 1998, Feedback: Purple star

If you're on a budget, you might want to limit your search to items within a certain price range. To perform a price-limited search, you need to use the Advanced Search page, shown in Figure 3.2. Open this page by clicking the Advanced Search link on the main search page.

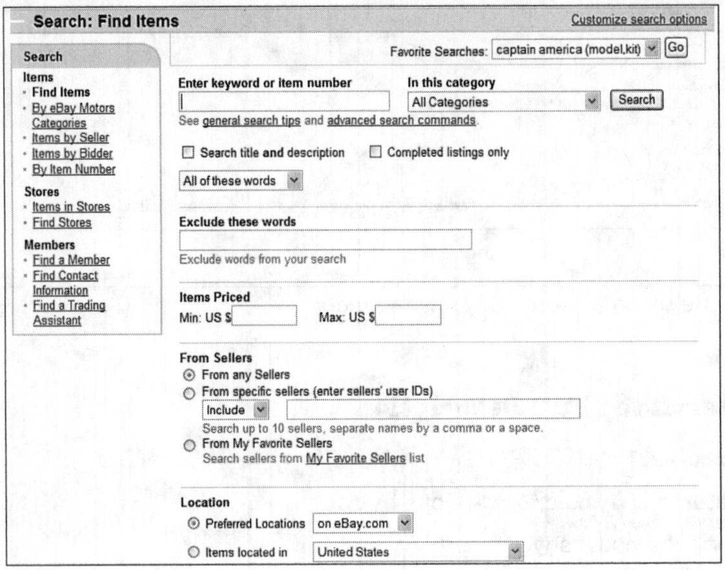

FIGURE 3.2

Use the Advanced Search to search by price range.

From the Advanced Search page, enter your query then enter the minimum and/or maximum prices you're willing to pay into the Items Priced boxes. This will return a list of auctions that not only match your query but also fall within your specified price range.

Trick #49: **Search for Items Near Your Home**

trapperjohn2000

stores.ebay.com/Molehill-Group-Store

Member since 1998, Feedback: Purple star

One of my favorite features of the Advanced Search page is the ability to search for items within a certain distance of your home ZIP code, which is great if you're shopping for large, hard-to-ship items. Open the Advanced Search page, scroll down to the Items Near Me section (shown in Figure 3.3), enter your ZIP code, and select a distance (in miles) from the Within list. Conduct your search, and only those items offered within your specified geographic range will be listed .

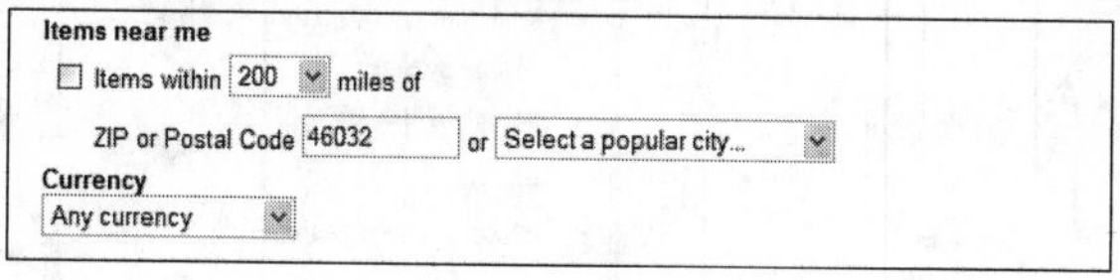

FIGURE 3.3

Use the Advanced Search page to find items in or near a specific ZIP code.

Trick #50: **Use the eBay Toolbar to Search**

> **trapperjohn2000**
>
> stores.ebay.com/Molehill-Group-Store
>
> Member since 1998, Feedback: Purple star

If you have the eBay Toolbar installed in your browser (see Trick #22), you don't have to go to the eBay site to do your searching. Instead, you can search directly from the toolbar.

To perform a basic search, just enter your query into the toolbar's empty search box, then click the Search button. To perform a more advanced search, click the down arrow to the right of the Search eBay button to display the list of search and browse options shown in Figure 3.4. You can search by title, by description, by item number, and so on, or you can click a category heading to browse all the listings in that product category. It's a great way to access eBay without always going through the home page!

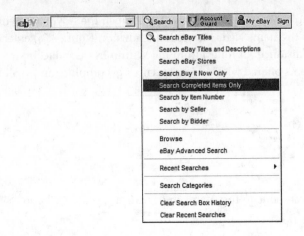

FIGURE 3.4
Perform a variety of searches from the eBay Toolbar.

Fine-Tuning Your Search

Whether you use the home-page search box, the dedicated Search page, or the search function on the eBay Toolbar, a successful search involves more than just entering a keyword or two. To make sure you find exactly what you're looking for—no more, no less—you need to fine-tune your query, using a variety of available tools.

Trick #51: **Conduct a More Specific Search**

> **trapperjohn2000**
>
> stores.ebay.com/Molehill-Group-Store
>
> Member since 1998, Feedback: Purple star

Many users, when searching for an item, enter a single search word—and then are buried under an overwhelming number of matching results. That's because some of the most popular categories on eBay list thousands of items on any given day.

The first step to fine-tuning your results is to use more than one keyword to describe what you're looking for—that is, to conduct a more specific search. For example, if you do a search on nba, you'll be overwhelmed by the results. Narrow your search to a more specific product category (to nba jerseys or nba tickets), and you'll better describe the specific item you're looking for and get more targeted results.

Be cautious, however, of making your query *too* precise. You need to pick a series of keywords that are specific but not overly restrictive. Get too specific in your query, and you'll end up excluding some auctions you might be interested in.

For example, it's easy enough to see that simply entering the word `model` is too general a query; you'll get thousands of results, most of which you won't care about. A more precise query would describe the type of model you're interested in, such as `star wars death star model`. Good so far, but if your search gets even more precise—searching for an `old star wars death star model partially assembled without instructions not painted`, to make a case—you probably won't return *any* matching results. The query is simply too specific; nothing fits all the parameters. So if your search generates few if any results, take some of the parameters out of your query to broaden your search.

Trick #52: **Narrow Your Search Results**

trapperjohn2000

stores.ebay.com/Molehill-Group-Store

Member since 1998, Feedback: Purple star

There's another way to narrow your search results—and it just so happens to be the method that eBay is officially pushing. eBay recommends you perform a general search, and then use the options along the left side of the page to narrow the results list.

If you enter a really broad search parameter—`books`, for example—the search results page displays a list of matching categories, in addition to a list of matching auctions, as shown in Figure 3.5. Your next step is to click the category in which you're interested.

Depending on the size of the category you select, you may next see another list of subcategories, or you may be taken directly to search results within a category or subcategory. However you get there, you'll eventually land on a page that includes a list of Matching Categories and Search Options in the left column. As you can see in Figure 3.6, the Matching Categories are just that, subcategories related to your main search. The Search Options, shown in Figure 3.7, let you fine-tune the results by listing only those items that you can buy with PayPal, that have a Buy It Now option, that are gift items, that are completed auctions, that are priced within a specified range, that are listed as multiple-item lots, that start or end today (or within the next five hours), or that offer fast shipping. Select the options that matter to you, then click the Search button again. This will generate a new, shorter, more targeted list of matching auctions.

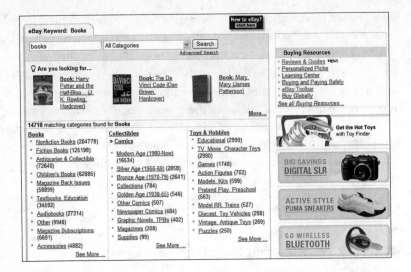

FIGURE 3.5
Some general searches require you to pick a more specific category.

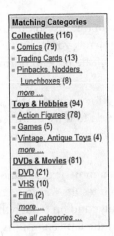

FIGURE 3.6
Use Matching Categories to narrow your search results to a specific product category.

FIGURE 3.7
Fine-tune your search results with eBay's Search Options.

Trick #53: **Search for an Exact Phrase**

> **artchick48**
>
> stores.ebay.com/Lee-Smith-Art
>
> www.leesmithart.com
>
> Member since 2001, Feedback: Turquoise star

When you enter two or more keywords in your query, eBay automatically assumes that you want to search for items that match all the words—but in no particular order. (This is the equivalent of putting the Boolean AND between the words.) So if you enter abraham lincoln, eBay will search for items that include both the words "abraham" and "lincoln"—which might include guys named Abraham who drive a Lincoln. That is, the two words don't have to be right next to each other, and they don't have to be in that order.

If you want to search for an exact phrase, put quotation marks around the words in your query. So in our example, to search for items about the former president, you'd enter "abraham lincoln". You won't get any results about cars!

Trick #54: **Don't Use AND, OR, or NOT**

> **trapperjohn2000**
>
> Member since 1998, Feedback: Purple star

Some experienced searchers like to use Boolean operators in their queries; this is a connecting word (AND, OR, NOT, and so on) that some search engines let you use to construct complex queries. Well, forget your ANDs and NOTs; eBay doesn't permit the use of Boolean operators in its search function. In fact, if you enter Boolean operators in your query, eBay will treat them as keywords—and search for them!

So you should only search for the words "and," "or," and "not" if they're actually part of an exact title that you're looking for. In other words, it's okay to search for batman and robin if you're looking for DVDs of the movie *Batman and Robin*. If you're looking for other items that include both Batman and Robin, drop the "and" from the search and enter this query instead: batman robin.

Trick #55: **Search for One Word *or* Another Word**

> **trapperjohn2000**
>
> stores.ebay.com/Molehill-Group-Store
>
> Member since 1998, Feedback: Purple star

If eBay won't let you use Boolean operators, then how do you create a complex search query? Fortunately, eBay has some alternate operators you can use to duplicate some Boolean functions.

First up is an operator that performs the OR function—that is, lets you search for auctions that include one word or another, as opposed to including both the words. To perform an OR search on eBay, enclose both the words within parentheses, separated by a comma, with no space after the comma. So to search for items that are either red or green (but not necessary both), enter the query (red,green). (Again, note that there's no space after the comma.)

Oh, and don't assume you can only use this trick with two keywords. You can link as many keywords as you want in this fashion, just keep adding commas and keywords, like this: (red,green,blue,purple,yellow).

Trick #56: **Exclude a Word from Your Search Results**

trapperjohn2000

stores.ebay.com/Molehill-Group-Store

Member since 1998, Feedback: Purple star

What if you want to search for all items within a particular category except those that match a particular parameter? In this instance, you want to use eBay's operator that excludes words from the search results—that is, lists all auctions except those that include a specific word. This operator is the simple minus sign (–), which you put in front of any word you want excluded from your results.

For example, if you want to search for all Scooby Doo-related items except Pez dispensers, put a minus sign in front of the word "pez," like this: scooby -pez.

Trick #57: **Use Wildcards**

trapperjohn2000

stores.ebay.com/Molehill-Group-Store

Member since 1998, Feedback: Purple star

Like many other search engines, eBay lets you use the wildcard character (*) to indicate one or more unknown letters at the end of a search keyword. Wildcards are great for when you're not sure of a word's spelling; the wildcard character replaces the letters in question in your query. For example, if you're not sure whether it's Barbie or Barby, enter barb* and your results will include both spellings.

Wildcards are also good for finding all variations on a keyword; just truncate the main word and add the wildcard character. For example, if you want Superman, Supergirl, and Superdog, enter super* to find all "super" words.

This is also a good way to search for items produced in a given decade. Many sellers put the date of manufacture or release in the title, as in **1966 Aurora Model Kit**. If you want to search for all kits manufactured in the 1960s, just drop the last digit of the date and insert the wildcard character instead, like this: 196*. This will return all items listed from 1960 to 1969.

Trick #58: **Use the Singular, Not the Plural**

> **trapperjohn2000**
>
> stores.ebay.com/Molehill-Group-Store
>
> Member since 1998, Feedback: Purple star

eBay actually does a little bit of wildcard searching on its own. In particular, it automatically searches for the plural form of any word you enter—assuming you enter the singular, of course. So to search for both singular and multiple items, truncate the main word to the singular form. For example, if you search for bears, your results won't include any auctions for a single bear. Instead, search for bear, and you'll get both singles and multiples in your results.

Trick #59: **Spell Out the Numbers**

New Trick

> **abc-books**
>
> stores.ebay.com/ABC-Books-by-Ann
>
> www.abcbooksbyann.com
>
> PowerSeller
>
> Member since 1999, Feedback: Red star

When dealing with a number in an auction title, some sellers enter the numeral, others spell out the number. So you might find a particular DVD listed as either *12 Angry Men* or *Twelve Angry Men*. That's why, when you're searching, it pays to search for both the numeral and the word—just in case.

Searching for Bargains

Okay, now you've learned lots of different ways to fine-tune your search results. But how do you use these tools to hunt down the best bargains on the eBay site? Read on to learn some bargain-hunting tricks, all using the basic search function.

Trick #60: **Search for Misspellings**

berties_house_of_horrors

stores.ebay.com/Berties-Emporium

PowerSeller

Member since 1999, Feedback: Red star

This is one of the best tricks in the entire book, a surefire way to find bargains that others have overlooked. It's a simple method, really, that takes advantage of other users' mistakes.

You see, some eBay sellers aren't great spellers—or are just prone to typing errors. Either they don't know how to spell a particular word, or they hit the wrong key by mistake. In either case, the result is an auction title with a misspelled word—a Dell personal *commuter*, an Apple *ipud*, or clothing by Tommy *Hilfigger*.

The problem for these sellers—and the opportunity for you—is that when buyers search for an item (using the correct spelling), listings with misspellings don't appear in the search results. If potential bidders can't find the listings, they can't bid on them, leaving these misspelled listings with few if any bidders. If you can locate a misspelled listing, you can often snap up a real deal without competition from other bidders.

The key, of course, is figuring out how an item might be misspelled. Let's say you're looking for a bargain on a toaster. Instead of searching for *toaster*, you might search for *toster*, *toastter*, *toastor*, and *toester*. Give it a try—you'll be surprised what you find!

And here's a trick within a trick. You can include multiple misspellings in your search by using the "or" technique from Trick #55. In this example, you could enter the following query: (toaster,toaster,toastor,toester).

Even better, try the Fat Fingers website (www.fatfingers.com). Fat Fingers lets you enter a proper keyword, and then generates the common misspellings and uses them to conduct a more comprehensive eBay search. It's a neat little timesaver!

Trick #61: **Vary Your Vocabulary—and Your Spelling**

> **trapperjohn2000**
>
> stores.ebay.com/Molehill-Group-Store
>
> Member since 1998, Feedback: Purple star

Misspelling aside, don't assume that everyone spells a given word the same way—or uses the same terminology. (A soda is a pop is a "coke," depending on what part of the country you're from.) Also, don't forget about synonyms. What you call pink, someone else might call mauve or salmon. What's big to you might be large to someone else. Think of all the ways the item you're looking for can be described, and include as many of the words as possible in an "or" query. To use our soda pop example, you'd enter the following query: *(soda,pop,coke)*.

Trick #62: **"Birddog" Other Bidders**

> **lludwig**
>
> stores.ebay.com/LLudwig-Books
>
> PowerSeller
>
> Member since 1998, Feedback: Green star

The term "birddogging" refers to the act of following the auctions of another eBay bidder. Find a user that always gets great merchandise, then birddog his or her other auction activity. Chances are you'll find something you like, and then you can get in on the bidding, too. As eBay member **lludwig** says:

> *People who bid on one great item often have very good taste, and bid on others.*

To birddog another member, you first have to find him, which is as easy as looking at the high bidder in a particular auction. Once you have a member identified, it's time to do the actual birddogging, using eBay's search function. Go to the Search page and click the Items by Bidder link. When the Items by Bidder page appears (shown in Figure 3.8), enter the bidder's user ID and click the Search button. (For the most possible results, you should also select the Even if Not the High Bidder option.) The results page lists all the other auctions your subject is bidding on, which amounts to your own personal shopping list. Bid away!

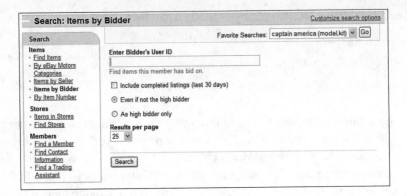

FIGURE 3.8
Use the Search by Bidder function to birddog other users.

Trick #63: **Search for Last-Minute Bargains**

trapperjohn2000

Member since 1998, Feedback: Purple star

When you search the eBay listings, be sure to display the results with auctions ending today listed first. Scan the list for soon-to-end items with no bids or few bids, and pick off some bargains that have slipped others' attention.

Trick #64: **Save Your Searches**

abc-books

stores.ebay.com/ABC-Books-by-Ann

www.abcbooksbyann.com

PowerSeller

Member since 1999, Feedback: Red star

On the topic of repeating your searches, here's a trick that lets you save your favorite searches and repeat them with a click of the mouse.

eBay actually makes it quite easy to save even the most complex search queries, if you know what to click. All search results pages include an Add to Favorites link at the top right of the page. Click this link, and you'll see an Add to My Favorite Searches page. Check the Create a New Search option, give the search a name, and click the Save Search button. This search is now saved and listed on the All Favorites page of My eBay.

To repeat this search, go to My eBay and click through to the All Favorites page, as shown in Figure 3.9. Your favorite searches are listed there; just click a search to execute the search.

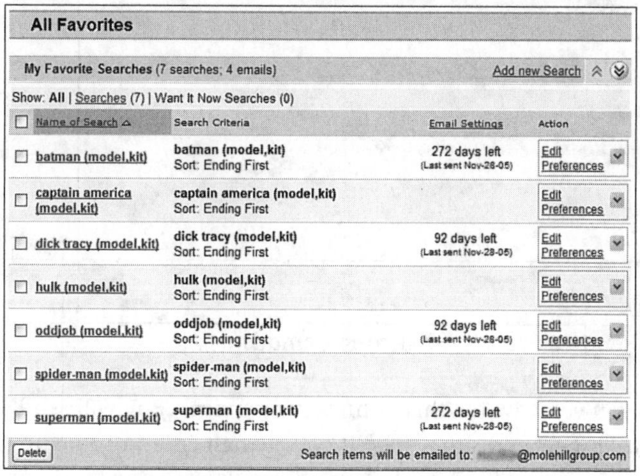

FIGURE 3.9

Repeat any saved search from the All Favorites page of My eBay.

Trick #65: **Get Notification of New Items That Match Your Search**

> **abc-books**
>
> stores.ebay.com/ABC-Books-by-Ann
>
> www.abcbooksbyann.com
>
> PowerSeller
>
> Member since 1999, Feedback: Red star

Here's an even better way to find out about new items that you're interested in. eBay can automatically notify you when new items that match your saved search come up for auction.

There are two ways to turn on email search notification. First, when you save your search, as described in Trick #64, you can click the **Email me daily** option. Second, you can navigate to the All Favorites page in My eBay and click the Edit Preferences link next to the search you want to be notified of. When the Edit

Favorite Search Preferences page appears, as shown in Figure 3.10, select the **Email Me Daily...** option, then pull down the list and select a duration. (Your options are for the notification service to last anywhere from 7 days to 12 months.)

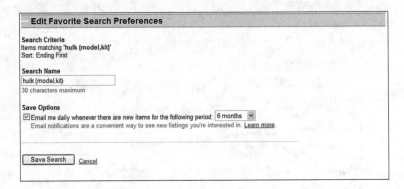

FIGURE 3.10

Configuring eBay to send you search notification emails.

When you've activated this notification service, eBay will send you an email (one a day) when new items that match your search criteria come up for auction. The email contains links for each new item in your search (see Figure 3.11); click a link to open your web browser and display the matching item .

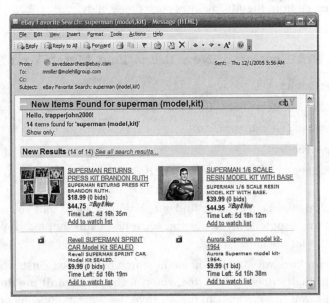

FIGURE 3.11

eBay sends you a daily email listing new items that match your search criteria.

Trick #66: **Expand Your Search to eBay Stores**

> **abc-books**
>
> stores.ebay.com/ABC-Books-by-Ann
>
> www.abcbooksbyann.com
>
> PowerSeller
>
> Member since 1999, Feedback: Red star

If you can't find an item for auction on eBay proper, you can opt to search items listed for sale in eBay Stores. You can sometimes find items for sale in eBay Stores that you can't find in eBay's normal auctions. All you have to do is go to the Search page and click the Items in Stores link, then conduct your search from there.

You can also expand a normal search to include eBay Stores items. Just scroll to the bottom of any search results page until you see the box labeled Get More Results in Other eBay Areas (shown in Figure 3.12). Click the See Additional Buy It Now Items link and you'll see a list of matching items from eBay Stores sellers .

> **Get more results in other eBay areas**
>
> ▪ See additional Buy It Now items from eBay Store sellers. Learn more.
> ▪ See all items including those available from non-English speaking countries/regions.

FIGURE 3.12

Expand your search to eBay Store sellers.

Trick #67: **Search for Items with Want It Now**

New Trick

> **selling4-u**
>
> stores.ebay.com/Selling-4-U-Consignment-Store
>
> www.selling4-u.com
>
> PowerSeller
>
> Member since 2002, Feedback: Purple star

If you can't find what you're looking for anywhere on eBay, now there's a way to put your requests in front of compatible sellers. eBay's Want It Now feature lets you create a "wish list" of items you want to buy, even if they're not currently listed on eBay. Sellers will see your request and notify you if they have similar items for sale. You can then make a purchase, if you want.

To use Want It Now, click the Want It Now link on the eBay home page. This takes you to the main Want It Now page, as shown in Figure 3.13. Click the Post to Want

It Now button, and you see the Want It Now: Create a Post page, shown in Figure 3.14. Enter a description of the item you're looking for, then click the Post to Want It Now button. Then sit back and wait for interested sellers to contact you!

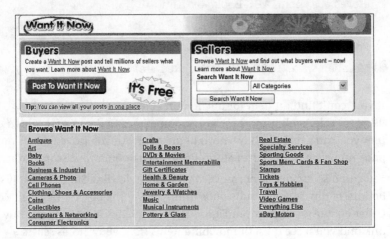

FIGURE 3.13
eBay's Want It Now page.

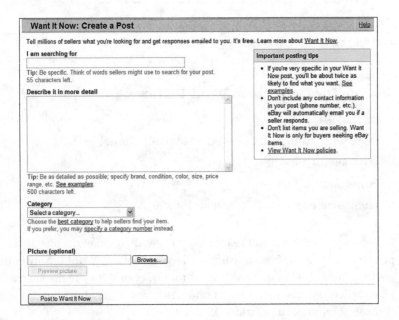

FIGURE 3.14
Entering your Want It Now request.

4

How to Be a Smarter–and Safer–Buyer

Any user can bid on an eBay auction, but only smart bidders get the best deals and avoid getting ripped off. There's no avoiding the simple fact that the smarter you are, the safer you'll be—and the better deals you'll get.

Wisdom comes from experience. But if you don't want to wait that long, get wise fast with these smart-bidding tricks from the eBay Masters.

Before You Bid

Smart bidders don't act impulsively. They take a little time to make sure they're well-informed before they bid and to make sure that they bid intelligently.

Trick #68: **Consult eBay's Reviews and Guides**

New Trick

trapperjohn2000

stores.ebay.com/Molehill-Group-Store

Member since 1998, Feedback: Purple star

eBay has recently added two new features that help eBay members share their collective expertise. eBay Reviews are product reviews written by other eBay members; Guides are more detailed how-tos that help you buy particular types of items or complete specific tasks. For example, you can find product reviews for CDs, home audio receivers, golf clubs, and so on. Guides are available for a number of different topics, and include both buying guides (Skis & Skiing Equipment Buying Guide, NASCAR Diecast Cars Buying Guide) and more informational guides (How to Identify a Powerbook G3, How to Plan the Perfect Vacation). You can find eBay's Reviews and Guides at reviews.ebay.com (shown in Figure 4.1).

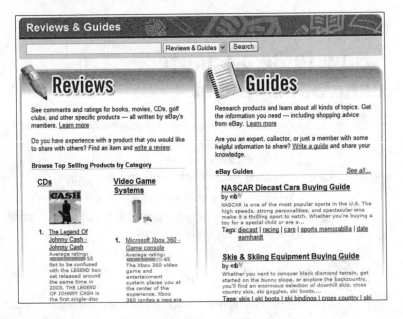

FIGURE 4.1

The main page for eBay's Reviews & Guides.

Not sure whether a particular CD is to your tastes? Then read the reviews (like the one in Figure 4.2). Don't know which PC games to buy? Then look for a Guide on buying PC games (like the one in Figure 4.3). Your fellow eBay members are not short of opinions; use those opinions (and their experience) to your advantage.

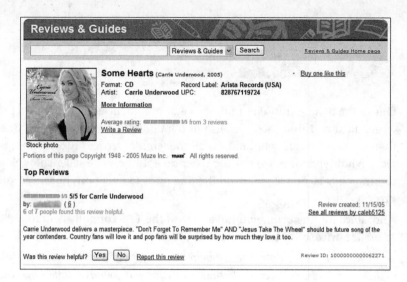

FIGURE 4.2
A typical eBay user review of a popular CD.

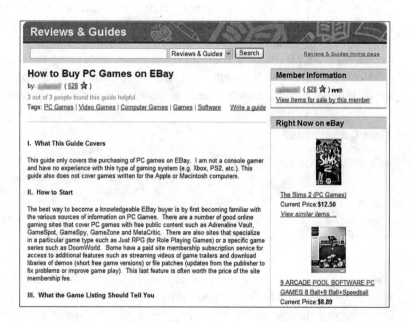

FIGURE 4.3
One of eBay's many Guides—this one on buying PC games.

Trick #69: **Read the Fine Print**

> ***samby***
> Member since 2001, Feedback: Turquoise star

One of the biggest mistakes that novice or impatient users make is to not read the entire auction listing. Good sellers put a lot of information into the "fine print" of their auction listings, what many call the *terms of service* (TOS). Here is where you'll learn what types of payments the seller accepts, how the seller ships, what their return policy is, and so on. Read the fine print to avoid any surprises later in the process.

And, since it's fine print, you have to read the TOS carefully. You might even want to read it twice. eBay member ***samby*** has this recommendation:

> *Have you read the entire description? Reading it out aloud to yourself sometimes helps you to be sure you understand everything. It sounds a little silly, but it does help, and I do it often. Small details can be easily missed by even the most experienced eBayer.*

Ignorance of a seller's TOS is no excuse. When you've placed a bid, you've entered in a contract to purchase that item, according to the terms set forth by the seller. Pay particular attention to the types of payment accepted; not all sellers accept PayPal, for example. (Beyond that, some sellers who accept PayPal won't accept payments from users with unconfirmed addresses.) It's your fault if you try to do something that the seller doesn't allow as stated in the TOS for that listing.

Trick #70: **Ask Questions**

> ***samby***
> Member since 2001, Feedback: Turquoise star

What do you do if something isn't explained in the seller's TOS or if you don't understand a particular point?

Simple. You ask the seller a question!

There's no reason *not* to ask questions of a seller. It's easy to do; just click the Ask Seller a Question link in the auction listing. (See Figure 4.4.) When the Ask Seller a Question page appears, as shown in Figure 4.5, select a type of question from the pull-down list, then enter your question in the text box. Click the Send button, and eBay forwards your question directly to the seller.

FIGURE 4.4

Click the link in the Seller Information section to ask the seller a question.

FIGURE 4.5

Use the form to ask the seller a question via email.

What types of question are common? Here are a few that ***samby*** notes:

What is shipping to my Zip? What does "fair" condition actually mean here? Are there any rips, tears, holes, cracks, chips?

As ***samby*** also recommends, don't place your bid until you get a satisfactory reply. And if you don't get a reply, don't bid!

Trick #71: **Find Out Shipping/Handling Costs Before You Bid**

peaches1442

stores.ebay.com/Peaches-Cards-and-Gifts-Shoppe

Member since 2002, Feedback: Red star

Another mistake that inexperienced buyers make is to not factor in the shipping and handling charges for items they win. As the winning bidder, you're responsible for not just the cost of the item (your high bid), but also the item's shipping and handling costs. As more experienced users know, these costs can add up—fast.

It's important to know what you'll pay for shipping and handling before you place your bid. Many sellers display a shipping/handling charge in their item listing; others use eBay's Shipping Calculator to help you figure out precise shipping to your location. If a seller doesn't list shipping/handling, email the seller to find out what the shipping/handling fees are before you bid.

As eBay member **peaches1442** advises:

> Always ask how much shipping is before *bidding*. Never *assume anything!*

Trick #72: **Beware Exorbitant Shipping/Handling Charges**

hortonsbks

stores.ebay.com/Hortonsbks

PowerSeller

Member since 2000, Feedback: Red star

You can't just assume that a seller is going to pass on his actual shipping costs. Many sellers add a reasonable handling fee to cover their costs of materials—boxes, peanuts, bubble wrap, and so forth. The key word here is "reasonable," and you want to watch out for those sellers that aren't. It's one thing to pay a $5.00 shipping/handling fee for something that has an actual shipping cost of $4.00; that extra buck is a reasonable overage for the seller's handling costs. It's quite another thing to pay $10.00 for $4.00 of shipping, however; that's just a rip-off.

Some less-than-scrupulous sellers use the handling fee as a profit center. You sometimes find this with ultra-low 99-cent auctions. How can a seller afford to sell an item for less than a buck? Simple—they make their profit on the handling fee. I'm not saying this is always the case, but it's definitely something to watch out for.

Bid Smart

Simply reading an auction's fine print won't make you a smarter bidder. To truly bid smart, you have to know how much to bid—so you can avoid overpaying for an item.

Trick #73: **Don't Bid on the First Item You See**

> **trapperjohn2000**
>
> stores.ebay.com/Molehill-Group-Store
>
> Member since 1998, Feedback: Purple star

Newbie bidders tend to get real excited when they first find an item they want to buy. They find the item and want to place their bid *now*. Of course, unless the auction is in its final minutes, there's no pressing need to bid at this exact moment. Better to take your time and keep looking for similar items. There's a good chance that there are several other items on eBay that are similar—if not identical—to the first item you found. Look at the entire list of items before you choose which one to bid on. Seldom is the first item you see the one you really want or the best deal.

And don't assume that you have to bid today to get that "one of a kind" item. In most auctions, that "one of a kind" item really isn't one of a kind. Some sellers will have multiple quantities of an item, which they release to auction in dribs and drabs over time. In addition, some collectibles are bought and sold and bought and sold by multiple buyers and sellers over time, continually changing hands via new auctions. If you don't get this particular item, there's a good chance you'll get to bid on something similar soon.

Trick #74: **Research the Item's Real Value**

> ***samby***
>
> Member since 2001, Feedback: Turquoise star

To avoid paying too much for an item, you need to know what the item is really worth—before you place your bid. There are several ways to research the value of an item. You can search for auctions of similar items; what prices are they going for? And don't neglect researching outside of eBay; sometimes, you can find what you're looking for at a discount store or in a catalog or at another online site.

eBay member ***samby*** has some additional recommendations:

> *What do past eBay bidders think it's worth? Search for the item and then click on the Completed Items link on the search results page. You'll see what like items have sold for in the past 15 days on eBay. That's the price that is probably going to be most relevant to you.*

Do your research, and don't assume that the price you see at an auction is always the best deal available.

Trick #75: **Check the Seller's Current—and Past—Auctions**

> **berties_house_of_horrors**
>
> stores.ebay.com/Berties-Emporium
>
> PowerSeller
>
> Member since 1999, Feedback: Red star

Here's a neat trick. Sometimes a seller is selling more than one of any given item. Just because the price is bid up on one item, the seller might have additional copies for auction with a lower current bid. Click the View Seller's Other Items link in the Seller Information section of the item listing page to see if other similar items are available.

And don't limit your search to a seller's current auctions. Search the seller's *completed* items to see if he's sold similar items in the recent past. If so, there's no need to get into a bidding war today if the same item is likely to come up for auction again next week.

Trick #76: **Check Out Buy It Now Items**

> **terrisbooks**
>
> stores.ebay.com/Terris-Books
>
> www.terrisbeads.com
>
> PowerSeller
>
> Member since 2002, Feedback: Red star

Along similar lines, look for auctions with Buy It Now options. You can often use Buy It Now to purchase an item *before* it gets bid up by other users.

And, besides, when you use Buy It Now, you get your item faster than if you have to wait until the auction is completed!

Managing Your Bids

You've found something you want to buy, done your homework, and figured out just how much you want to pay. What comes next?

Trick #77: **Watch, Don't Bid**

losboyi

Member since 2000

It's important that you realize that you don't have to place your bid immediately. In fact, as you'll learn in Chapter 5, "How to Win More Auctions," there are definite benefits to *not* bidding early in the auction process. If you decide to hold off on bidding for the time being, how do you remember which auctions you're interested in?

eBay makes it easy to watch the progress of individual auctions without first placing a bid. All you have to do is click the Add to Watch List link in the top right corner of the item listing, and eBay adds this item to your own personal watch list. Then you view the auctions you're watching from the All Buying page of My eBay, shown in Figure 4.6. Keep a daily watch on your auctions, and place your bids when you want. (The later the better, as you'll soon learn.)

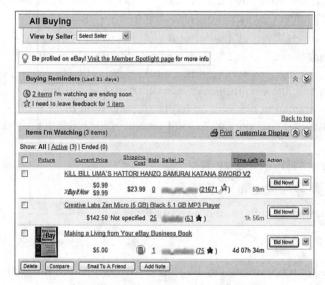

FIGURE 4.6

View auction progress—without bidding—from the Items I'm Watching section of the My eBay page.

Trick #78: **Use My eBay to Track Your Bids**

trapperjohn2000

stores.ebay.com/Molehill-Group-Store

Member since 1998, Feedback: Purple star

You can also use My eBay to track *all* your auction activity, including those auctions in which you've already placed a bid. Again, it's the All Buying page you want; the auctions you're participating in will show up in the Items I'm Bidding On section.

Trick #79: **Don't Let the Proxy Bid Things Up**

trapperjohn2000

stores.ebay.com/Molehill-Group-Store

Member since 1998, Feedback: Purple star

Smart bidding means not letting the bid price get out of hand, which can sometimes happen when you use eBay's proxy bidding system. If two or more people are bidding on the same item, eBay's proxy bidding software can automatically (and quickly) rocket up the price until the bidder with the lower maximum bid maxes out. It's kind of an automated bidding frenzy conducted by two mindless robots.

All of which is yet another good reason not to participate in early-process proxy bidding. (See Chapter 5 for late-process bidding advice.) If you insist on bidding early, you can get more control over the process by *not* bidding your maximum amount right away. Instead, make sure your bid amount is the same price as the next incremental bid, and no higher. It takes a bit more work, but this manual bidding method does put you in total control of the bidding process.

Trick #80: **Know When to Say No**

trapperjohn2000

stores.ebay.com/Molehill-Group-Store

Member since 1998, Feedback: Purple star

However you choose to bid, it's important to set your limits and stick to them. If you do your homework and decide that an item is worth a certain price, don't let your bidding go over that amount. If the bidding goes higher, just drop out. It's okay to lose an auction; in fact, it's preferable to lose than to overpay.

Let's face it; it's much too easy to get caught up in the excitement of a fast-paced auction and find yourself in the middle of a bidding war. Learn how to keep your cool; know when to say no.

After the Auction

Your obligations as a buyer don't stop when you win the auction. Naturally, you have to pay the seller, but there are also a few tricks to keep in mind to make sure that the end of the transaction goes as smoothly as possible.

Trick #81: **If You Haven't Heard from the Seller, Make Contact Yourself**

samby

Member since 2001, Feedback: Turquoise star

You'd think that all sellers would be really interested in contacting you to arrange payment. Unfortunately, not all sellers are diligent about their end-of-auction communications. (This includes some really big sellers who sometimes get overwhelmed with all the transactions they have to manage.)

Give the seller a fair amount of time to contact you—24 hours, let's say—and then, if you still haven't received a message, take the reigns yourself and send your own email to the seller, using either the Contact Seller or Ask Seller a Question links on the closed listing page. Identify yourself, ask for a total price (including shipping/ handling), and tell them how you intend to pay. You should receive a quick response.

Trick #82: **Pay Now with a Single Click**

trapperjohn2000

stores.ebay.com/Molehill-Group-Store

Member since 1998, Feedback: Purple star

These days many buyers and sellers bypass the traditional end-of-auction emails by using eBay's checkout service. If the seller has specified a flat shipping/handling charge, or incorporated eBay's Shipping Calculator, a Pay Now button will appear on the closed item listing page after the auction ends and in eBay's end-of-auction email notification, as shown in Figure 4.7. Click this button to initiate the checkout process, and its just like buying from an honest-to-goodness online store—especially if you use PayPal to pay via credit card. Your payment information is automatically sent to the seller, no additional email communication necessary.

FIGURE 4.7

One-button checkout, from eBay's end-of-auction email.

Trick #83: **Ask If the Seller Will Insure the Item**

mrsdocy2k1

Member since 2000, Feedback: Red star

If you're buying a rare or fragile item, you may want to insure the item during shipping. Many sellers offer the insurance option upfront, but even those sellers who don't explicitly offer insurance are often willing to insure if you ask. It's best if you do your asking before you bid, of course, but if you're willing to pay for it, most sellers will handle it for you.

Trick #84: **Include the Item Number When You Pay**

regans*closet

stores.ebay.com/Regans-Closet

Member since 2001, Feedback: Red star

Okay, this is a big one. As a seller, I can't tell you how many times I've received a check or money order in the mail as an auction payment but with no other information in the envelope—no name, no address, no mention of the auction item or number, nothing! It's difficult for even small sellers to link anonymous payments with auction items; for heavy sellers, the task can be virtually impossible. Think of it this way—you wouldn't just send a check to L.L. Bean without including your personal information. The same goes for auction payments; you definitely want the seller to know who you are!

One of the easiest ways to do this is to simply print out the closed item listing page. Write your name and address at the top, and the seller will have all the information she needs to make sure you get what you paid for.

Trick #85: **Be a Considerate Buyer**

> **gothgirlscloset**
>
> PowerSeller
>
> Member since 1999, Feedback: Red star

Just as you like to deal with polite, efficient sellers, sellers like to deal with considerate customers. It's in both your best interests to make the transaction go as smoothly as possible, with a minimum of fuss and muss on both your parts.

To that end, eBay PowerSeller **gothgirlscloset** has put together a list of things you can do to be a considerate buyer. These items include:

- **Don't pester the seller.** Most sellers actually work for a living (outside of their eBay auctions) and can only handle so much bother. Don't email the seller four times a day asking where your package is, especially if you were already given a delivery confirmation number. Remember, you're not their only customer—so even if they're doing their best to please everyone, you may not get your emails answered right away.

- **Don't try to change the terms after you've won.** This goes back to Trick #69, about reading all the fine print before you bid. It isn't fair to the seller to ask her to change things after the fact.

- **Don't expect a refund just because you don't like what you get.** Most sellers are individuals, not merchants, and can't be expected to offer iron-clad money-back guarantees like the kind you get at Sears or Macys. When you bid on an item, you assume some responsibility for adhering to your purchase.

- **Don't demand special shipping.** Most sellers have a preferred method of shipping that works best for them; anything outside of this method can dramatically interfere with the seller's established routine. Most sellers state their shipping method upfront in the auction listing. Know this before you bid, and accept it if you win.

- **Don't expect same-day shipping.** Again, you're dealing with an individual, not with L.L. Bean. Many sellers simply don't go to the post office 24/7, instead grouping their items to ship on specific days of the week. Give the poor seller a break, and give them time to pack your item and take it to the post office—on their schedule.

A few more things. If you paid by personal check, remember that your item will more than likely be held for at least 10 days while your check clears. And take into account the vagaries of particular shipping methods; in particular, know that media mail can take up to two weeks to arrive. Don't pester the seller about these types of things; wait a reasonable amount of time before you start firing off the emails!

Trick #86: **Inspect It When You Receive It**

> **trapperjohn2000**
>
> stores.ebay.com/Molehill-Group-Store
>
> Member since 1998, Feedback: Purple star

When you receive the item you paid for, open it up and inspect it—*immediately!* Don't wait a month before you look at it and then expect the seller to rectify a situation that was long considered closed. Okay the item, and then send the seller an email saying you got it and it's okay. (Leaving positive feedback is another way to indicate to the seller that you're happy with your purchase.) If you sit on an item too long, it's yours—no matter what might be wrong with it.

How to Shop for Cars

All of the tricks so far in this chapter apply to any type of product you might be bidding on. But there's one category of product that carries some unique risks—and some big tickets. Read on to learn some tricks for getting your money's worth when bidding on automobiles via eBay Motors.

Trick #87: **Question the Buyer First**

> **mainedog70**
>
> PowerSeller
>
> Member since 2001, Feedback: Turquoise star

More so than any other category, it's important to know that you're dealing with a reputable seller before you bid on an expensive vehicle. One good way to do this is to contact the bidder before bidding, either via email or the phone. (User **mainedog70** recommends phone contact for these types of big-ticket items.) Ask questions about the vehicle for sale and about the business they run; see what their procedures are. Try to come to some sort of opinion about their professionalism and honesty—as best as you can, under the circumstances.

Trick #88: **Have the Vehicle Inspected Before You Bid**

> **rapparts**
>
> Member since 1999, Feedback: Red star

Buying a car via eBay Motors doesn't relieve you of the same responsibilities you'd have if you bought the vehicle from a traditional car dealer. It's your responsibility to make sure the car is in good working condition—before you buy, not afterward.

As eBay member **rapparts** states:

> *Would you go to a used car lot, pay for a car, and* then *ask questions/test drive it/have a mechanic check it out? Of course not.*

Before you place a bid on a vehicle, do your homework. At the very least, order the car's vehicle history report. And for even more peace of mind, schedule a vehicle inspection. Obviously, you can't do the inspection yourself, but you can arrange for a professional to do the inspection for you.

While "buyer beware" is the operative motto when buying anything online, at least eBay provides some assistance to help you check out a vehicle before you make a bid. To order a vehicle history report, all you have to do is click the VIN number in the Item Specifics section at the top of the listing page. Each report you order costs $7.99. The service is provided by AutoCheck.

To set up a vehicle inspection, go back to the main eBay Motors page (motors.ebay.com) and click the Buyer Services & Protection tab. From here, go to the Bidding & Buying Services section and click the Vehicle Inspection link. This takes you to a page where you can order an inspection from SGS Automotive, for $99.50.

If you're satisfied with the way the history report and inspection check out, then go ahead and place your bid. Better to spend a little money upfront—especially when you're potentially making such a big purchase sight unseen.

Trick #89: **Factor In Vehicle Transport**

> **mainedog70**
>
> PowerSeller
>
> Member since 2001, Feedback: Turquoise star

Chances are the car you want to buy isn't located just down the street. That means you'll have to arrange to have the vehicle shipped from the seller's location to your driveway, and vehicle transportation isn't a small cost. eBay offers vehicle shipping via Dependable Auto Shippers (the link is in the Shipping section of the item information at the top of the item listing page), or you can call toll-free 866.327.3229. Get a shipping quote before you bid, and factor the cost into your total budget.

How to Protect Yourself from Fraud

One of the biggest fears of newbie users is getting ripped off in an auction transaction. Well, it can happen (remember, your transaction is with an individual, not with eBay), but there are things you can do to minimize the risk. Read on to learn some tricks that the eBay Masters use to ensure safer auction transactions.

Trick #90: **Check the Seller's Feedback**

> **2ndhand4u**
>
> Member since 1998, Feedback: Red star

This trick is so important I devoted an entire chapter to it (see Chapter 2, "How to Deal with Feedback"). I won't repeat all the specific advice here, but suffice it to say that a high feedback score, combined with a high feedback percentage (over 90%) and positive feedback comments, should make you feel comfortable dealing with a particular seller. On the other hand, a seller with a low feedback score, a low feedback percentage, and multiple negative comments is probably someone you don't want to deal with.

Bottom line is that eBay's feedback system is your first and best defense against disreputable sellers. Here's how member **2ndhand4u** uses seller feedback:

I seldom buy from anyone with fewer than 25 transactions, as their track record or history of how they do business on eBay is insufficient. If someone has 5 or more negatives or a like amount of neutrals, it would not be prudent to buy from this person. Reputable sellers take pride in the kind of feedback they receive. Anyone with even a 90% rating may be questionable.

If, after reading a seller's feedback ratings and comments, you feel unsure about buying from that seller, then don't. There are many, many sellers out there, and you can probably find a similar item for sale from a seller with a better feedback rating.

Trick #91: **If the Deal Seems Too Good to Be True, It Probably Is**

mainedog70

PowerSeller

Member since 2001, Feedback: Turquoise star

Trust your nose. If something doesn't smell right, there's probably a reason. If a deal seems too good to be true, it probably is. Not that you can't find some terrific deals on eBay, but you have to be real about it. As user **mainedog70** relates:

I bought a $30,000 truck for $24,000. But to expect the same truck to sell for $15,000 is unrealistic and not very smart. There are a few scammers out there and they prey on believing souls who want the world for nothing.

Let your instincts be your guide—and don't be afraid to step away from any auction that feels wrong to you in any way.

Trick #92: **Beware Fraudulent Auctions from Hijacked Accounts**

trapperjohn2000

stores.ebay.com/Molehill-Group-Store

Member since 1998, Feedback: Purple star

Here's something nasty to watch out for—hijacked eBay accounts. This happens when a hacker somehow gains access to a legitimate member's user ID and password, and then takes over that member's identity to launch a series of fraudulent auctions. Everything looks good about the user—because the hijacker is hiding behind the original user's actual feedback—but the auction is a complete sham. When you send away your payment, that's the last you hear of it.

Obviously, eBay does its best to shut down these fraudulent auctions and hijacked accounts. But how can you identify a fraudulent/hijacked auction before you place a bid?

Here are some telltale signs of a fraudulent auction from a hijacked account:

- The auction is for a very high-priced item, but the starting price or Buy It Now price is considerably below typical retail price.
- Payment doesn't include PayPal or credit cards, instead insisting on money order, cashiers check, or Western Union cash transfer (more on this in Trick #94).
- The seller's feedback is primarily for buying items, not for selling.
- The seller hasn't completed any transactions for several months. (Inactive accounts are more likely to be hijacked.)
- While the seller's account is listed in the United States, if you contact the seller you'll find out he's actually in another country. (Eastern Europe is a popular haven for scammers.)

Remember, even if the address and contact info look legit (because they're from the original user), they'll be false. When it comes to sending payment, you'll be instructed to mail it to somewhere else—typically in another country.

To further confuse the issue, many of these scammers will send you a follow-up email that claims to be from eBay, vouching for the seller's veracity, or even offering additional insurance to cover the seller's buyers. Since eBay doesn't endorse individual sellers or sell such insurance, you'll know this is a scam.

Bottom line: If you think there's something fishy about a particular auction, don't bid! And if you *know* something is fishy, report it to eBay.

Trick #93: **Don't Send Cash in the Mail**

trapperjohn2000
stores.ebay.com/Molehill-Group-Store
Member since 1998, Feedback: Purple star

This one appears to fall in the blatantly obvious file, but you never know. There's nothing riskier than sending cash in the mail. Not only is it easily stolen, it's not traceable. If the seller says he never received your cash, it's your word against his— and his word probably wins.

Trick #94: **Don't Pay via a Cash Wire Transfer Service—Including Western Union**

trapperjohn2000

stores.ebay.com/Molehill-Group-Store

Member since 1998, Feedback: Purple star

If you find a seller that demands payment through Western Union or a similar cash wire transfer service (MoneyGram, eGold, and so on), run away as fast as you can. These services are designed to let you send money to family and friends—people you trust. They're *not* to be used to pay for auction items.

(Note that this warning applies to Western Union cash transfers, not to Western Union Auction Payments—now known as BidPay—which operates much like PayPal and is perfectly legit.)

Scammers like to receive payment through Western Union and similar cash transfer services, because it's essentially the same as wiring them cash, no questions asked. Cash wire transfers are particularly vulnerable to criminal abuse because they're not traceable, don't offer any verification procedures, and make it difficult to identify the recipient. In other words, these services offer virtually no protection against fraud—which makes them the payment method of choice for fraudulent sellers, especially those in certain European nations.

Even Western Union warns against abuse of their cash transfer service:

> … we don't recommend that you use a money transfer service to pay for online auction purchases. Money transfer services are fast, easy and convenient ways to send funds to people you know. They are not designed to be a payment vehicle when doing business with a stranger.

So if a seller only accepts payment by Western Union money transfer, chances are you're looking at a real honest-to-goodness scam. And if you get taken in this fashion—if you send cash to a stranger who cuts and runs—eBay won't be able to help you much, outside of their normal $200 Buyer Protection Program guarantee.

In short, when you see Western Union cash transfer in the payments accepted of an auction listing, don't bid—and report the auction to eBay.

Trick #95: **Pay via Credit Card—Using Paypal**

morning_lark

Member since 2001, Feedback: Turquoise star

The safest way to pay for an auction item is with your credit card. When you pay by credit card, you're protected by the Fair Credit Billing Act, which gives you the right to dispute certain charges and limits your liability for unauthorized transactions to $50. That's right; if anything goes south, just contact your credit card company and they'll absorb all but $50 of the cost. That's a safety net you don't have with any other payment method.

In addition, if you use your credit card to pay via PayPal, you have the additional coverage of PayPal's Buyer Protection Plan or (if the individual auction isn't covered under the Buyer Protection Plan) the Buyer Complaint Process. This one isn't a lock, because PayPal investigates each claim individually, but if they agree that you've been taken, you may be eligible for a full refund. Go to the PayPal site (www. paypal.com) for more details or to file a claim. My recommendation is to file with PayPal first (since you could receive a 100% refund), then if that doesn't work file with your credit card company.

Trick #96: **Use an Escrow Service for Higher-Priced Items**

trapperjohn2000

stores.ebay.com/Molehill-Group-Store

Member since 1998, Feedback: Purple star

There's another payment option you might want to use if you're buying at a particularly high-priced auction. An escrow service acts as a neutral third party between you and the seller, holding your money until you receive the seller's merchandise. If you don't get the goods (or the goods are unacceptable), you get your money back; the seller gets paid only when you're happy.

When you and the seller agree to use an escrow service, you send your payment (by check, money order, cashier's check, or credit card) to the escrow service, not to the seller. After your payment is approved, the escrow service instructs the seller to ship the item. When you receive the item, you notify the escrow service that you're satisfied with the transaction. At that point, the escrow service pays the seller.

The cost of using an escrow service is typically paid by the buyer. eBay recommends the use of Escrow.com (www.escrow.com), as there have been some fraud problems with lesser-known escrow sites.

What to Do If You Get Ripped Off

Even the most cautious buyers can have a bad auction. If you ever find yourself on the fuzzy end of the lollypop, here are some tricks to help you recover some of your money.

Trick #97: **Submit a Claim to eBay's Buyer Protection Program**

samby

Member since 2001, Feedback: Turquoise star

eBay's Buyer Protection Program is designed to help you recover some of your money if you're the victim of a fraudulent auction. Assuming you meet the criteria, you're insured for up to $200 (with a $25 deductible) for items with a final value over $25. (If you paid less than $25, you're out of luck.) You'll be reimbursed only for the final bid price, not for any other fees such as shipping, handling, or escrow fees. And you can only file a maximum of three claims in any six-month period.

You submit your claim as part of eBay's Item Not Received or Significantly Not As Described Process. (That's a mouthful!) You can learn more about the process at pages.ebay.com/help/tp/inr-snad-process.html, but in general it works like this.

If you don't receive an item you paid for, even after contacting the seller directly, go to your My eBay page and click the Security & Resolution Center link at the bottom left. When the Security & Resolution Center page appears, check the Item Not Received option, click the Report Problem button, and follow the onscreen instructions from there.

eBay will now contact the seller, encouraging him to resolve the problem. If the seller still doesn't ship the item, return to the Dispute Console and complete the process to file a claim under eBay's Standard Purchase Protection.

You can initiate this process up to 60 days after the end of an auction. You have to wait a minimum of 10 days before you can file a complaint.

And, of course, when submitting your claim, it pays to be civil. eBay member ***samby*** recommends the following:

> Make it concise, short, and factual. Your web form complaint will stand a much better chance if written in concise, economical language. Avoid emotional, inflammatory, and accusatory language. It won't help your case and will more likely muddy your argument. Just stick to the facts.

With any luck, you'll get some of your money back.

Trick #98: **Use a Mediation Service to Resolve Conflicts**

trapperjohn2000

stores.ebay.com/Molehill-Group-Store

Member since 1998, Feedback: Purple star

Sometimes who's right and who's wrong isn't so clear-cut. You may think you've been wronged, but the seller might disagree. In this sort of situation, a good recourse is to engage SquareTrade (www.squaretrade.com), an online dispute resolution service.

SquareTrade settles these types of disputes through a two-part process. You start out with what SquareTrade calls Online Dispute Resolution; this free service uses an automated negotiation tool to try to get you and the seller to neutral ground. The process helps to cool down both parties and let you work out a solution between the two of you.

If the two of you can't work it out in this manner, you have the option of engaging a SquareTrade mediator to examine the case and come to an impartial decision. This will cost you $20, and both parties agree to abide with the results. If the SquareTrade mediator says you're owed a refund, the seller has to pay you. If the representative says there's no basis for your claim, it ends there.

Trick #99: **Report Fraud to the Authorities**

trapperjohn2000

stores.ebay.com/Molehill-Group-Store

Member since 1998, Feedback: Purple star

If mail fraud is involved in a bad auction (which it is if any part of the transaction—either payment or shipping—was handled through the mail), you can file a complaint with your local U.S. Post Office or state attorney general's office. If you've had a large amount of money ripped off or if your credit card number was stolen, you should also contact your local police department.

You can also register a complaint with the National Fraud Information Center (www.fraud.org), which is a project of the National Consumers League. This site will transmit the information you provide to the appropriate law enforcement agencies.

Finally, you can file a complaint about any fraudulent auction transaction with the Federal Trade Commission (FTC). Although the FTC doesn't resolve individual consumer problems, it can and will act if it sees a pattern of possible law violations. You can contact the FTC online (www.ftc.gov) or via phone (877-FTC-HELP).

How to Win More Auctions

When you find something you want to buy on eBay, you really want to buy it—you don't want the disappointment that comes from losing an auction. To increase your odds of winning those important auctions (without overpaying, of course), it helps to know the tricks that the eBay Masters use, which is what this chapter is all about. Read on to learn the secrets of successful bidding!

Win with Proxy Bidding

There are two primary methods of bidding you can employ in an auction: eBay's standard proxy bidding and time-conscious proxy bidding—more commonly known as *sniping*. We'll talk about sniping later in this chapter, but let's start out with the standard method of bidding and why many eBay Masters prefer it over a last-second snipe.

Trick #100: **Bid Now, Not Later**

terrisbooks

stores.ebay.com/Terris-Books

www.terrisbeads.com

PowerSeller

Member since 2002, Feedback: Red star

Many users prefer to place their bids as early as possible in the auction process. There's no reason not to bid early, as eBay's automatic proxy bidding system keeps raising your bid to fend off any subsequent bids by other users. As long as you bid the maximum amount you want to pay, you won't get beat until somebody bids a higher amount.

There are several advantages to bidding early. By placing a preemptive bid, you stake your claim and let other potential bidders know that you're serious about buying the item in question. In addition, in the case of a tie bid, the early bidder wins, which gives you a distinct advantage over late-auction snipers. In essence, the earlier you bid, the better your position.

In addition, when you bid early, you get it out of the way. There's no chance of you forgetting to bid, or of your bid being interrupted by any eBay system problems. eBay member **terrisbooks** relates some very real problems that can occur if you *don't* get your bid in early:

> Buyers have emailed me that they intended to bid on my item, to "snipe" as it's called, at the last minute, but forgot. They are so sad when they miss out on a rare, one-of-a-kind piece. Invariably something will happen and they won't be at their computer the hour a piece of my jewelry is selling and they'll lose the auction. I just wish they had bid early, entering the highest bid they were willing to pay from the outset.

Trick #101: **Bid High—Don't Nibble**

james900rr

Member since 2002, Feedback: Blue star

When you place your bid, don't weasel around. Make your bid the maximum amount the item is worth to you, and be done with it. Remember, the high bid always wins, no matter when its placed. You can't get outbid by a sniper if you bid more than he does.

Some users try to get by on the cheap, by placing one low-ball bid after another, incrementally raising the bid price on an item. This is called "nibbling," and it doesn't do you much good in the end. A nibbler will always be beat by a bidder willing to bid what an item is really worth. Snipers win a lot of auctions from nibblers, because they bid so late in the process the nibbler doesn't have a chance to respond. Better to bid a higher amount earlier, rather to risk a low-ball bid later.

And remember, no matter how high your maximum bid, eBay's proxy bidding system ensures that your stated bid is only as high as it needs to be to beat the next-lowest bidder. If you bid $10 and the next-lowest bidder bids $5, you don't have to pay the full $10; you'll win the auction with a proxy-generated bid of $5.50.

Win with Sniping

What's a sure-fire way to win more eBay auctions? It's all about saving your best bid for the final seconds of the auction, a technique that's called *sniping*.

Trick #102: **Make a Last-Second Bid**

> ***samby***
>
> Member since 2001, Feedback: Turquoise star

The most effective bidding method is the snipe, a literal last-second bid. One of the advantages of sniping is that you don't give away your interest beforehand, which keeps other bidders from nibbling the price up. You place one bid, as late as possible, for the maximum amount you're willing to pay. It's a last-chance hail Mary play, all your chips on one card. You have one chance to win, but it's a good one.

Of course, there are other advantages to waiting until the closing seconds of the auction to place your bid. eBay member ***samby*** outlines some of these benefits:

> *You spend the week researching the item, both on eBay and off. You work out the true value of the item for you, you research your seller, his selling history, his positive comments, and his negs. If you're a collector, your competition won't have time to search your bidding history and follow you from auction to auction, using you to find their goodies for them. You have all the time you need to email the seller about anything that concerns you before you bid.*

Even better, by bidding so late in the auction process, you don't leave other bidders any time to respond to your bid. Obviously, the later your bid, the better. A snipe with five seconds to go is going to be more successful than one that leaves a full minute for other bidders to respond.

Trick #103: **Don't Wait Until the Literal Last Second**

New Trick

> **blueab**
> Member since 1999, Feedback: Purple star

Some buyers recommend placing your bid with just 5 or 10 seconds left on the auction clock. But **blueab** points out that this approach isn't always the best way to go. That's because if you place your snipe bid but then find out it wasn't high enough, you don't have enough time to respond with a second, higher bid. For this reason, you might want to place your snipe at the two-minute mark, which gives you time to raise your bid if necessary.

Trick #104: **Sign In First**

> **trapperjohn2000**
> stores.ebay.com/Molehill-Group-Store
> Member since 1998, Feedback: Purple star

This sounds like a no-brainer, but you'd be surprised how many people forget, and lose precious seconds entering their user ID and password. Several minutes before you make your snipe, click the Sign In link at the top of the eBay page. You don't want to waste valuable seconds entering your ID and password when it's time to place your snipe.

Trick #105: **Snipe in Two Windows**

> **tiptie**
> Member since 1996, Feedback: Purple star

How do you place a successful snipe? eBay sniping expert **tiptie** recommends using the tried-and-true "two-window" method. Simply put, you open two instances of your web browser, then resize and reposition them so they're side-by-side on your screen, as shown in Figure 5.1.

You should get everything set up a few minutes before the end of the auction. Open the first browser window to the item listing page, scroll down to the bid section, and enter your bid amount. After you've entered your bid amount, stop—do *not* click the Place Bid button yet!

Now open the second browser window to the same item listing page, and then click the bid count link in the History section to display the Bidding History page. This page shows the standing of the bids and the current time, without a lot of extraneous information. As the seconds tick by, reload this browser window so that the bid and time information is continually refreshed.

Count down the seconds until there are just 15 seconds left to the end of the auction. Now move to the first browser window and click that Place Bid button. Follow through to confirm your bid, and then return to the second window and hit reload as many times as you want. You should see your bid registered in the bid count—and hopefully as the high bid!

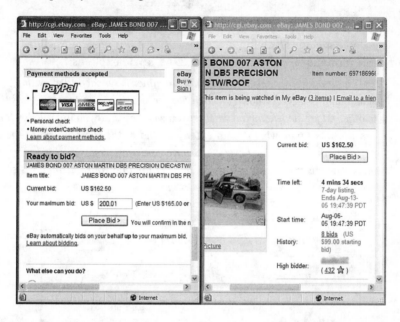

FIGURE 5.1

Positioning your desktop for two-window sniping.

Trick #106: **Get in Synch**

To perfectly time your last-second snipe, you want to be sure you're in synch with eBay's official clock; if you're a few seconds slow, you could lose a sniping contest. You can access eBay's official time at cgi3.ebay.com/aw-cgi/eBayISAPI.dll?TimeShow.

It's also convenient to place a countdown clock on your desktop while you're waiting to snipe. Sniping expert **tiptie** recommends TClockEx (www.5star-shareware.com/Business/ClocksAlarmsReminders/tclockex.html) to supplement the standard Windows clock.

Trick #107: **Let AuctionTamer Manage the Bid Process**

tiptie

Member since 1996, Feedback: Purple star

The whole synching/sniping process is easier if you use the AuctionTamer bid management program, shown in Figure 5.2. As **tiptie** explains:

You can mark any number of auctions, the timer is synched to eBay time, the individual item clocks click down on each auction you mark, and the auctions shift over to other pages, depending on whether you won or lost. If you use AuctionTamer you can use this single window and enter your bid in the top part, go to the confirm page and then watch the lower countdown clock and place your bid in the final seconds. There is no need to refresh in the last minute; your maximum is set and all you do is confirm your bid and hope for a win.

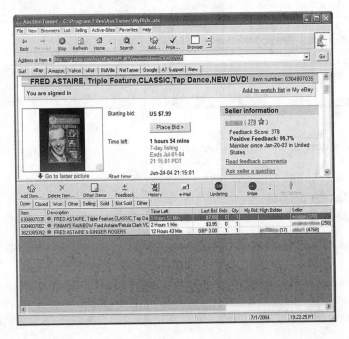

FIGURE 5.2

Use AuctionTamer to manage the bidding process.

AuctionTamer offers a 14-day free trial. The buyer access plan costs $24.95 for a
12-month subscription. Find out more, and download the program, at www.
auctiontamer.com.

Trick #108: **Use Other Sniping Software and Services**

> ***samby***
> Member since 2001, Feedback: Turquoise star

To make a snipe, you need to be present at your computer at the end of an auction.
If you can't be available at the end of every important auction, you can use sniping
software and services to automatically do your sniping for you. These programs and
websites let you enter your bid amount ahead of time; then they connect to eBay at
the proper time and place a literal last-second bid.

Table 5.1 lists some of the most popular sniping programs:

Table 5.1   **Sniping Software**

Software	Price	Website
Auction Sentry	$14.95	www.auction-sentry.com
Cricket Power Sniper	$24.99	www.cricketsniper.com
Merlin AuctionMagic	$14.95	www.merlinsoftware.com

The only problem with using sniping software is that your computer has to be
turned on and connected to the Internet for the snipe to take place. Another, possibly more reliable, alternative is to use a web-based sniping service. Just sign up,
and enter your eBay ID, auction number, and maximum bid amount. The sniping
service will place your bid for you in the final seconds of the auction.

Most of these sniping services charge either a monthly fee, a fee for each bid, a percentage of the final bid amount (for winning bids), or some combination of the
above. Table 5.2 provides the details.

Table 5.2   **Sniping Services**

Tool	Pricing	Website
AuctionSniper	1% of final price; minimum $0.25, maximum $9.95	www.auctionsniper.com
AuctionStealer	$8.99–$11.99/month	www.auctionstealer.com
Bidnapper	$9.95/month	www.bidnapper.com

continues

Table 5.2 **Continued**

Tool	Pricing	Website
BidRobot	$10.00/month	www.bidrobot.com
BidSlammer	$0.10/losing bid or 1% of final price, maximum $5.00	www.bidslammer.com
eSnipe	1% of final price; minimum $0.25, maximum $10.00	www.esnipe.com
HammerSnipe	Free	www.hammertap.com/ HammerSnipe.html
Vrane Sniper	Free	www.vrane.com

All of these programs and services provide a certain amount of peace of mind about the entire sniping process.

Trick #109: **Snipe Similar Auctions with eSnipe Bid Groups**

> **gothgirlscloset**
>
> PowerSeller
>
> Member since 1999, Feedback: Red star

eSnipe, shown in Figure 5.3, is the most popular of the sniping services, and for good reason. Member **gothgirlscloset** describes why she likes the service:

> *eSnipe rocks! It also keeps me from forgetting about auctions that end when I'm not around, and keeps me from getting caught up in a bidding war and paying way too much for something.*

FIGURE 5.3

Let eSnipe do your sniping for you.

Above and beyond normal sniping, eSnipe also offers a feature that lets you snipe multiple similar items, to make sure you win one of them. With eSnipe Bid Groups, you identify a number of auctions for the same type of item. You enter a single bid price, and eSnipe goes to work. First, it automatically dismisses those auctions that have already exceeded your maximum bid. Second, it places a snipe for the auction that ends first. If you lose that auction, it places a snipe in the next-ending auction, and so on and so on until you win one. The first auction you win, eSnipe cancels your bids in the other auctions.

It's a great feature, and it really increases your chances of winning *something*.

Other Tricks for Winning Auctions

Many buyers focus on sniping and neglect some of the other tricks you can use to increase your odds of winning. Not me. Here are a few of my favorite non-sniping tricks you can use when bidding to win.

Trick #110: **Bid in the Off Season**

> **trapperjohn2000**
>
> stores.ebay.com/Molehill-Group-Store
>
> Member since 1998, Feedback: Purple star

You already know that the final minute of the auction is the best time to place your bid. But are there specific times of the year that offer better bargains for bidders?

The answer, surprisingly, is yes. Although there is some category-specific seasonality, the best overall time of the year to pick up bargains on eBay is during the summer months. Summer is the slowest period on eBay, which means fewer people bidding—and lower prices for you.

Trick #111: **Look for Off-Peak Auctions**

> **trapperjohn2000**
>
> stores.ebay.com/Molehill-Group-Store
>
> Member since 1998, Feedback: Purple star

Believe it or not, some sellers set their auctions to end in the wee hours of the morning, when there aren't a lot of bidders awake to make last-minute snipes. And when there aren't a lot of snipers, prices often stay lower. So if you want some competition-free bidding, look for auctions ending between midnight and 5:00 a.m. Pacific time. The bargains lie in the wee hours of the morning!

Trick #112: **Look for Items with Bad Pictures**

New Trick

> **lady-frog-vintage-jewelry**
>
> stores.ebay.com/SOMETHING-TO-RIBBIT-ABOUT
>
> www.ladyfrog-vintage-jewelry.com
>
> Member since 2000, Feedback: Red star

I know, this one sounds a little counterintuitive, but hear me out. As you no doubt have discovered on your own (or will discover in Chapter 10, "How to Display Better Product Photos"), items with more and better photos sell better, and at higher prices. So doesn't it make sense that the converse is true—that items with no or lousy pictures will have fewer bidders? And, of course, the fewer bidders, the more likely it is that you can win the item without overpaying.

So if you actively look for items with really bad photos, you'll probably be able to pick up some bargains. Here's what member **lady-frog-vintage-jewelry** found:

> *As a buyer, I find that I actually look for items with bad pictures, because I can get jewelry at a better price if the pictures are so bad.*

It doesn't seem fair that you should be able to take advantage of the mistakes of sloppy sellers, but if you don't, somebody else will.

Trick #113: **Bid in Odd Numbers**

> **trapperjohn2000**
>
> stores.ebay.com/Molehill-Group-Store
>
> Member since 1998, Feedback: Purple star

We'll end this chapter with my very favorite bidding trick, one that's won me more than a few auctions over the years. It's a simple trick and lets you win auctions without wildly overbidding.

Here's the trick. When you bid, don't bid an even amount. Instead, bid a few pennies more than an even buck. Follow this advice, and you can win an auction by pennies!

For example, if you want to bid $10 for an item, bid $10.03 instead. That way, your bid will beat any bids at the same approximate amount—$10.03 beats $10 any day—without your having to place a new bid at the next whole bid increment.

It works!

Part III:

Tricks for More Successful Selling

6

How to Find Merchandise to Sell

When you're first starting out, you can find lots of stuff to sell just sitting around the house. Clean out the garage, the basement, the attic; it's all sellable on eBay.

Sooner or later, however, you run out of stuff. That's when you get serious about this online selling business and go looking for more merchandise to sell on eBay. Where do you find items to sell? Just follow the advice of the eBay Masters!

Doing the Research

Before you determine what you want to sell on eBay, it pays to do your homework. I'm talking research here—research about what's selling, what's not, and for what price. Let's listen to some of the eBay Masters tell you how they get smarter about what they sell.

Trick #114: **Check the Guide Books**

tradervic4u

stores.ebay.com/LeeWardBooks

Member since 2002, Feedback: Red star

It's always good to know a little bit about what you're selling, especially if you're dealing in collectibles. To that end, it pays to familiarize yourself with the key guide books in a given category. You can find tons of guide books on Amazon.com or at your local library.

Trick #115: **Don't Rely on the Guide Books Exclusively**

RAC

Member since 1998, Feedback: Yellow star

As useful as the guide books are, realize that online auctions don't always operate in a purely rational fashion, particularly when it comes to pricing. On eBay, items can sell for a lot more—or a lot less—than the guide books recommend, depending on the mood of eBay's buyers on any given day. As the name implies, take any pricing info in these books as a guide only.

Trick #116: **Search eBay's Closed Auctions**

tradervic4u

stores.ebay.com/LeeWardBooks

Member since 2002, Feedback: Red star

Of course, the best way to discover the market value of an item is to find out what other recent buyers have been willing to pay. For this, you want to search eBay's closed auctions for items similar to what you're thinking of selling. Examining the final results can tell you not only how popular an item is (how many bids it received—if any), but also the true worth of the item, as evidenced by the final high bid. (Looking at bid prices on current auctions doesn't give you the final picture—you're only looking at demand mid-auction.) Just make sure you click the Completed Listings box on the search page, as shown in Figure 6.1, and the results of your query will be closed auctions only.

FIGURE 6.1

Click the Completed Listings box to research the results of successful auctions.

Here's how **tradervic4u** describes the process:

When you scroll through the hundreds of completed auctions, you will immediately start to notice patterns. Most auctions die a lonely death; however, several have many bids. These you study for the clues you need. The only trouble is, you need to learn to recognize things about that auction that drew bids. Was it the headline, the item, the description, the price, and so on? Once you learn this technique you can study various products and get a good grasp of what's going on. Everything successful on eBay is hangin' out there for all to see.

When you research successful auctions, here's the information you want to analyze:

- Starting price
- Length of auction
- Ending time/day
- Is it a regular auction, auction with Buy It Now, or a straight fixed price auction?
- Is it a regular or reserve price auction?
- Category
- Title
- Condition
- Description

- Number and quality of pictures in the listing
- Seller's terms of sale
- Seller feedback
- Shipping costs
- Number of bids and number of bidders (not always the same)
- Timing of the bids—were they early in the auction, or were they all last-minute snipes?

Trick #117: **Use eBay's Hot Categories Report**

New Trick

> **trapperjohn2000**
>
> stores.ebay.com/Molehill-Group-Store
>
> Member since 1998, Feedback: Purple star

When you want to find out the best types of merchandise to sell, it helps to know which product categories are hot. Fortunately, eBay makes this relatively easy, with its monthly Hot Categories Report. As you can see in Figure 6.2, this list details the hottest product categories on the eBay site—which are the best categories in which to sell.

Cameras & Photos

Super Hot

Level 2	Level 3	Level 4
Film Camera Accessories	Camera Body Accessories	For 35mm Rangefinder

Very Hot

Level 2	Level 3	Level 4
Projection Equipment	Accessories	Slide Tray
Lighting & Studio Equipment	Booms, Stands & Supports	Lightstands & Boom Accessories
Film Cameras	35mm Rangefinder	Leica
Film	35MM	Color
Manuals, Guides & Books	Camera Manuals	Nikon
Digital Camera Accessories	Accessories	Underwater Housings
Printers, Scanners & Supplies	Scanners	Scanners
Film Cameras	Medium Format	Hasselblad
Film Processing & Darkroom	Hardware, Lighting & Setup	Clocks & Timers
Film Camera Accessories	Camera Body Accessories	For Medium Format

Hot

Level 2	Level 3	Level 4
Flashes & Accessories	Film Camera Flash Units	Vivitar
Professional Video Equipment	Cameras	Sony
Flashes & Accessories	Digital Camera Flash Units	Nikon
Digital Cameras	Point & Shoot	4.0 to 4.9 Megapixels
Wholesale Lots	Cameras	Film Cameras
Lighting & Studio Equipment	Light Controls & Modifiers	Softboxes
Digital Camera Accessories	Memory Cards	Sony Memory Stick

FIGURE 6.2

Find out the hottest product categories with eBay's Hot Categories Report.

To access the Hot Categories Report, click the Sell link on the eBay Navigation Bar to open the Sell hub, and then click the The Hot List link. Remember, the report is updated every 30 days—so check it monthly!

Trick #118: **Search eBay's Marketplace Research Database**

> **trapperjohn2000**
>
> stores.ebay.com/Molehill-Group-Store
>
> Member since 1998, Feedback: Purple star

The Hot Categories Report isn't eBay's only research tool. eBay pulls together other essential sales statistics in its Marketplace Research database, which you can search (for a fee). What sort of information are we talking about? Here's a sample, for any given item:

- Average sold price
- Sold price range
- Start price range
- Average BIN price
- BIN price range
- Average shipping cost
- Last sold price
- Last sold date/time
- Number successfully sold
- Average bids per item

Then there are the charts, including trend charts for average sold price, number successfully sold, and average bids per item; and distribution charts for average start price and number successfully sold. You can search the entire database, or filter your results by date, specific sellers, specific stores, country, and so on.

eBay's Marketplace Research can be accessed at pages.ebay.com/ marketplace_research/. Three different packages are available—the Fast Pass provides $2.99 for two days' access; the Basic plan costs $9.99 per month; and the more robust Pro plan (which offers more search options) costs $24.99 per month.

Trick #119: **Use Ándale's Research Tools**

> **griffin_trader**
>
> stores.ebay.com/Naturally-In-New-Orleans-Mardi-Gras
>
> Member since 1999, Feedback: Green star

You can supplement eBay's search tools with those from Ándale (www.andale.com), a popular third-party site. Ándale's key reports include

- **What's Hot** ($3.95/month) provides detailed reports about the hottest-selling eBay items; it's an excellent tool for identifying what types of products to sell.

- **Ándale Research** ($7.95/month) provides detailed pricing reports for any specific product or category on eBay; it's good for tracking pricing trends over time and determining what day of the week to list and what initial price to set.

- **Sales Analyzer** ($5.95/month) is designed to help you better understand your own eBay sales. It provides a detailed analysis of your total sales, sell-through rate, return on investment, and other key metrics.

Figure 6.3 shows the What's Hot report, which is similar to but more detailed than eBay's Hot Categories Report. I find this and the Ándale Research reports worth the money, especially if you're a high-volume seller.

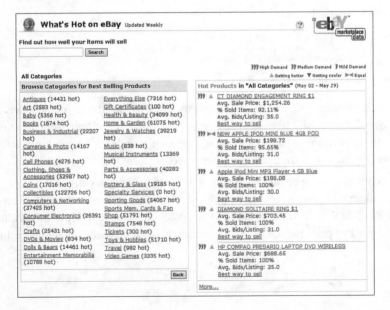

FIGURE 6.3

Ándale's What's Hot report.

Trick #120: **Check Out Other Third-Party Research Tools**

> **trapperjohn2000**
>
> stores.ebay.com/Molehill-Group-Store
>
> Member since 1998, Feedback: Purple star

As I just mentioned, Ándale Research is my favorite research tool, but it's not the only one out there. The eBay Masters recommend other third-party tools for you to to check out.

The first tool, AuctionIntelligence (www.certes.net/AuctionIntelligence/), is an auction analysis program available on a subscription basis. Downloading the software is free; you have to pay $9.99 per month to use it. The second tool is DeepAnalysis 2, a software program from HammerTap (www.hammertap.com) that performs basic auction sales analysis, with a license fee of $17.95 per month. They're both good adjuncts to your basic analysis, particularly suited for high-volume sellers.

Picking the Right Merchandise to Sell

During the course of your research you'll no doubt find lots of different types of items that could prove profitable to sell. But which items should you decide on?

Trick #121: **Specialize**

> **torreyphilemon**
>
> PowerSeller
>
> Member since 1999, Feedback: Red star

It's tough for any individual seller to stand out among the millions of other sellers on eBay. One way to make a name for yourself is to specialize. If you establish your own niche, you can appeal to a special interest group of buyers. Build your reputation among this group, and you'll generate lots of return business. Plus, it sets you apart from everyone else, the big boys included. Discover your niche, then mine it.

Trick #122: **Sell a Variety of Items**

> **clact**
>
> stores.ebay.com/Once-Upon-A-Bid
>
> PowerSeller
>
> Member since 2002, Feedback: Red star

Specializing isn't the only way to go, of course. Many eBayers recommend the opposite approach, selling a variety of items. One advantage to not specializing is that you won't be affected when a particular type of item goes out of fashion or if a category is impacted by eBay changes. If you sell in a variety of categories, you can weather any category-specific downturns. It's nice to have the safety net.

Trick #123: **Sell Stuff No One Else Sells**

berties_house_of_horrors

stores.ebay.com/Berties-Emporium

PowerSeller

Member since 1999, Feedback: Red star

Do you want to sell the same items that hundreds (or thousands) of other sellers offer, or do you want to sell something that is a little harder to find? Selling common items forces you into competition, which can lower your selling price. Selling unique items relieves that price pressure and can be quite rewarding. Here's what **berties_house_of_horrors** recommends:

> Unless you are Wal-Mart, it is hard to compete on most items. But if I am the only person in the universe who has that cap or pin you want, then you will come to me.

Trick #124: **Sell Things You Know and Love**

puglover2000

Member since 2000, Feedback: Red star

You can analyze products and categories till you're blue in the face, but at the end of the day are you having fun? Selling on eBay can be a business, but businesses don't have to be impersonal. Let your own personal likes and interests drive what you sell. Do you have a hobby? Do you collect things? These are natural directions to go with your eBay sales. As **puglover2000** says:

> One thing I tell people who ask me, "What should I sell on eBay?" I always tell them, sell what you like and know a little about.

Trick #125: **Trade on Regional Scarcity**

griffin_trader

stores.ebay.com/Naturally-In-New-Orleans-Mardi-Gras

PowerSeller

Member since 1999, Feedback: Green star

Here's a trick I really like. Not all items are equally available in all areas of the country. Some products are only distributed regionally, and many national retailers vary their product mix by locale. With this in mind, you can often find items in your local stores that aren't available in other areas of the country—a perfect opportunity for selling on eBay. Identify these items, and you can make some easy bucks.

Trick #126: **Buy the Whole Thing, Sell the Parts**

tradervic4u

stores.ebay.com/LeeWardBooks

Member since 2002, Feedback: Red star

Sometimes the parts are worth more than the whole. That is, you can often make more money selling component parts than you can by selling the complete item. I've seen this with musical instruments, where you can sometimes make more money selling the parts of a drum (lugs, heads, rims, and so on) than you can selling the whole drum. There are lots of categories where this is true; **tradervic4u** points out another example:

> One fellow I know buys junk motorcycles, then disassembles them and sells the parts—and gets 50–100x his cost!

It's true!

Trick #127: **Sell Higher-Priced Items**

mgr1969

Member since 2001, Feedback: Purple star

When planning your eBay selling strategy, you have to make a choice. Do you try to sell lots of relatively low-priced items, or go with higher-priced items that you have to sell fewer of to make the same profit? Of course, it may be harder to sell a

$50 item than a $5 item. But then again, you have to sell ten of those $5 items to generate the same revenue as one $50 sale. eBayers go back and forth on this, and there's no one right approach, but it's certainly the case that there's less work involved (listing, emailing, packing, shipping) in that one $50 sale than in the ten $5 sales.

Trick #128: **Take Advantage of Home Page Promotions**

clact

stores.ebay.com/Once-Upon-A-Bid

PowerSeller

Member since 2002, Feedback: Red star

When deciding what to list in your eBay auctions this week, take notice of what items and categories eBay is promoting on its home page. It's like piggybacking on a promotion, and it doesn't cost you a thing.

Here's an example of how **clact** took advantage of this type of piggyback promotion:

> When I noticed eBay kept promoting 1-cent CDs on page one, I said OK, let me try that. I sold a ton, because anyone clicking on that link from page one was coming to my listings and those of others selling at 1 cent.

I discuss eBay's home page promotions in more depth in Trick #219. Read ahead to learn more!

Where to Find Merchandise

All that advice is well and good, but I know what you're begging to ask: Where do I find merchandise to sell? There are lots of places you find sellable items (including in your own basement or attic), so let's see what the eBay Masters recommend.

Trick #129: **Shop at Estate Sales**

satnrose

PowerSeller

Member since 1998, Feedback: Green star

We'll start our shopping trip at the house down the road—the one hosting an estate sale. Estate sales, often held in the form of live auctions, can be a great source of all kinds of merchandise. You can buy as little as you want, or buy a lot and sort through what's valuable afterward.

When shopping estate sales, I like the advice that **satnrose** offers:

You can't tell what's inside a house from the outside. Estate sales are unpredictable. You cannot really judge the quality of the sale from the ad, the neighborhood, the house itself, the person running the sale, etc. And it only takes one good item to make it all worthwhile.

Trick #130: **Shop the Thrift Stores**

kattinsanity

Member since 2000, Feedback: Red star

Here's another popular source of eBay merchandise—your local thrift store. Some eBayers prefer smaller thrift stores to the larger Goodwill and Salvation Army stores, but bargains abound at just about any thrift store. In addition, many sellers report that shopping at thrift stores is a lot of fun, regardless of what they find.

Trick #131: **Shop Garage Sales, Yard Sales, and Tag Sales**

clact

stores.ebay.com/Once-Upon-A-Bid

PowerSeller

Member since 2002, Feedback: Red star

Buying used items from individuals is always a good way to fuel your eBay inventory. Where are the best places to pick up used goods? You know what they are—garage sales, yard sales, tag sales, flea markets, and the like. Just make sure you get there early; chances are other eBayers will be racing you to pick up the good stuff first!

Trick #132: **Shop the Antique Malls**

bushellcollectibles

stores.ebay.com/Bushells-Collectibles

Member since 1999, Feedback: Red star

If you're selling antiques and collectibles, you can sometimes pick up good deals at your local antique mall. This isn't always a sure thing, as items here are often over-priced, but if you keep your eyes open you can sometimes pick up a deal. Member **bushellcollectibles** notes the following:

> I have found some great finds in [antique] shops. Not everyone can know every-thing, and on the items a dealer does not know well enough, you can get quite a bargain.

Trick #133: **Buy at a Live Auction**

ghostwritersmith

stores.ebay.com/GhostWriterSmith

Member since 2003, Feedback: Turquoise star

You're familiar with how an online auction works, but what about a live auction? Every city has at least one, and they're great places to pick up items to sell on eBay. Just make sure you know what you're doing, or else you'll either get outbid or end up paying too much. (Just like on eBay!)

To that end, I relay some extremely useful live auction advice from member **ghostwritersmith**:

> If you haven't been to a live auction before I would suggest just going to watch. Go ahead and get a bidder's number, but don't go thinking you need to get something.

> Don't be intimidated by grumpy big guys. You're not there for them to like you. You are there to make money, just like they are. If you are a newbie, show them some respect for their experience, but don't let them scare you off if there is something you really want.

> The best bargains are usually the first units auctioned. Many people figure they will wait and see what's coming up before making their bids. Then, as the number of available units goes down, the prices go up and up.

Trick #134: **Buy from a Liquidator**

rosachs

stores.ebay.com/My-Discount-Shoe-Store

home.midsouth.rr.com/rosachs/RKS/

PowerSeller

Member since 1997, Feedback: Red star

Many eBay sellers get their merchandise from professional liquidators. These are companies that purchase surplus items from other businesses, in bulk. These items might be closeouts, factory seconds, customer returns, or overstocked items—products the manufacturer made too many of and wants to get rid of.

Just as liquidators purchase their inventory in bulk, you also buy from them in bulk. That means buying 10 or 20 or 100 units of a particular item. You get a good price for buying in quantity, of course, which is part of the appeal. (You also have to manage that large inventory, and inventory storage can be both a lot of work and somewhat costly. Just something to keep in mind.)

Some liquidators sell their lots at a fixed price; others auction off the merchandise, in eBay fashion. The most popular liquidation sites (all of whom claim to be "the world leader," if that's possible) include:

- America's Best Closeouts (www.abcloseouts.com)
- American Merchandise Liquidators (www.amlinc.com)
- AmeriSurplus (www.amerisurplus.com)
- Bid4Assets (www.bid4assets.com)
- Liquidation.com (www.liquidation.com)
- Luxury Brands (www.luxurybrandsllc.com)
- My Web Wholesaler (www.mywebwholesaler.com)
- Overstock.com (www.overstock.com)
- Salvage Closeouts (www.salvagecloseouts.com)
- TDW Closeouts (www.tdwcloseouts.com)

Probably the most popular of these liquidators, on a wholesale level, is Liquidation. com. As you can see in Figure 6.4, this site liquidates bulk merchandise using an eBay-like auction model—that is, you have to bid for the lots you want. Win the auction, arrange delivery, and you'll have a *ton* of merchandise to resell!

Also very popular is Overstock.com, shown in Figure 6.5; it's an easier place to pick up bargains on onesies and twosies, as opposed to big pallet quantities. (Although there are some larger lots available on the Bulk Buys & Business Supplies tab.) Seller **rosachs** says that he often finds merchandise for considerably less on Overstock.com than he does on eBay, which makes it a good source of inventory. He relates:

> Overstock.com is a great place for bargains. I just bought seven copies of Windows XP Pro for an average $52 a copy, delivered. The same thing on eBay sells for twice that, or more. You can pick up a few at Overstock.com and resell them on eBay for a decent markup.

FIGURE 6.4

Buy bulk merchandise from Liquidation.com.

FIGURE 6.5

Buy clearance and overstock items from Overstock.com.

The key to purchasing from any of these liquidators and clearance sites is to know what you're buying and what it's really worth, and be sure you can easily and quickly resell the merchandise on eBay for a decent markup.

Trick #135: **Buy from a Wholesaler**

tradervic4u

stores.ebay.com/LeeWardBooks

Member since 2002, Feedback: Red star

Another alternative for obtaining new merchandise is to purchase from a wholesale distributor. The distributor purchases their merchandise direct from the manufacturer, who in many cases doesn't deal directly with retailers, and then resells it to retailers and other third parties.

There are thousands of wholesalers out there, most specializing in specific types of merchandise. Most wholesalers are set up to sell in quantity to authorized retail locations, but many also handle smaller orders and smaller buyers, making them ideal for eBay sellers. Many of these distributors operate over the Internet, which makes the process even easier for you.

Where do you find wholesalers? Here's what **tradervic4u** recommends:

You can find wholesalers in your Business-to-Business Yellow Pages at your local library. Most want to deal with a genuine business with a State Tax resale number.

You can also find directories of wholesalers at the following web directories:

- Buylink (www.buylink.com)
- goWholesale (www.gowholesale.com)
- Wholesale Central (www.wholesalecentral.com)
- WholesaleQuest (www.wholesalequest.com)
- Wholesale411 (www.wholesale411.com), shown in Figure 6.6

FIGURE 6.6

Use Wholesale411 to find wholesalers and drop shippers.

Trick #136: **Consider Using a Drop Shipper**

> **rsgold13**
>
> Member since 1999, Feedback: Turquoise star

Want to buy merchandise for resale but don't have enough space to warehouse the merchandise? Then use a drop shipper—a wholesaler or manufacturer that inventories the merchandise for you and ships directly to your customer when you make a sale.

While not all distributors offer drop ship services, many do. Check with your wholesaler to see what services are available, or check out this short list of popular drop shippers and drop ship directories:

- 123DropShip.com (www.123dropship.com)
- #1 Accessory.com (www.1accessory.com)
- Bookliquidator.com (www.bookliquidator.com)
- DropshipDesign.com (www.dropshipdesign.com)
- MegaGoods.com (www.megagoods.com)
- Wholesale Marketer (www.wholesalemarketer.com)
- Worldwide Brands, Inc. (www.worldwidebrands.com)

In addition, Wholesale411 and the other wholesaler directories listed in Trick #135 often note whether a particular wholesaler drop ships.

When shopping for a drop shipper, make sure you know the company you're dealing with and what kind of service they offer. Seller **rsgold13** relates that using the right drop shipper can be a good experience:

> *The two drop shippers I use ship the same day they receive the order (if they get it in time); if not, the next day. They enclose my invoice and business card in the order and their name is not on there anywhere.*

Trick #137: **Think Carefully About Using Drop Shippers**

> **loblollygifts**
>
> stores.ebay.com/LoblollyGifts
>
> PowerSeller
>
> Member since 2001, Feedback: Purple star

While drop shipping might sound attractive from an inventory management standpoint (you have none to manage) as noted in Trick #136, it might not always be the best deal for your customers—especially if your supplier isn't always a speedy shipper. Remember, your customers hold you responsible for shipping the products they purchase, and if a drop shipment isn't prompt, you are the one who'll get the complaints (and the negative feedback). If, for whatever reason (like they're temporarily out of stock), your supplier drops the ball and never ships the merchandise, you're on the hook. If this happens too often, you could get the boot from eBay.

Some sellers, such as **loblollygifts**, use drop shippers on occasion, but warn of the inherent dangers:

> *I drop ship from the manufacturer from time to time when I am out of inventory. There a couple reasons I don't like to do it, though.*
>
> *(1) When I drop ship I don't get any quantity discount, so it cuts into my margin significantly.*
>
> *(2) Around the end of the month when they do inventory, shipping slows down a little. They might not ship for as long as a week. I guess that's not bad by eBay standards, but I hate to put buyers off about the shipping date.*
>
> *Okay, there is another reason I don't like to do it. I'm a control freak.*

That last point is important. When you outsource two essential components of your business (inventory and shipping), you cede control over those components—and thus have less say in the end results to your customers.

That said, other sellers find drop shippers quite reliable, and use them either as a primary or supplementary source of inventory. Use your own best judgment.

Trick #138: **Buy Direct from the Manufacturer**

griffin_trader

stores.ebay.com/Naturally-In-New-Orleans-Mardi-Gras

Member since 1999, Feedback: Green star

Depending on what type of merchandise you sell, you may be able to cut out the middleman and buy directly from the manufacturer. Use Google to find out who manufactures the type of product you're interested in, and then query them to see if they sell direct. It could amount to a considerable savings!

Trick #139: **Use Ándale Suppliers**

trapperjohn2000

stores.ebay.com/Molehill-Group-Store

Member since 1998, Feedback: Purple star

If you're not sure where to find specific types of merchandise, you're in luck. Ándale Suppliers (www.andale.com) is a free service that helps you find suppliers of various types of merchandise for resale. It does a good job of matching resellers with suppliers by keeping a big database of both. When you sign up for the service, you fill out the sourcing profile that includes the categories of merchandise in which you're interested. Ándale Suppliers will automatically match you with suppliers who match your criteria.

You can choose to receive your leads by email or via the site's Leads Dashboard. Each listing includes the supplier's location and eBay feedback rating, so you can judge their trustworthiness. Click the supplier's name to display a detailed Sourcing Profile, which includes the supplier's phone number and email address. You can then contact the supplier at your discretion.

And here's the best thing about Ándale Suppliers—it's free for anyone looking to buy merchandise for resale.

Trick #140: **Go Dumpster Diving**

> **milehiauctionaction**
>
> Member since 2000, Feedback: Turquoise star

This might be sinking a little too low for some of you, but you never know what you can find in the trash. People throw out all sorts of stuff, including items that might be sellable on eBay. Here's a neat story from member **milehiauctionaction**:

> *My mom manages a condo high-rise smack in the middle of downtown Denver. Anyway, the homeowners that live in this building are, should we say, rich and snooty. My mom's office is close to the dumpster area, and you wouldn't believe the stuff these people throw out! They are constantly redecorating, and we call my mom "queen of the dumpster divers." Lamps, microwaves, furniture, VCRs, computers, tons of knickknacks and statues…All in great condition!*

And it doesn't have to be a rich neighborhood. My sister lives in a suburb of Chicago, and once a year the trash collectors have an "anything goes" day, where you can put anything out in the trash to be hauled away for free. My nephews always love this day; they cruise the neighborhoods picking up all sorts of good stuff just sitting by the curb. You never know what you'll find!

Trick #141: **Buy It on eBay**

New Trick

> **torreyphilemon**
>
> PowerSeller
>
> Member since 1999, Feedback: Red star

Let's not forget that the place you sell can also be the place you buy. It's possible to buy merchandise on eBay for resale on eBay, if you're smart about it. The key, of course, is to buy low and sell high. You can do this if you time your buying correctly. Buying during the off-season (July and August are always slow months) lets you save a few bucks, that you make back when you sell in higher-traffic months (November and December).

In addition, you can watch eBay's auctions all through the year to try to pick up some bargains on specific types of merchandise. Here's what **torreyphilemon** recommends:

> *Keep a watch with eBay's favorite search emails for chances to acquire items at a lower cost—or check Froogle (froogle.google.com) to find the merchandise even cheaper outside of eBay.*

Trick #142: **Make Contacts at Trade Shows**

New Trick

bobbibopstuff

stores.ebay.com/BobbiBopStuff

www.bobbibopstuff.com

PowerSeller

Member since 1998, Feedback: Red star

Another good place to find merchandise suppliers—both wholesalers and manufacturers—are at industry trade shows. Read the industry magazines for the product categories you specialize in, and then attend the major shows. You'll find aisle after aisle of potential suppliers—and make lots of great contacts.

For example, **bobbibopstuff** sells stationery, greeting cards, and scrapbooking and craft supplies. He has made a lot of valuable contacts by attending various gift industry trade shows, in particular the Associated Surplus Dealers/Associated Merchandise Dealers show, held in Las Vegas every August. (You can find out more about the ASD/ASM trade show at www.merchandisegroup.com.)

Trick #143: **Don't Buy More Than You Can Sell in a Reasonable Time**

trapperjohn2000

stores.ebay.com/Molehill-Group-Store

Member since 1998, Feedback: Purple star

When you're buying from liquidators, wholesalers, and clearance sites, you're often presented with the option (or requirement) of buying large quantities of a given item. A large lot might seem attractive, especially if it comes with a low per-unit cost. But the problem is, you have to find someplace to store all that merchandise you order—and you also need to sell it. You don't want to get suckered into buying large lots that will take forever to sell!

Here's a small example from my own experience. I found a site that sold close-out toys and model kits at wholesale prices. I purchased a lot of 12 Dick Tracy models for $4 apiece. This seemed like a good deal, as I could probably sell each model for $8–$10.

The problem is, the models didn't sell. Oh, I sold one every few weeks or so, and for considerably less than that ideal $10 price. But that lot of a dozen models ended up taking almost six months to sell, which was not a good investment. Smart sellers want to turn their inventory much more often than that.

So heed my advice: Avoid buying more merchandise than you think you can sell in a month or two. Buy too large a lot, and you have to eat the excess!

How to Maximize Your Sales

When you're selling on eBay, you want to sell more stuff, at higher prices. Well, it's not that easy—unless you employ some of these effective tricks of the eBay Masters. Be warned: There are a ton of tricks in this chapter. You don't have to try them all—just one might make all the difference in the world for your auctions!

Setting the Initial Price

The first key to closing more auctions is to attract more attention. One way to do this is with your initial listing price.

Note, however, that there is no single strategy for setting the "perfect" initial bid price. That's because eBay isn't a single marketplace; it's a global collection of hundreds of different marketplaces. For one user, eBay might be a giant clothing store; for other users, it might be an antiques store, or an electronics store, or even a car dealership. As you can imagine, pricing strategy is often quite different from one category to another.

Pricing strategy is also highly individualistic. What works for one seller might deliver horrible results for another. Some sellers really like low-ball initial pricing; others find this too risky and prefer a higher starting price. Personal preference definitely plays a hand in setting price.

So read on to learn what the eBay Masters recommend—but know that everybody has their own individual strategies, which sometimes are contradictory.

Trick #144: **Start the Bidding at 99 Cents—or a Penny**

quadaxel83

stores.ebay.com/Buttons-And-Beads

Member since 2001, Feedback: Red star

One of the most popular pricing tricks is to set an extremely low initial price. This attracts a lot of buyer attention and gets the bidding started sooner. Obviously, you hope that all this attention will result in the price being bid up from the starting level.

When it comes to low prices, many successful sellers swear by 99-cent pricing. Even if you actually end up selling a few items at this price, it can drive traffic to your other auctions or your eBay store. It's a loss leader, and you make it up with other sales.

Here's what **quadaxel83** says about it:

> I start most of my items at a dollar or less. This may not be practical for a lot of sellers, but for me it works. I figure as long as there's more than one person who's interested, the item will go for the market price and I won't lose out by setting a price floor and listing my item too high. Of course it won't work if you're selling items that usually just get one bid. But people are more likely to bid on something with a low starting price thinking they are getting a better deal.

And if 99 cents is a good starting bid, why not go even lower—like a penny? Setting a one-cent initial price really attracts a lot of attention. It's an especially effective strategy for items that have a lot of competition or are otherwise overexposed.

Trick #145: **Don't Do Penny—or 99-cent—Pricing**

puggybelle

stores.ebay.com/Soap-Opera-World

Member since 1999, Feedback: Red star

For all the supporters of low-ball pricing, there are an equal number of sellers who avoid it like the plague. The problem, of course, comes when you only get a single bid and actually have to sell that item for a penny (or 99 cents or whatever). It's a huge amount of work to sell and ship an item, and to do it for a buck or less probably isn't worth your time.

And then there are the fees. Take your dollar profit, then subtract eBay's standard listing and final value fees—as well as the PayPal fee, if the buyer pays by credit card. There's nothing left to speak of.

Here's what member **puggybelle** has to say about it.

> Well, I'll be the voice of dissention here and say NO! NO! Do not run 99-cent auctions! I learned the hard way when I began selling years ago. I would start bidding on my things (I sell magazines) at $1.00. And I ended up selling most of it for one lousy dollar. Throw in eBay listing fees and final auction value fees and—God forbid—the buyer pays via PayPal...Holy smokes! All of my time and effort to pocket pennies. I don't think so.
>
> My experience is that buyers who will bid one dollar would probably be very content and happy to bid, say, 3 or 4 dollars for that same item. So my advice is this: Do not start the bidding at one penny less than you'd be happy to sell that item for.

Another argument against low-ball initial pricing is that you might actually scare some buyers away. If you put too low a price on a valuable item, buyers might think there's something wrong with it. Something to think about...

Trick #146: Set a Low Initial Price...But Make It Up in Shipping/Handling

disneyshopper

stores.ebay.com/Your-Own-Disneyshopper

PowerSeller

Member since 2000, Feedback: Red star

One option to under-a-buck pricing is to set a low initial price, but then balance that with a higher (but not excessive) shipping/handling (S/H) charge. I know that most buyers like lower S/H fees, but that low initial price still attracts a lot of attention. If you add a few bucks into your S/H fee, you protect yourself if the bidding never rises above the basement level. As **disneyshopper** says:

> Most sellers would say that you get more bids with a low starting bid and higher S/H fee than if you start with a high starting bid and low S/H. However, I would

suggest that you clearly state the shipping/handing in larger, bolder print than the rest of your TOS so there are no problems later on.

Trick #147: Set Your Initial Price High Enough to Cover Your Costs

erika*n.company

PowerSeller

Member since 2003, Feedback: Purple star

All this talk about low initial bid prices ignores the fact that most sellers would actually like to recoup all the fees they have to pay. And there are lots of fees, as you're well aware. So you might want to set an initial price that's high enough to cover the cost of the item and all your other costs—including your eBay fees, PayPal fees, and expected packing/shipping costs. This way, if you get only one bid, you at least cover your costs.

While this means you might be starting at a higher price than some competing sellers, it doesn't necessarily mean you'll get fewer bids. Just listen to what **Erika*n.company** experienced:

In the past, I offered extremely low opening bids, only to lose a lot of money when my item didn't sell as high as expected. I found that by combining all my out-of-pocket expenses in the starting price, and then offering free to minimal shipping, I have gained more interest from buyers. I no longer lose great amounts of money in the event my items only receive one bid, because everything was covered in the beginning. For example, I buy a rare comic book for $20. My starting price will be $30–$32, which is still very low for this item, but in the event there is only one interested buyer I have lost nothing.

Trick #148: Price One Item Really High—to Make Your Other Auctions Look Like Steals

satnrose

PowerSeller

Member since 1998, Feedback: Green star

Here's a neat little trick that makes it look as if you're really offering a deal. When you're selling multiple similar items, price one of those items considerably higher than the others. This draws attention to your other auctions and makes it look as if they're real bargains.

Trick #149: **If You're Selling Something Expensive, Create a Critical Mass**

satnrose

PowerSeller

Member since 1998, Feedback: Green star

It's easier to sell something expensive if you have a bunch of other expensive items up for auction at the same time. As **satnrose** points out, bidders will thus have more confidence in bidding:

> This goes along with the "critical mass factor," where items of a type tend to do better if clustered. So it's a good strategy to hold stuff back until you can list all of a kind on the same day.

Trick #150: **Set Your Price Just Below the Listing Fee Cutoff**

berties_house_of_horrors

stores.ebay.com/Berties-Emporium

PowerSeller

Member since 1999, Feedback: Red star

When you're trying to decide the perfect listing price, don't forget to take into account eBay's fee structure. When you're up against the next tier of the fee structure, a penny difference in price can result in an extra dollar or more in fees. You want to set your price *just under* the next tier, if that's where you're at.

And, just so you know, Table 7.1 lists insertion fees, as of February 2006:

Table 7.1   **eBay's Insertion Fee Breaks**

Price Point	Fee
$0–$0.99	$0.20
$1.00–$9.99	$0.35
$10.00–$24.99	$0.60
$25.00–$49.99	$1.20
$50.00–$199.99	$2.40
$200.00–$499.99	$3.60
$500.00 and up	$4.80

This is why you never want to list an item for $1.00 (listing at $.99 saves you 15 cents) or $10.00 (listing at $9.99 saves you a quarter). It's all about beating the fees!

Trick #151: **Make Sure Your Initial Price Is Well Below Retail**

> **tradervic4u**
>
> stores.ebay.com/LeeWardBooks
>
> Member since 2002, Feedback: Red star

Don't get carried away by how much you think an item is worth. In particular, pay attention to the item's retail price, and keep your initial bid price well under this level. As **tradervic4u** points out:

> *Nobody likes to bid on items priced at retail, unless the item is very collectible.*

Using Buy It Now

One pricing option that eBay offers is Buy It ow (BIN). BIN lets you sell your item to the first bidder who offers a specific fixed price. It's a great way to get money faster; the auction ends when a buyer pays the BIN price.

Buy It Now is very popular among high-volume sellers, especially those selling commodity items where you pretty much know what the item is going to sell for. In many ways, setting a BIN price is like sticking a retail selling price on the item; it's going to sell for X amount, whatever happens. And—here's the good part—when you end a seven-day auction in one day with a BIN purchase, you get your money sooner. Instant gratification.

Trick #152: **Use the Buy It Now Option**

> **boutiqueannemarie**
>
> PowerSeller
>
> Member since 2002, Feedback: Turquoise star

BIN is good for high-volume sellers and for buyers who want their merchandise in a hurry. When they use the BIN option, they don't have to wait for a 7-day auction to end; they get their stuff as soon as they pay for it, just like normal retail.

If you've never used BIN before, you might be surprised at the response. Here's what **boutiqueannemarie** found:

> *I always use BIN, and most of my auctions end with a BIN. Very rarely do people bid on my auctions vs. just buying immediately.*

Trick #153: **BIN Isn't Right for All Auctions**

> **trapperjohn2000**
>
> stores.ebay.com/Molehill-Group-Store
>
> Member since 1998, Feedback: Purple star

When is BIN *not* a good deal? It may work against you when you're selling a unique item, like many collectibles. With this type of item, you want the bidding to carry the item to the highest possible price—which could be considerable, depending on who's doing the collecting. If you set a BIN price, you limit your upside.

Trick #154: **Use BIN in the Summertime**

> **betty*blackbent**
>
> stores.ebay.com/betty-blackbents-world-of-stuff
>
> PowerSeller
>
> Member since 2002, Feedback: Red star

For some reason, many eBay sellers find that BIN is a particularly effective option during the normally slow summertime months. As **betty*blackbent** notes:

> *BINs are a good summer sales motivator for me. People seem more impatient for their stuff in the summertime.*

Using the BIN option is also a good idea during the Christmas holiday season, as you'll learn in Trick #225, later in this chapter.

Trick #155: **Only Use BIN If You Check Your Auctions Frequently**

> **torreyphilemon**
>
> PowerSeller
>
> Member since 1999, Feedback: Red star

BIN is only a good option if you really stay on top of your auctions. Buyers use BIN because they want immediate gratification. If you don't check your auctions frequently, you could really disappoint these eager buyers. Here's what **torreyphilemon** recommends:

> *I always tell sellers that if they don't check their auctions and email at least every 12 hours, they shouldn't do Buy It Now. Buyers will get very impatient with a seller when they don't hear from him/her within 12 hours after a sale.*

Trick #156: **Don't Be Afraid to Set a High BIN Price**

> **brewcity_bob**
>
> stores.ebay.com/Brew-City-Limited
>
> PowerSeller
>
> Member since 1998, Feedback: Red star

If you're going to use Buy It Now, make sure that it's worth your while. You defi-nitely *don't* want to set a BIN price lower than what you think your item will even-tually sell for. In fact, you probably want to set the BIN price at some point *higher* than the expected high bid price. If somebody really wants to buy it now, they'll pay a premium for the privilege. If not, bidding will proceed as normal until a (presumably lower) high bid is realized. As **brewcity_bob** points out:

> *A BIN should be the price you truly want, and the start bid is supposed to attract bidders looking to get a deal. You want the buyers to be torn between outright buy-ing the item or risking a bidding war in an attempt to "steal" the item from the seller.*

Trick #157: **Offer an Incentive for BIN Purchases**

> **2ndhand4u**
>
> Member since 1998, Feedback: Red star

Those sellers who really like Buy It Now—you get your money faster, remember—offer incentives to drive buyers to use the BIN option. One particularly popular incentive is free shipping when the buyer uses Buy It Now. It works!

Using Reserve Pricing

A reserve price auction is one in which you set a low starting price to get the bid-ding started, but keep a higher, hidden reserve price that serves as the lowest price you'll sell the item for. Should you use reserve pricing? Read on to learn what the eBay Masters recommend.

Trick #158: **Set a Low Initial Price...But Add a Reserve**

> **art_by_eileen**
>
> Member since 2002, Feedback: Blue star

Reserve price auctions let you set however low a starting price you want. And, as you now know, low starting prices get a lot of buyer attention—and get the bids flowing. You're not obligated to sell at that low price, of course; that's why you have the reserve, as protection in case the bids don't go high enough. This is why many eBayers—especially those selling higher-priced items—recommend the strategy of setting a low initial price and a higher reserve price. It offers the benefit of looking like you're offering a steal but with the reserve price safety net.

Trick #159: **Don't Set a Reserve Price**

mrsdocy2k1

Member since 2000, Feedback: Red star

On the downside, reserve auctions confuse a lot of potential bidders—newer users, in particular. They also foster a bit of suspicion from bidders, because you're not telling them the whole truth. (The reserve price is always hidden.) So you're apt to have fewer bidders on a reserve price auction, in spite of the lower starting price. As **mrsdocy2k1** notes, the reserve price often does more harm than good:

> *Most buyers like to know what your reserve is and shy away from reserve auctions.*

I've certainly experienced this. Many buyers simply refuse to bid on items with a reserve price because they have no idea what that price is—and they don't want to play guessing games. This is why many experienced sellers don't use the reserve price option. If there's an absolutely positively minimum price you have to get out of a particular item, set that price as your starting bid price. There's no need—and little to be gained—by setting a hidden reserve.

Trick #160: **Use Reserve Pricing for Higher Value Items Only**

New Trick

sellerdropoff

stores.ebay.com/SellerDropoff

PowerSeller

Member since 2004, Feedback: Turquoise star

Reserve pricing isn't for every type of item. In particular, there's little advantage to using reserve pricing for low-priced items. Here's what **sellerdropoff** recommends:

> *Reserve pricing should mainly be used on cars, expensive cameras, and other luxury goods. If the item is an in-demand mass-market item, you don't need the reserve price. The market will take care of the price for you.*

Think about it. What would you gain by listing a specific toner cartridge for auction with a reserve price? There are probably dozens of similar items listed on eBay, all within a general price range. Going reserve on this type of item simply doesn't make sense. On the other hand, if you're selling a one-of-a-kind expensive collectible, where there isn't an established price, setting a reserve might work to your advantage. Use common sense, and you'll make the right decision.

Trick #161: **Reveal Your Reserve Price If Asked**

> **going1nceamc**
>
> stores.ebay.com/GOing1nceAMC
>
> www.going1nce.com
>
> PowerSeller
>
> Member since 1999, Feedback: Red star

What do you do if you're running a reserve price auction and a potential bidder emails you, asking what the reserve price is? Well, there's really no harm in revealing the reserve price. As **going1nceamc** notes:

> *Think about how you may react if you wanted something you saw listed—you'd want to know that you have to bid at least $X to get it. I would either list the reserve in the auction description or just respond to the email that the "reserve is $X."*

In fact, if there's no real reason to keep the reserve price a secret, why not list it in your item description? Just something to consider—it lets everybody know the minimum that they actually have to bid to win.

Choosing the Right End Time

What time of day your auction ends is important. That's because of sniping. The more potential bidders who'll be home at the end of your auction, the higher the final bid is likely to be. End your auction when nobody's at home, and you lose out on potential bidders.

That said, when is the best time of day for your auction to end? As the eBay Masters point out, that all depends...

Trick #162: **End When You're Awake**

New Trick

> **scifi4me2004**
>
> stores.ebay.com/Needle-In-a-Haystack-Treasures
>
> Member since 2003, Feedback: Turquoise star

Given all the talk about the "perfect" end time for your auctions, which we'll get into shortly, keep one important thing in mind: Make sure to end your auctions when *you* are home and awake. It's possible that you'll get last-minute questions from bidders right before the auction ends, and you'll need to be there to answer them. More importantly, you want to send out your invoices as soon as possible after each auction closes. As **scifi4me2004** advises:

> *I list all my items to end when I am awake. When they end I immediately send an invoice and a "thank you for your purchase" note. My eBay office hours are 9 a.m. to midnight.*

Trick #163: **Don't End Your Auctions in the Middle of the Night**

trinkettrauma

Member since 2003, Feedback: Purple star

Along the same lines, don't end your auctions when all your bidders are asleep! The absolute worst time to end your auction is in the middle of the night; not even the most dedicated sniper will stay up all night to bid on your item. As seller **trinkettrauma** points out:

> *If a seller ends their auction at 3 or 4 in the morning, the likelihood that I will be awake to bid is nil. Even at 6 in the morning...nil. What you lose out on are last-minute bidders; they are nowhere but in bed.*

Given that such a high percentage of bids come from last-minute snipers, you want those snipers to be awake when your auction ends. If it's too late, a large number of potential bidders will be sound asleep—which does your auction no good at all.

Trick #164: **End Your Auction in Prime Time**

trapperjohn2000

stores.ebay.com/Molehill-Group-Store

Member since 1998, Feedback: Purple star

So if the middle of the night is the worst time to end your auction, when is the best time? You want most bidders to be at home, but still awake. And you have to make a bit of a compromise between time zones—which means dealing with the three-hour time-zone gap between the East and the West coasts.

Do the math, and it's easy to see that the best times to end your auction are between 9:00 p.m. and 11:00 p.m. EST, or between 6:00 p.m. and 8:00 p.m. PST. That way you'll catch the most potential bidders online for the final minutes of your auction—and possibly generate a bidding frenzy that will garner a higher price for your merchandise!

Trick #165: **End in the Daytime**

meloearth

Member since 2001, Feedback: Turquoise star

That general advice might not apply to all types of auctions, however. What you need to do is figure out who is the audience for what you're selling and when you're most likely catch them at home. For example, if you're selling an item that appeals to grade-school or high-school kids, try ending your auction in the late afternoon, after the kids get home from school and before they head off for dinner. Items with appeal to homemakers do well with a late morning or early afternoon end time. And business items sell best when they end during normal business hours.

Trick #166: **Use eBay's Start Time Feature**

bushellcollectibles

stores.ebay.com/Bushells-Collectibles

Member since 1999, Feedback: Red star

What do you do if you want to end your auction at a particular time of day, but you can't be home in front of your PC at that time to start the listing? eBay lets you pay an extra dime to schedule your auction to start (and stop) at a specified time different from when you created the item listing. Just select this option from the Sell Your Item page, and you can post all your auctions at your convenience—and have them end at the best times possible.

Trick #167: **Don't End Your Auctions All at Once**

New Trick

peaches1442

stores.ebay.com/Peaches-Cards-and-Gifts-Shoppe

Member since 2002, Feedback: Red star

If you're offering several items for sale that the same bidder might be interested in, it's difficult for that bidder to make last-minute bids on all of them if they all end at the precise same second. (Which can happen if you use eBay's start time feature or an automated listing service.) It's better to put a few minutes between each auction, so that interested bidders can track and bid in each of the auctions separately. As **peaches1442** puts it:

When you are listing several items, space out the time they end, at least by a few minutes each. Having dealt with this recently, nothing is more frustrating than wanting several items from the same seller that end so close together—or, worse yet, end at the exact same time. It's terrible for people like me, who like to manually snipe an auction at the end!

Choosing When to List

If the ending time is important, the ending day is no less so. Some days of the week have more traffic than others, and the more traffic, the more potential buyers for your items. Here's what the eBay Masters have to say about it.

Trick #168: **End on Sunday Evening**

griffin_trader

stores.ebay.com/Naturally-In-New-Orleans-Mardi-Gras

Member since 1999, Feedback: Green star

Among experienced eBay sellers, the generally agreed-upon best day to end your auction is Sunday. Sunday is a great day to end auctions because almost everybody is home—no one is out partying, or stuck at work or in school. In addition, when you end your auction on a Sunday, you get one full Saturday and *two* Sundays (the starting Sunday and the ending one) for a seven-day item listing.

Trick #169: **End on Tuesday or Wednesday Evening**

debijane12000

stores.ebay.com/Debijanes-Music-and-More

Member since 2002, Feedback: Red star

Of course, not everybody adheres to the always-on-a-Sunday rule. Some eBayers swear by a middle-of-the-week auction ending, as **debijane12000** recommends:

> *A fellow eBay seller advised me that the majority of e-buyers are online midweek evenings around 6:00-7:00 p.m., not on weekends as I'd presumed. So scheduling an auction to end on a Tuesday or Wednesday evening around 7:00 p.m. (Pacific time) may help increase last-minute bidding.*

There's some logic to this, particularly on specific types of items. For example, if you're selling an item of interest to college students, you'll catch more of them in their dorms mid-week, as a lot of them travel home for the weekend. In addition, religious items targeted at churchgoers might also be better ending during the week, so that you don't catch them when they're at Sunday evening church services.

Trick #170: **Don't End on Friday or Saturday Nights**

edlinlac

Member since 2001, Feedback: Turquoise star

Whatever you do, definitely do *not* end your auctions on a Friday or Saturday night. That's because a lot of eBay users (a lot of people, period) are out dining and drinking on these non-school/non-work nights. End an auction for any item (especially youth-oriented items) on a Friday or Saturday night, and you eliminate a large number of potential buyers.

Trick #171: **Don't End on a Holiday**

raeosenbaugh

stores.ebay.com/OLD-BOOKS-NEW-BOOKS

Member since 2001, Feedback: Red star

It's also good to avoid ending your auctions on a holiday, such as Easter or Thanksgiving or Christmas Day, when people are likely to be away from their computers. (The same goes for three-day weekend holidays when people are apt to be traveling away from home.) Schedule your auctions around these holidays, or you risk having very few—if any—last-minute bids.

This also means you should avoiding ending during blockbuster sporting events or award shows. And definitely don't end any auction on Super Bowl Sunday!

Trick #172: **Space Out Your Auctions Throughout the Week**

New Trick

trapperjohn2000

stores.ebay.com/Molehill-Group-Store

Member since 1998, Feedback: Purple star

This one's for high-volume sellers. If you're listing only a few items at a time, it's okay for them to all end on the same day of the week. But when you're listing 100 items, if they all end on the same day, that means you have hundreds of items to pack and ship simultaneously. It's a whole lot easier if your 100 listings are spaced out to end over the course of a week; this way, you'll only have a dozen or so items to deal with on any given day.

You have to manage your workflow. Do you want to do all your work (listing, packing, shipping, and so on) on one day and then have nothing to do the rest of the week, or do you want to even out your work so that you do a little bit every day?

Trick #173: **Avoid the First Week of the Month**

mikeology

Member since 2002, Feedback: Purple star

Here's one you might not have thought of. Auction activity slows down the first week of every month. Why? Because that's when, for many people, rent is due. You want people to bid when they actually have some money in their pockets!

Trick #174: **Avoid the Tax Season Slump**

mikeology

Member since 2002, Feedback: Purple star

Speaking of having money in your pocket, another slowdown comes every year around the end of March/beginning of April. That's tax time, people, and it's a definite slow period on eBay. The tax season slump particularly affects sellers of high-priced and collectible items, so plan for it. And, as **mikeology** notes:

It is also the time I see the majority of no pays or late pays (as you can guess why).

Trick #175: **Avoid the Summer Doldrums**

> **puggybelle**
>
> stores.ebay.com/Soap-Opera-World
>
> Member since 1999, Feedback: Red star

The absolute worst time of year to sell, however, is during the summer. Lots of potential buyers are on vacation, and even more are outside enjoying the sunshine. How bad does it get? Here's what **puggybelle** found:

In my experience, summer has always been a rough time to sell on eBay. I've been selling for several years, and summer is absolutely the slowest season of the year. I have a store and it's been doing very well...until June hit. I sold 120 store items in the month of May. So far in June, I've sold a whopping seven items.

Fortunately, things start to pick up again in late August and early September, just in time for the back-to-school selling season.

Trick #176: **Christmas Season Is the Greatest**

> **tradervic4u**
>
> stores.ebay.com/LeeWardBooks
>
> Member since 2002, Feedback: Red star

If summer's the worst time of year to sell, when's the best? No surprise; it's the Christmas season, from November through January. (I include January because there's a heavy after-Christmas effect on eBay that you don't want to miss.) I know a lot of sellers who save up their best stuff to sell during this period—the higher buyer traffic results in significantly higher selling prices.

Trick #177: **Pick the Right Season for the Merchandise**

> **powershopper**
>
> Member since 1998, Feedback: Purple star

In addition to the general selling seasons, you also need to take into account the selling seasons for particular types of merchandise. For example, selling bikinis in January probably isn't that great of an idea. (Unless you're in Australia, of course.) In fact, the best time to sell most items is early in that particular selling season, when the demand is just peaking; selling late in the season will find far fewer interested buyers.

Here's what **powershopper** recommends:

> *When you list certain items you will typically garner the best prices right before and during the season it will be used. For example, scuba items sell spring through summer; Christmas items sell in the fall; ski items sell fall through winter. Many sellers list right at the beginning of the season before there is a lot of competition.*

Trick #178: **Even When It's Slow, Keep a Few Active Listings**

bushellcollectibles

stores.ebay.com/Bushells-Collectibles

Member since 1999, Feedback: Red star

Okay, so things slow down in the summertime. Does this mean your eBay business goes on vacation for three months? Not necessarily. Most experienced sellers try to keep one or two active listings every week of the year. This lets buyers know you're still there and still in business—and they will keep your listings bookmarked for future reference.

Trick #179: **When It's Slow, Promote!**

pins-n-needles

stores.ebay.com/Pins-n-Needles-Sewing-Emporium

www.ditzyprints.com

PowerSeller

Member since 2000, Feedback: Red star

Just because business is slow for everyone else doesn't mean it has to be slow for you. You can combat the summer doldrums by upping your promotions and offering better deals to attract more buyers. There may be fewer buyers out there, so you want to get more of the ones who are left.

Here's something that worked for seller **pins-n-needles**:

> *Last year I tried a promotion with patterns starting in June—free shipping to U.S. or Canada on sewing patterns. It worked so well for me, I've kept it year round! Summer weather doesn't stop us all!*

Trick #180: **Summer in the U.S. Is Winter in the Southern Hemisphere**

pins-n-needles

stores.ebay.com/Pins-n-Needles-Sewing-Emporium

www.ditzyprints.com

PowerSeller

Member since 2000, Feedback: Red star

Here's one more thing to keep in mind. Just because it's summer here in the U.S. doesn't mean it's summer everywhere. When things slow down during our summer months, it's approaching winter for the southern hemisphere. This means you can actually expect *increased* international sales from South America and Australia. Plan for it!

Listing Options

eBay offers all sorts of ways to spice up your auctions, in the form of extra-cost listing options. How effective are these listing options? Here's what the eBay Masters say.

Trick #181: **List for Seven Days**

jakki01

Member since 2000, Feedback: Purple star

With all the listing options available, the big choice you have to make is how long you want your auctions to run. The default auction length is 7 days, and it's also the best option. What's nice about a 7-day auction is that it guarantees that your item is listed over a weekend; a 1-, 3-, or 5-day auction won't necessarily hit the busy weekend days, depending on the day you start the auction. Besides, the 7-day auction is what users expect, and it allows for bidding on each day of the week— without taking *too* long to get the process over with.

Trick #182: **Get an Extra Weekend with a 10-Day Auction**

tradervic4u

stores.ebay.com/LeeWardBooks

Member since 2002, Feedback: Red star

Thinking about heavy weekend traffic, some sellers prefer a 10-day auction, starting on a Friday or Saturday, to get *two* weekends into the bidding schedule. There's some logic in that; just one extra bid will probably offset the extra $0.40 cost. However, a longer auction like this also means that you have to wait longer before you collect your money, so that needs to be figured in, as well.

Trick #183: **Don't List in Two Categories**

trapperjohn2000

stores.ebay.com/Molehill-Group-Store

Member since 1998, Feedback: Purple star

In the past, choosing the best category was extremely important. But then eBay got really big, so any given category became too crowded to browse. Today, most bidders find items by searching, which is why spending the money to list in a second category doesn't make a lot of sense. If a buyer is searching for an item, it doesn't matter which category it's listed in—so don't waste your money with the second category option.

Trick #184: **Don't Pay for Subtitles**

trapperjohn2000

stores.ebay.com/Molehill-Group-Store

Member since 1998, Feedback: Purple star

The subtitle is another listing option that most sellers find pointless. The option doesn't do anything for you that you can't get from a powerful title and a decent item description. The only exception might be those categories where many sellers are offering the same items for sale; in this instance, all the titles on a search results page might look the same, but you can use the subtitle to distinguish your item from the others or to provide additional information.

Trick #185: **Use the Gallery**

sunfarmer

stores.ebay.com/Sunfarmers-Wild-Bird-Seeds

Member since 2002, Feedback: Purple star

One listing option that some sellers find effective is the Gallery. While few buyers access the Gallery directly, the Gallery option also displays your item with a photo in any browsing or search results page. It's this photo in the search results that makes a difference. As **sunfarmer** points out:

> *The picture makes the search easier and faster. Time is important to people. The Gallery pictures show them what they are going to get.*

The Gallery picture is particularly important for more visual items, such as paintings and artwork. An item in these categories *without* a Gallery picture is likely to be overlooked.

Trick #186: **Don't Use the Gallery for Certain Items**

mississippi*mercantile
Member since 2003, Feedback: Turquoise star

If you're selling an item that isn't highly visual—and most of your competitors don't include Gallery pictures either—then there might not be any advantage to paying for the Gallery option. Here's what **mississippi*mercantile** found out:

> *I quit using it and my sell rate stayed the same, about 40 percent. Yes, I agree it helps but peeps that are using search tools are gonna look without a pic. That's why I don't put up items in Gallery that have no point being there.*

If you don't need the Gallery picture option, don't pay for it.

Trick #187: **If You Use the Gallery, Use a Different Photo**

quiltworks
Member since 1999, Feedback: Turquoise star

If you do choose to use a Gallery photo, you might as well get the most use out of it—which means using a different photo for the Gallery than you do in your main product listing. Remember, it's a smaller photo, so you need to display a shot that works best in that size. Here's what **quiltworks** recommends:

> *One has to take very special care with the photos used in the Gallery. I never use the same picture as my main photo; I always take a different one—a close up, or details that will look good as a small image. I also make sure that it is extra sharp using photo editing tools, since eBay reduces it and it loses some sharpness. A blob will not be helpful at all!*

Trick #188: **Don't Use eBay's Listing Designer**

> **bluemagnoliablossoms**
>
> Member since 2003, Feedback: Yellow star

Sellers always like to make their listings "pop" as much as possible, and one way to do this is by using special listing templates. In the old days, you had to create your own templates using HTML, but now eBay offers a Listing Designer option with a variety of prepared templates you can choose from. The problem is, these listing templates are kind of lame, and they cost 10 cents per listing. Savvy sellers use their own HTML to design their listings, or use third-party listing creation tools that provide better-looking results. Learn more in Chapter 9, "How to Enhance Your Product Listings with HTML."

Trick #189: **Use a Hit Counter**

> **sunfarmer**
>
> stores.ebay.com/Sunfarmers-Wild-Bird-Seeds
>
> Member since 2002, Feedback: Purple star

When you're creating your item listing, eBay gives you the option of including a hit counter at the bottom of your listing, provided for free by Ándale. Most sellers like incorporating a hit counter, as it tells you whether anyone is looking at your item. It's also useful to bidders, as it tells them how many people are interested in that item. (That might not be a good thing for you, the seller, however—which we'll cover in the next trick.)

Trick #190: **Hide Your Counters**

> **quiltworks**
>
> Member since 1999, Feedback: Turquoise star

As a seller, do you really want potential buyers to know how many other people are looking at your auctions? If the counter count is low, bidders might be inspired to bid low—if at all. For that reason, you might want to choose the invisible counter option, which shows the count to you (the seller) but not to potential bidders. As **quiltworks** points out:

> *A hit counter, in my opinion, is a tool for the seller. It helps determine interest in the item, or if there is something wrong with the listing. The best counters for that purpose are hidden. I see no benefit to the seller for the bidder to know the hit count.*

Trick #191: **Use Third-Party Counters**

lesley_feeney

stores.ebay.com/Lesleys-Auction-Template-Designs

www.zoicks.com

PowerSeller

Member since 2000, Feedback: Purple star

One of the most consistent beefs on the part of expert sellers is how often Ándale's counters malfunction. Half the time they don't show up in the listing, and half of that time the count doesn't register correctly. Many high-volume sellers prefer to pass on the Ándale counters and use another third-party counter. To that end, seller **lesley_feeney** offers the following list of free counters you can add to your eBay auction listings:

- Amherst Robots/Vrane (www.vrane.com/counters.html)
- BoingDragon's Lair (www.boingdragon.com/counters.html)
- Bravenet (www.bravenet.com/webtools/counter/)
- CounterBot (www.counterbot.com)
- Shoporium.com (www.shoporium.com/counters/)
- ZCounter (www.zcounter.com)

Trick #192: **Don't Use the Slideshow**

berties_house_of_horrors

stores.ebay.com/Berties-Emporium

PowerSeller

Member since 1999, Feedback: Red star

At just 25 cents, you might think that eBay's picture slideshow option is a good deal, especially if you have a bunch of photos to accompany your product listing. It's not an option I'd recommend, however, and that's not just because of the price. The simple fact is that many eBay buyers are still on slow-poke dial-up Internet connections, and for them it takes an eternity for a six-picture slideshow to load. As **berties_house_of_horrors** notes:

The average eBay buyer spends five seconds in a listing before moving on. It is much more effective to host your own photos and use smaller thumbnail images.

In other words, if you force buyers to download too many large pictures, they're apt to click back and skip your auction completely. Not a good thing.

Trick #193: **Track Your Fees with ecal**

trapperjohn2000

stores.ebay.com/Molehill-Group-Store

Member since 1998, Feedback: Purple star

One of the problems with all of eBay's listing options is that they cost money. Choose one from column A and two from column B, and pretty soon those extra fees start to add up—especially if you're selling a low-priced item. And eBay, of course, doesn't go out of its way to let you know when you're spending too much.

Fortunately, there's a third-party fee calculator available to help you track the costs of eBay's various listing options. As you can see in Figure 7.1, The ecal auction fee calculator lets you select any and all listing options you want, and then input your starting price and expected selling price. Click the Calculate button and ecal displays the analysis page shown in Figure 7.2. You'll see what your costs are if your item doesn't sell, if it sells for the initial bid price, and if it sells for your expected final prices. The calculator even tells if your fees will run higher than your selling price—which is something you want to avoid!

FIGURE 7.1

The ecal auction fee calculator factors in all the listing options and information about your auction.

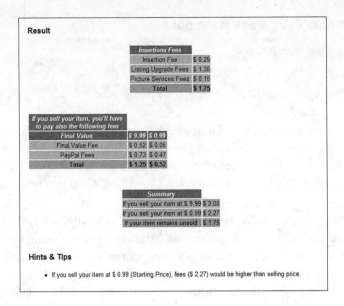

FIGURE 7.2

Let the ecal auction fee calculator analyze how much you're spending to list and sell items on eBay.

And the best thing about ecal is that it's completely free. Try it for yourself at ecal.altervista.org/en/.

Offering Incentives

Many sellers find they can increase their close rate by offering incentives to their auction buyers. Here are some of the most effective of these auction incentives.

Trick #194: **Offer Additional Services**

New Trick

| **kyderbyfan** |
| PowerSeller |
| Member since 1999, Feedback: Red star |

When you offer additional services above and beyond normal packing and shipping, you give bidders a unique incentive to purchase from you, and not from your competitors. What kinds of additional services am I talking about? Here's what **kyderbyfan** suggests:

Some customers will purchase from sellers who offer extra services like gift wrapping, direct shipping to gift recipient, discounts on shipping of multiple items purchased, free gift card with purchase, small gift (like a pen, mints, or free product coupons), or other such bonus services with the purchase. This is especially useful around the holidays, for baby gifts, wedding gifts, Mother's Day gifts, military care packages, and other special occasion purchases. The added services you choose to include in any of your auctions are totally up to you, the seller, but may make the difference in someone purchasing your item or another similar item from a different seller.

Trick #195: **Offer a Discount for Multiple Purchases**

michelelise

Member since 2001, Feedback: Yellow star

When you want buyers to buy more stuff, make it worth their while. One popular incentive is to offer a discount on multiple purchases. This is particularly popular among sellers who run their own eBay Stores, but any seller can do it, by manipulating payment-due amounts at the end of an auction to override eBay's automatically-generated invoices. Here's what seller **michelelise** offers:

I sell mostly books and offer 10% off final bid price after your first book win.

Trick #196: **Offer Free/Discounted Shipping on Multiple Purchases**

thecountrybaker

stores.ebay.com/THE-COUNTRY-BAKER

Member since 2000, Feedback: Red star

Another effective incentive is free or discounted shipping on multiple purchases. Here's what **thecountrybaker** offers:

I offer free shipping on some items and discounted shipping when they purchase three or more items.

Trick #197: **Bundle Slow Sellers Together**

623merlin

Member since 2002, Feedback: Red star

If you have a handful of items that haven't moved in multiple auctions, try bundling them together into a single lot. This approach kind of hides the dogs in a pack and offers a good deal to potential buyers—especially when a dodgy item is paired with something a bit more attractive. Here's what **623merlin** recommends:

> *If I am having trouble selling an item, I will put it with another item and sell it as a set, increasing its perceived value. People like to get more for less. This way I can move out slow-selling items and buy more of what sells.*

Trick #198: **Blitz Multiple Auctions with a Similar Theme**

torreyphilemon

PowerSeller

Member since 1999, Feedback: Red star

This next trick really isn't an incentive per se, but it does help drum up interest in what you have to sell. If you have multiple items available, sell them all (in individual auctions, batch) under a similar theme—and make sure you reference all the auctions in each listing. For example, you might list a dozen auctions of Star Wars merchandise, or a group of auctions somehow related to "summer fun." Pick the right selling theme, and you can really increase buyer interest. As **torreyphilemon** notes:

> *It really helps to create the time—the right time—to do a real blitz of auctions on a related theme, and to create some anticipation in regard to it.*

Mid-Auction Strategies

Okay, you have your auctions started, and you're waiting it out through the 7-day process. But what do you do if your auctions aren't generating any bids?

Trick #199: **If You Don't Have Any Bids, Extend the Auction**

debijane12000

stores.ebay.com/Debijanes-Music-and-More

Member since 2002, Feedback: Red star

The first thing to do, if you can, is to extend the length of your auction. As long as there aren't any bids, you can extend the auction. If you're running a 7-day auction, extend it to 10 days. If you're running a 3- or 5-day auction, extend it to 7 or

10 days. In fact, some sellers start with a 1-day auction, then lengthen it to 3 days, then to 5 days, then to 7 days, then to 10 days, if necessary.

Here's what **debijane12000** recommends:

I always start with 7 days. Then if there are watchers but no bids by day 6, I extend to 10 days. Why pay the extra 40 cents up front when you might make a great sale in 7 days?

Trick #200: **Create Multiple Ending Days**

> **emedia-direct**
>
> stores.ebay.com/Emedia-Direct-Shop
>
> Member since 2003, Feedback: Red star

The previous trick can become a deliberate strategy, as many sellers search only for items ending today. If you can manipulate your auction so that it ends on multiple days (after 1 day, after 3 days, after 5 days, and so on), you show up in more search results.

The strategy is simple:

1. List an item as a 1-day auction.
2. When there are just over 12 hours left in the auction, revise the listing and change the duration to 3 days. Your listing now has 2 1/2 days left.
3. On the third day, when there are just over 12 hours left again, revise the listing and change the duration to 5 days. Your listing now has another 2 1/2 days left.
4. On the fifth day, once the listing gets down to just over 12 hours left again, revise the listing and change the duration to 7 days. Your listing now has yet another 2 1/2 days left.
5. Finally, on the seventh day, once the listing gets down to just over 12 hours left again, revise the listing and change the duration to 10 days. Your listing now has another 3 1/2 days left.

Of course, you can only make these changes if there are no bids on your item, and if there are more than 12 hours left in the auction. This is why you make the revisions with just over 12 hours left; if you wait past the 12-hour mark, eBay won't let you extend the auction.

Trick #201: **Add a BIN If You Have a Lot of Watchers but No Bidders**

> **clact**
>
> stores.ebay.com/Once-Upon-A-Bid
>
> PowerSeller
>
> Member since 2002, Feedback: Red star

Use My eBay to watch how many watchers your auction has. If you have a lot of watchers but no bidders, consider adding Buy It Now to your auction mid-stream. If you do this, make the BIN price really low and attractive—you might turn one of those watchers into a buyer!

Trick #202: **Change the Item Title Mid-Auction**

> **satnrose**
>
> PowerSeller
>
> Member since 1998, Feedback: Green star

If nobody's bidding, change something! Wait a few days, and then change the item title to something a little more attention-grabbing. It certainly won't hurt!

If It Doesn't Sell

Even the best sellers have unsuccessful auctions. (Some estimates place the successful close rate at less than 50% of all auctions.) If your auction closes without a sale, here are some tricks on what to do next.

Trick #203: **If It Doesn't Sell the First Time, List It Again**

> **trapperjohn2000**
>
> stores.ebay.com/Molehill-Group-Store
>
> Member since 1998, Feedback: Purple star

If at first you don't succeed, try again. You just might have hit an off week; the same item listed at a different time might draw lots of bidders. Fortunately, eBay makes it easy to relist an unsold item. So if it doesn't sell the first time, relist it—and see who's interested the next week.

Trick #204: **When You're Relisting, Change Things Up**

lludwig

stores.ebay.com/LLudwig-Books

PowerSeller

Member since 1998, Feedback: Green star

Of course, maybe your item didn't sell because of something you did. Maybe the title was unexciting. Maybe the description was uninformative. Maybe you didn't include a picture. Maybe it was listed in the wrong category. Whatever the case, take this opportunity to review all aspects of your item listing, and change it for the better!

And when you're looking at changing your item at relist time, definitely reevaluate the starting price. If the item didn't draw any bids, it's quite possibly because it was overpriced to begin with. Definitely consider lowering the price when you relist. Seller **shellyscloset** recommends the following strategy:

> *Once it's been listed a couple times I'll start dropping the price so I can sell it and recoup my costs.*

Trick #205: **Use the Second-Chance Offer to Sell Additional Items**

afwhited

Member since 2003, Feedback: Turquoise star

Here's a trick you can use when you successfully sell an item but have additional quantities available. eBay's Second Chance Offer feature lets you offer additional items to the non-winning bidders in your auction. It's a great way to sell more items without running additional auctions—and paying additional listing fees. (And if you use the Second Chance Offer option, give your bidders one day to respond; the three-day option tends not to work as well.)

Promoting Your Auctions

Once you have a bunch of auctions running, how do you get the word out? Read on to learn how the eBay Masters do it.

Trick #206: **Find Prequalified Buyers with Want It Now**

New Trick

selling4-u

stores.ebay.com/Selling-4-U-Consignment-Store

www.selling4-u.com

PowerSeller

Member since 2002, Feedback: Purple star

A good way to find interested buyers is to go directly to those eBay members who want to buy what you have for sale. You can do this with eBay's Want It Now feature, where buyers create "wish lists" of specific items. You search the Want It Now listings, and when you find a match, you offer the item for sale to the interested buyer. (eBay still takes their normal cut, of course.)

Browsing these ads is a great way for you to focus on potentially hot products that buyers want and are in short supply. Start by clicking the Want It Now link on eBay's home page. When the Want It Now page appears, you can browse through the listings by category, or use the Sellers search box to search for specific items that might be listed in the database. When the search results are displayed, as shown in Figure 7.3, click a particular listing for more detail from the interested buyer. From the listing page, as shown in Figure 7.4, you can then click the Respond button to let the buyer know that you have the item they're interested in.

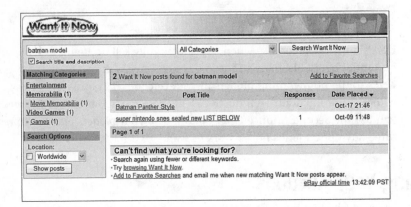

FIGURE 7.3

Searching for interested buyers via Want It Now.

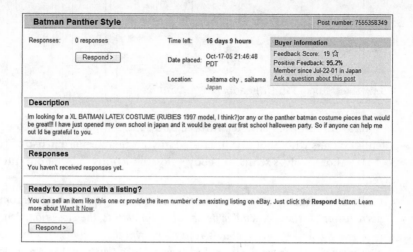

FIGURE 7.4

Getting ready to contact a potential Want It Now buyer.

The interested buyer is now emailed a message containing a link to your item listing. To place a bid on your item, all the recipient has to do is click a button.

Trick #207: **Inform Past Buyers of Upcoming Auctions**

kyderbyfan

PowerSeller

Member since 1999, Feedback: Red star

Savvy sellers keep good records of all their past auctions—and past buyers. Then you can create a list of buyers who want to be contacted when you have similar merchandise for sale. (Make this an opt-in list; you don't want to spam anyone!) When you have new items for auction, send out emails to interested customers, and watch the bids arrive!

Here's what **kyderbyfan** does:

> I often will send email alerts to customers who purchase items from me regularly, to let them know I am about to list an item they may be interested in. This gives them a little more time to watch for an item to become available. I also may ask if they are looking for other specific items that I may be able to list the same week. By listing items of interest to my buyers concurrently, it will allow me to combine shipping for multiple items that are purchased.

Trick #208: **Inform Other eBay Buyers of Your Auctions**

New Trick

> **rufusduff**
>
> PowerSeller
>
> Member since 1999, Feedback: Turquoise star

Let's take that last trick one step further, and consider how you can contact other potential buyers who might be interested in your item. Seller **rufusduff** offers a neat trick that involves searching eBay's closed auctions to ferret out interested buyers:

I call this one Precision Market Targeting. Before posting an item, search completed auctions for identical or similar items. Click through to the closed auction listing and note the underbidders' eBay screen names via the "bid history" link. Use the eBay member search feature to contact them with an "Auction Alert" message containing the URL of your current auction. This informs them that an item, similar or identical to the one they missed, is now on the market, and where to find it. Often, very surprised underbidders will thank you profusely for alerting them, bid on your current item (creating a healthy competitive situation), and very often win.

And, in case you're wondering, eBay does not consider this "auction stealing" (which is not allowed) because these auctions have already ended. eBay allows up to 10 of these messages to members per day.

Trick #209: **Inform Bidders in Older Auctions of Your Auctions**

New Trick

> **rufusduff**
>
> PowerSeller
>
> Member since 1999, Feedback: Turquoise star

Here's a neat variation on the previous theme. As you'll no doubt discover, the searching eBay approach limits you to auctions that closed within the past 21 days. (That's all the longer eBay keeps historical auction info.) To find interested buyers from before the 21-day mark, try this technique from **rufusduff**:

Use Google to search the same-named item plus the word "eBay." Many older auctions will appear, well past eBay's own 21-day limit. When you get Google's results, click the "cache" link, because that item will no longer appear on the eBay site. The cache link will open the long-closed auction and color-highlight the item name. Once open, the "bid history" link will reveal those underbidders from weeks, months, sometimes even one or two years back. (Note, however, that the results are variable; not every old auction will pop up in Google's results.)

Trick #210: **Inform Other Interested Parties of Your Auctions**

New Trick

rufusduff
PowerSeller
Member since 1999, Feedback: Turquoise star

Seller **rufusduff** has one more trick for finding interested buyers. When you do your research on an item before you list it for sale (you do do your research, don't you?), you'll discover the community most interested in that item. Just do a little Googling and you're likely to find websites, webrings, message forums, and the like all devoted to the type of item that you're selling. For example, if you're selling an antique radio, I know you'll find a half-dozen sites devoted to the hobby. Visit these sites and let them know about your upcoming auction, by posting on their message boards, using their contact forms, or just emailing them. Chances are, they'll be very interested in the item you have for sale!

Trick #211: **Offer Discounts to Repeat Buyers**

clact
stores.ebay.com/Once-Upon-A-Bid
PowerSeller
Member since 2002, Feedback: Red star

While you're sending out customer emails, make it worth their while. Offer some sort of discount to your repeat customers—maybe a coupon worth a few bucks off a future purchase. The right incentive will bring them back!

Trick #212: **Promote Duplicate Items**

New Trick

trickie636
Member since 2000, Feedback: Purple star

If you're selling similar or identical items in other auctions, make sure you mention that in each of your auction listings. This way you let people know they can bid on similar items in case they get outbid in the current auction.

Trick #213: **Link to Your Other Auctions**

kyrn

stores.ebay.com/The-Art-of-Meredith-Dillman/

www.meredithdillman.com

Member since 1998, Feedback: Turquoise star

Of course, it makes sense to promote all your auctions in each of your item listings. The standard eBay View Seller's Other Items link is fine, but you can put a fancier link in your auction description with the following HTML code:

<a href="http://cgi6.ebay.com/ws/eBayISAPI.dll?ViewSellersOtherItems& userid=*YOURID*&include=0&since=-1&sort=3&rows=50& sspageName=DB:OtherItems" target=_blank>Check out my other items!</a>

Naturally, replace YOURID with your eBay user ID.

Trick #214: **Include Photos of Your Other Auction Items**

New Trick

slfcollectibles2

stores.ebay.com/A-Gift-for-Her

PowerSeller

Member since 2001, Feedback: Red star

What's better than linking to your other auctions? Cross-promoting those auctions with pictures of the items for sale!

While you could insert all those photos manually, using HTML code, there's an easier method. All you have to do is use the Thumbnail Cross-Selling Links Tool found at www.egocentral.com/cgi-bin/ebay_cross_sell.cgi. As you can see in Figure 7.5, you enter the item numbers of your current auction, and this tool generates the appropriate HTML code to insert into your item listings. It's easy enough that anyone can do it!

And, if you have an eBay Store, this type of auction cross-promoting is even easier, thanks to eBay's Cross-Promotions feature. See Trick #552 to learn more.

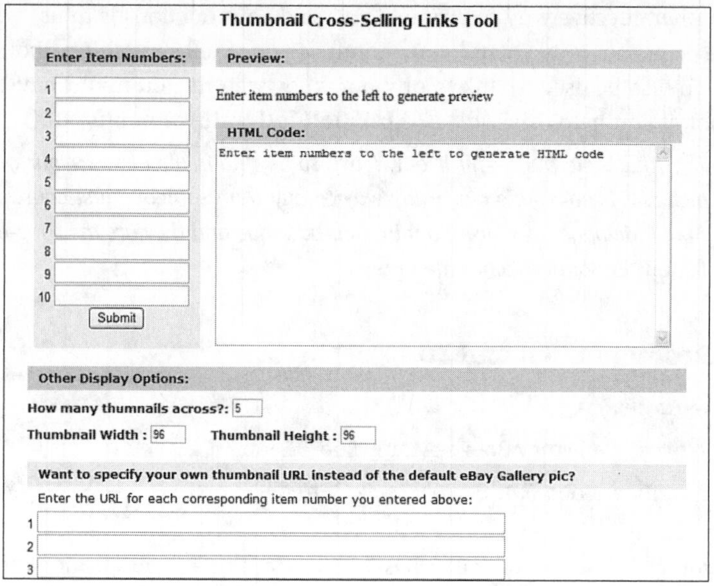

FIGURE 7.5

Generate your own cross-promotional pictures with the Thumbnail Cross-Selling Links Tool.

Trick #215: **Link to Other Items in Your eBay Store**

artchick48

stores.ebay.com/Lee-Smith-Art

www.leesmithart.com

Member since 2001, Feedback: Turquoise star

If you have an eBay Store, you should definitely mention (and link to) your store within each of your auction listings. Use your store to drive add-on sales—typically less expensive items that are accessory to the main item for auction. (Learn more about eBay Stores in Chapter 18, "How to Sell More Products in an eBay Store.")

Trick #216: **Use Your About Me Page for Promotion**

bushellcollectibles

stores.ebay.com/Bushells-Collectibles

Member since 1999, Feedback: Red star

Another effective way to promote you and your auctions is to use your eBay About Me page. Not only should your About Me page tell something about you as a seller, it can also be used to link to any non-eBay website you might have. If you do it right, it can help drive sales, as **bushellcollectibles** points out:

> The About Me page—fill it out. Have some tidbits about you, your interests, and pictures! I have gone out of my way to buy from someone just cause I loved their About Me page. I feel like I am in their boutique and they are the shop-owner whom I know. Personal touches mean a lot.

Trick #217: **Promote a Second ID**

swlakat
stores.ebay.com/Books-Along-The-Bayou
Member since 2003, Feedback: Purple star

If you use two separate eBay IDs, buyers from one ID might not know about the items you have for sale under your second ID. (Same deal if you're operating dual eBay Stores.) To this end, include an invoice or business card in each package you ship out, listing both your IDs/Store addresses, and a description of the merchandise sold under each ID. You never know what kind of additional sales you might drum up!

Trick #218: **Tag Along on eBay's Promotions**

rosachs
stores.ebay.com/My-Discount-Shoe-Store
home.midsouth.rr.com/rosachs/RKS/
PowerSeller
Member since 1997, Feedback: Red star

Even if you're a big eBay seller, you're still a small business when compared to the Wal-Marts and Amazons of the world. You do what you can to maximize your sales within the eBay community, but there's no way you can afford to compete with the big boys in real-world advertising.

Fortunately, you don't have to. That's because eBay does your advertising for you. eBay runs a ton of advertising and promotions, and they target both the mass market and specific markets with ads that the average eBay seller could never afford.

And here's the best part: eBay tells you about their plans, so that you can join in on the promotions—if you're selling the right products.

PowerSeller **rosachs** provides the following real-world example:

> *My current product line is primarily women's shoes. eBay runs four "Fashion Blowouts" a year—Spring, Summer, Fall, and Winter. Invariably, during these promotional periods, my sales increase. The Spring 2005 blowout bumped my monthly sales from just over 100 sales per month to well over 200! With sales doubled for nearly six weeks (the length of the promotion), I was hard pressed to keep up with the volume. And this cost me nothing—eBay would have run the promotion anyway. All I had to do was follow the guidelines to ensure my products would be picked up by the promotions page and presented to buyers; eBay took care of getting them to the site.*

How do you find out about eBay's promotions? Simple. Just go to the Merchandising Calendar page in eBay's Seller Central (pages.ebay.com/sellercentral/calendar.html). As you can see in Figure 7.6, the Merchandising Calendar lists all of eBay's upcoming home page promotions. Match the merchandise you're selling to the categories promoted, and you'll come out ahead.

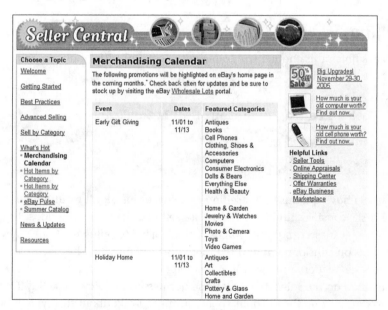

FIGURE 7.6

Track upcoming promotions with eBay's Merchandising Calendar.

Trick #219: **Cross-Promote with Another Seller**

New Trick

trapperjohn2000

stores.ebay.com/Molehill-Group-Store

Member since 1998, Feedback: Purple star

eBay's Cross-Promotion Connection lets you team with other eBay sellers to market your auctions at the bottom of each other's item listings. You can work with friendly sellers you know, or request to work with other sellers whose auctions you like.

The cross-promoted items from other sellers appear at the bottom of all your active items, just like your own cross-promoted items from your eBay Store. Your own cross-promoted items will be displayed first, followed by items from connected sellers.

To form a cross-promotion connection with another seller, go to the My Accounts page in My eBay and click the Cross-Promotion Connections link. Click the Request New Connection button, then enter the user ID or eBay Store name of the seller with which you want to cross-promote. If the seller accepts your request, the cross-promoting begins.

Other Selling Tricks

Let's finish this chapter with a few more general tricks that can help you maximize your eBay sales.

Trick #220: **Let a Trading Assistant Sell It for You**

mikeology

Member since 2002, Feedback: Purple star

If you have qualms about selling on eBay, or just don't want to bother with all the hassle, consider having someone else sell your items for you. Most localities now have businesses that function as "middlemen" for eBay auctions. They take your goods on consignment and sell them on eBay for you. They create the listings, manage the auction, and even handle the packing and shipping, in return for a commission on the sale. Officially these businesses are known as eBay Trading Assistants, and they're doing good business. I talk about this type of business more in Chapter 19, "How to Make Money as a Trading Assistant"; turn there to learn more.

Trick #221: **Check Out the Trading Assistant Before You Sign the Contract**

New Trick

> **ourstuff4you**
>
> stores.ebay.com/OurStuff4You
>
> PowerSeller
>
> Member since 1998, Feedback: Red star

If you're looking for someone to sell your merchandise on consignment, know that not all Trading Assistants (TAs) are created equal. When you search the Trading Assistant Directory for a TA near you, as shown in Figure 7.7, you'll probably find that you have several sellers to choose from. (Just go to pages.ebay.com/tahub/, and then click the Find a Trading Assistant link.) At this point, it's time to do a little research to find out which of the available TAs is best for what you want to sell.

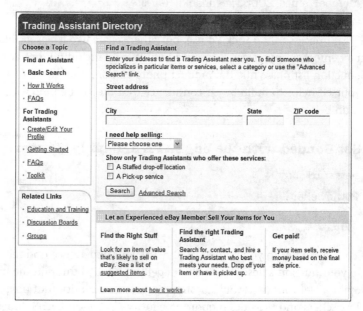

FIGURE 7.7

Searching the Trading Assistant Directory.

Here's some advice on how to pick a Trading Assistant, from experienced TA **ourstuff4you**:

> *When researching Trading Assistants, be sure to check more than the fee structure. Look to see how many listings the seller has placed on eBay over the last few weeks. Look at their listings. Are they professionally done? Do they list reasonable shipping*

fees? Do they ship outside the country? Do they have experience selling a variety of items, or do they specialize in a very specific area?

Also, ask the TA if they have a contract for you to sign. Ask to see a sample of their reporting form from previous contracts. After all, you want to know how you're going to receive your money! A good reporting system, and a good contract, will be signs of a quality Trade Assistant. And be sure the contract has spelled out the timing for you to receive your profits.

Trick #222: **Include a Photo of Yourself in the Listing**

emedia-direct

stores.ebay.com/Emedia-Direct-Shop

Member since 2003, Feedback: Red star

This isn't necessarily a trick I'd use, but other sellers like it—especially if they're photogenic. Let buyers get to know you a little by including a photo of yourself in the auction listing. While the product photo is more important, a subsidiary photo of yourself helps to build buyer confidence that they're dealing with a real live human being.

Trick #223: **Get Bonded with the buySAFE Shopping Network**

newstartoday

PowerSeller

Member since 2000, Feedback: Red star

Of course, anything you can do to play up your experience and reliability will only help your auction sales. That includes getting bonded through the buySAFE Shopping Network (www.buysafeshopping.com), a service that prequalifies "safe" online sellers and provides a guarantee for the buyer on each bonded purchase. Seller **newstartoday** swears by it:

I have noticed a big difference since being bonded with buySAFE. Plus, now my auctions are not only listed on eBay, but also on the buySAFE website—so I get twice the bang for my auction money!

To become a bonded seller, you'll need to provide some detailed financial information, as well as agree to pay 1% of the final sales price of each bonded transaction. After that, you can display the buySAFE logo in all your auctions, and be listed in buySAFE's merchant directory.

Trick #224: **Include a Phone Number in the Listing**

emedia-direct

stores.ebay.com/Emedia-Direct-Shop

Member since 2003, Feedback: Red star

If you're selling bigger-ticket items, some buyers might want to contact you person-ally before placing a bid. That's why seller **emedia-direct** recommends including your phone number in the auction listing. Not your personal phone number, of course, but if you have a separate phone for your eBay business, what's the harm? (And if you don't have a business phone, invest in a low-cost prepaid cell phone and use that for your incoming eBay calls.)

Know, however, that eBay's policy warns against including this sort of direct contact info in your auction listings. That's not to say that some seller's don't do it, but it's not eBay's policy.

Trick #225: **Adapt Your Strategies During the Christmas Season**

trapperjohn2000

stores.ebay.com/Molehill-Group-Store

Member since 1998, Feedback: Purple star

Whatever your normal selling strategies, you might need to adapt them during the holiday selling season. In particular, consider the following:

- Add the Buy It Now option, for buyers who don't want to (or can't) wait for the full auction period to end.
- Schedule your auctions to end at least a week before Christmas, to allow time for the package to arrive in time.
- Consider shorter (3- or 5-day auctions) for those last-minute items you have to sell.
- Ship everything Priority Mail, for faster holiday delivery—and consider offer-ing even faster express shipping, via either the Postal Service or FedEx. (And definitely avoid Media Mail, which slows way down over Christmas.)
- Offer gift-wrapping services, either for free or for an additional charge.
- Offer to ship directly to the gift recipient rather than to the buyer.
- Make sure you're stocked up on boxes and other shipping supplies; you don't want to hold up shipping while you go out to buy more Styrofoam peanuts.

Finally, you'll need to adapt your own personal schedule and put in some long hours during the holiday season. Not only will you have more orders during the Christmas season, you'll need to pack and ship those orders out faster than normal. It's a lot of work, but the increased seasonal sales should be worth it!

Trick #226: **Use Sellathon to Analyze Your Auctions**

scifi4me2004

stores.ebay.com/Needle-In-a-Haystack-Treasures

Member since 2003, Feedback: Turquoise star

Sellathon ViewTracker (www.sellathon.com) is a little different from the other research tools we discussed back in Chapter 6, "How to Find Merchandise to Sell." Instead of analyzing other auctions, it analyzes *your* auctions—to help you fine tune your listings. As you can see in Figure 7.8, ViewTracker provides detailed analysis of all the visitors to your auction listings, including number of visitors, time of visit, visitor's location, how much time was spent viewing your auction, what search terms the visitor used, and so on.

Sellathon offers several levels of service, including Basic Seller ($4.99/month), Advanced Seller ($8.95/month), and Enterprise Seller ($19.95/month). The Basic Seller package lets you track up to 50 simultaneous auctions; the Advanced Seller package lets you track 250 simultaneous auctions; and the Enterprise Seller package lets you track an unlimited number of auctions.

FIGURE 7.8

Analyzing your auction visitors with Sellathon ViewTracker.

How to Write Better Titles and Descriptions

One of the keys to running more successful auctions is the ability to write powerful item titles and informative item descriptions. The best eBay sellers know that an item listing has to function much like a traditional advertisement—it has to pull in the potential buyer, grab his attention, tell him everything he needs to know to make his purchase, and then close the sale. Learn to write more effective item listings, and you're on your way to becoming an eBay Master!

Writing a More Powerful Title

The first thing potential buyers see is your listing's title. In fact, when they're searching or browsing for an item, that's all they see. Most buyers search rather than browse, and close to 90% of all buyers search titles only—not the item description. So the most important part of your entire auction listing are those 55 little characters at the top, because that's all that most browsers will ever see.

Writing a great title isn't all that easy, however, unless you happen to have a day job as a professional copywriter. I like the way eBay Master **satnrose** puts it:

> *Haiku is easy*
> *compared to choosing the right*
> *Item title, no?*

Trick #227: **Use Keywords Buyers Will Be Searching For**

amrell

stores.ebay.com/The-Hot-Mannequin

Member since 2002, Feedback: Turquoise star

First things first. Most buyers find items by searching, so you want to include all the important words that someone might be searching for. Put popular search words in your title, and your item will pop up on more search results pages.

The key thing, then, is to think like the people who will be looking for your item. Use the words that they are likely to use. Include the name of the item—both the "official" name and any more common name it might have. Use the model number. Use the series name. Use the year manufactured. Use the color, the size, the condition. Include whatever terms you typically use to describe the item. The more search words you can include, the better.

Trick #228: **Be Creative—Think Like a Copywriter**

2ndhand4u

Member since 1998, Feedback: Red star

I find that the best way to approach a listing title is as if you're writing the headline for an advertisement. In other words, think like an advertising copywriter. Ask yourself, what words almost always stop consumers in their tracks? That means punching up your title with attention-getting words such as FREE and NEW and BONUS and EXTRA and DELUXE and RARE—as long as these words truly describe the item you're selling and don't mislead the potential bidder. After all, what's more appealing, East of Eden by John Steinbeck or RARE FIRST EDITION East of Eden by John Steinbeck? As **2ndhand4u** recommends:

> *Be creative, fair, and honest. If what you are selling is rare, say so.*

And if the item isn't rare, don't refer to it as such.

Trick #229: **Use a Synonym Finder**

New Trick

> **newstartoday**
>
> PowerSeller
>
> Member since 2000, Feedback: Red star

If you're having trouble finding words that make your auctions snap, invest in a synonym-finder program or reference book. (The book is called a *thesaurus*, which is a synonym for "synonym finder.") Synonyms also help you avoid using the same tired verbiage as found in other auctions, and sometimes find a shorter word to fit in that 55-character title limit.

Trick #230: **Use the Entire Phrase or Title**

> **satnrose**
>
> PowerSeller
>
> Member since 1998, Feedback: Green star

When describing an item in your title, use the full phrase or title for the item. After all, that's how most people will be searching. Leave out a word—even if it's the word "and"—and your item won't come up as a hit on the search. For example, if you're selling a copy of Robert Browning's *The Ring and the Book*, enter the entire book title in the title field; if you only enter Ring and Book, you'll be excluded from the results of anyone seaching for the exact phrase "The Ring and the Book". Along the same line, include the entire author or artist name when you're listing books and CDs.

Trick #231: **Use the Common Word**

> **satnrose**
>
> PowerSeller
>
> Member since 1998, Feedback: Green star

Here's another search-oriented tip. Whenever possible, use the common form of a word in your title—even if doesn't make sense grammatically. For example, you'll get more hits with the title Argentina poet than you will with Argentine poet.

Trick #232: **Sometimes Less Is More**

satnrose

PowerSeller

Member since 1998, Feedback: Green star

Master seller **satnrose** reminds us that sometimes less is more. When the "official" name of an item is too long for eBay's 55-character title limit, paraphrase or abbreviate it. This happens a lot with books, CDs, and movies. As **satnrose** notes:

> In this circumstance, your only recourse is to supply a title that is both generic and specific to your most likely audience for the item. And in many other instances, a minimalist approach allows you to carefully choose your words.

Trick #233: **Avoid Superlatives**

quadaxel83

stores.ebay.com/Buttons-And-Beads

Member since 2001, Feedback: Red star

Yes, you should think like an advertising copywriter when composing your item title. But that doesn't mean you should write like a carnival barker. State the facts, but don't exaggerate or overuse superlatives. There's no need to say that you're selling a HUGE HUGE LOT! Let the facts speak for themselves; don't unnecessarily pump them up.

Trick #234: **Avoid Nonsense Characters**

samby

Member since 1998, Feedback: Turquoise star

Along the same lines, many overeager sellers include a lot of non-alphanumeric characters, such as *!!!* or *###* or W@W! or C@@L@, in their titles. Other sellers use these nonsense characters as separators in the title, like this: **Brand New Widget *** Great Bargain - Low Price**.

I strongly recommend against using these characters in your title, for a number of reasons. First, eBay's search engine sometimes tosses out titles that include these nonsense characters, which is the exact opposite of what you want to accomplish. Second, too many nonsense characters make your listing look a little tacky, like a late-night TV used car salesman. Finally, and perhaps most importantly, these non-sense characters waste valuable space that could be better used to tell more about your item. So don't use them.

And, along the same lines, try not to overuse exclamation points, both in your title and in your item description. As ***samby*** so elegantly puts it:

> *The exclamation point (!) is a useful literary tool. But only one is required in any given sentence. More than one is overkill. More than ten is diabolical.*

Trick #235: **Avoid "Not" Comparisons**

trapperjohn2000

stores.ebay.com/Molehill-Group-Store

Member since 1998, Feedback: Purple star

You should also avoid putting words into your title that don't have anything to do with your item—words designed to mislead eBay's search engine and potential bidders. I like to call these "not" titles, where the item is described in terms of what it is not.

For example, if you're selling a Superman poster, but would also like to attract Batman and Spider-Man fans, you might be tempted to use the following "not" title: Superman Poster NOT Batman Spider-Man. It's not a lie; the Superman poster definitely is *not* a Batman or Spider-Man poster. But that's not why the seller put those words in the title. He put those words there so that anyone searching for a Batman or Spider-Man model would find his listing in their search results. He might think he's increasing the visibility of his listing, but what he's really doing is ticking off potential buyers of Batman and Spider-Man merchandise. What at first seems clever is annoying and misleading, and should be avoided. Do *not* use "not" titles!

Trick #236: **Use Accepted Acronyms and Abbreviations**

lesley_feeney

stores.ebay.com/Lesleys-Auction-Template-Designs

www.zoicks.com

PowerSeller

Member since 2000, Feedback: Purple star

When dealing with some item categories, collectibles in particular, you often can use accepted abbreviations and acronyms in your titles. This lets you provide a more complete description without using a lot of valuable characters. For example, you can use the abbreviation MISB to stand for *mint in sealed box*. True collectors will know what this means, and it saves precious real estate in your title and item description.

If you don't know all the TLAs and FLAs (three-letter and four-letter acronyms) you can get really confused really fast. To that end, eBay member **lesley_feeney** has prepared a comprehensive list of acronyms and abbreviations, as detailed in Table 8.1. Note that some acronyms have multiple meanings, depending on the type of product involved.

Table 8.1   **eBay Acronyms and Abbreviations**

Acronym	Definition
1E	First edition
1st	First edition
2E	Second edition
ABM	Automatic bottle machine (bottles prior to 1910)
ACC	Accumulation (stamps)
ACL	Applied color label (bottles)
ADV	Adventure (books/movies)
AE	American express
AG	About Good (coins)
AIR	Air mail (stamps)
AMEX	American Express
ANTH	Anthology (books)
AO	All original
ARC	Advance reader's copy (usually a paperback edition of a book put out before the trade edition for publicity)
AU	About Uncirculated (coins)
AUTO	Autographed
BA	Bronze Age
BB	BB-sized hole drilled through record label Beanie Baby
BBC	Bottom of back cover
BC	Back cover Blister card
BCE	Book club edition

Acronym	Definition
BIM	Blown in mold (bottles prior to 1910)
BIN	Buy It Now
BIO	Biography
BJ	Ball jointed body (dolls)
BK	Bent knee (dolls)
BKL	Booklet (stamps)
BLB	Big Little Book
BLK	Block (stamps)
BOMC	Book of the Month Club edition
BP	Blister pack Booklet pane (stamps)
BTAS	Batman the Animated Series
BU	Brilliant Uncirculated (coins)
BU	Built up (for models and other to-be-assembled items; indicates that the item has already been assembled)
BW	Black and white (photos, illustrations, drawings)
C & S	Creamer & sugar Cup & saucer
C	Cover (stamps) Cartridge only (videogame—no instructions)
CART	Cartridge (videogame—no instructions)
CB	Club book (stamps)
CC	Carbon copy Cut corner (books, magazines, records) Commemorative cover (stamps) Credit card
CCA	Comics Code Authority
CCG	Collectable card game
CDF	Customs declaration form (stamps)
CF	Centerfold (magazines)
CFO	Center fold out (magazines)
CI	Cartridge and instructions (videogames, computer equipment)
CIB	Cartridge/instructions/box (videogames, computer equipment)
CIBO	Cartridge/instructions/box/ overlay (videogames, computer equipment)

continues

Table 8.1 **Continued**

Acronym	Definition
CLA	Cleaned/lubricated/ adjusted (cameras)
CM	Customized
CO	Cut out (close-out item)
COA	Certificate of authenticity
COC	Cut out corner
COH	Cut out hole
COL	Collection
CONUS	Continental United States (ship-to destination)
CPN	Coupon
CPP	Colored picture postcard
CS	Creamer & sugar Cup & saucer
CTB	Coffee table book
CU	Crisp Uncirculated (currency)
D	Denver mint (coins)
DB	Divided back (postcards)
DBL	Double (2-in-1: paperbacks)
DG	Depression glass
DJ	Dust jacket Disk jockey copy (records)
DOA	Dead on arrival (item in non-working order when received)
DUTCH	Dutch auction (multiple quantities available)
EAPC	Early American Prescut (Anchor Hocking glass c. 1960+)
EAPG	Early American pattern glass
EC	Excellent condition
EF	Extra Fine condition Extremely Fine (coins)
EG	Elegant glass (Depression-era)
EP	Extended Play (records, videotapes)
ERR	Error
EX	Excellent (condition) Extra Except

Acronym	Definition
EXLIB	Ex-library book From the library of
EXT	Extended
F/E	First edition (books)
FC	Fine condition Front cover
FDC	First day cover (stamps)
FE	First edition (books)
FFC	First flight cover (stamps)
FFEP	Free front end page/Paper (1st blank page of a book, usually an extension of the part pasted down on the inside front cover)
FFL	Federally licensed firearms (dealer)
FN	Fine condition
FOR	Forgery
FPLP	Fisher Price Little People
FS	Factory sealed
FT	Flat top (beer cans)
FVF	Final value fee (fee charged by eBay based on the final price of auction)
G	Good condition
GA	Golden Age
GD	Good condition
GF	Gold filled
GGA	Good girl art (paperback book covers)
GP	Gold plate Gutter pair (stamps)
GSP	Gold sterling plate
GU	Gently used
GW	Gently worn (clothes)
GWTW	Gone with the Wind
HB	Hardback or hardbound (book)
HB/DJ	Hardback (book) with dust jacket
HC	Hand colored (maps/engravings) Hard cover (book)
HE	Heavy gold electroplated
HIC	Hole in cover

continues

Table 8.1   **Continued**

Acronym	Definition
HIL	Hole in label
HIST	Historical (books)
HM	Happy Meal (McDonald's)
HOF	Hall of Famer (baseball memorabilia/autograph/ trading cards)
HP	Hard plastic (dolls) Hand painted Hewlett Packard
HS	Hand stamp (stamps)
HTF	Hard to find
IBC	Inside back cover
IFC	Inside front cover
ILLO	Illustration
ILLUS	Illustration Illustrated
INIT	Initial Initials Initial issue
IRAN	Inspect and repair as decessary
ISH	Issue
JUVIE	Juvenile delinquency theme
L	Large
LBBP	Large bean bag plush (Disney)
LBC	Lower back cover
LCD	Liquid crystal display
LE	Limited edition
LED	Light emitting diode
LFC	Lower front cover
LFT	Left
LLBC	Lower left of back cover
LLFC	Lower left of front cover
LP	Little People (Fisher Price toys) Long-playing record
LRBC	Lower right on back cover

Acronym	Definition
LRFC	Lower right on front cover
LSE	Loose
LSW	Label shows wear (records)
LTBX	Letterbox (video that re-creates a widescreen image)
LTD	Limited edition
LWOL	Lot of writing on label (records)
M	Medium Mint Mono (records)
MA	Madame Alexander (dolls)
MAP	Map back (paperback books)
MC	Miscut
MCU	Might clean up
MEDIC	Medical genre (paperbacks)
MIB	Mint in box (box not necessarily mint—email the seller and ask!)
MIBP	Mint in blister pack
MIJ	Made in Japan
MIMB	Mint in mint box
MIMP	Mint in mint package
MIOJ	Made in occupied Japan
MIOP	Mint in opened package
MIP	Mint in package
MISB	Mint in sealed box
MIU	Made in USA
MM	Merry Miniatures (Hallmark) Mounted Mint (Stamps)
MMA	Metropolitan Museum of Art
MNB	Mint—no box
MNH	Mint never hinged (stamps)
MOC	Mint on card
MOMA	Museum of Modern Art
MOMC	Mint on Mint card
MONMC	Mint on Near Mint card
MONO	Monophonic (sound recordings and equipment)

continues

Table 8.1   **Continued**

Acronym	Definition
MOP	Mother of pearl
MOTU	Masters of the Universe
MP	Military post (stamps)
MS	Miniature sheet (stamps)
	Mint state (coins—usually followed by a number from 62 to 70; that is, "MS62" or "MS-62")
	Microsoft
MWBMT	Mint with both mint tags
MWBT	Mint with both tags
MWBTM	Mint with both tags mint
MWMT	Mint with mint tags
MYS	Mystery (books/movies)
N/R	No reserve
NAP	Not affected play (records)
NARU	Not a registered user
NASB	Nancy Ann story book
NBW	Never been worn (clothes)
NC	No cover
ND	No date
	No dog (RCA record labels)
NDSR	No dents, scratches, or rust (tins)
NIB	New in box
NIP	New In package
NL	Number line (books—a means of telling the edition; occurs on copyright page and reads "1234567890"; lowest number indicates the edition)
NM	Near Mint
NORES	No reserve
NOS	New old stock
NP	Not packaged
NR	No reserve
NRFB	Never removed from box
NRFSB	Never removed from sealed box
NRMNT	Near Mint
NW	Never worn (clothes)

Acronym	Definition
NWOT	New without tags
NWT	New with tags
O	New Orleans mint
O/C	On canvas (paintings)
OB	Original box
OC	Off center Off cut On canvas
OEM	Original equipment manufacturer
OF	Original finish
OJ	Occupied Japan
OOAK	One of a kind
OOP	Out of package Out of print Out of production
OP	Out of print
OS	Operating system (computers)
OST	Original soundtrack
P	Poor condition Philadelphia mint (coins)
P/O	Punch-out (inventory that has been "declassified" with a hole punch)
P/S	Picture sleeve (records)
PB	Paperback or paperbound (books)
PBO	Paperback original
PC	Picture postcard
PC	Poor condition Postcard
PD	Picture disk (a record with a photo or image on it)
PF	Proof coin
PIC	Picture
PM	Post mark (postcards; first day covers) Postal markings (postcards; first day covers) Priority Mail
POC	Pencil on cover
POPS	Promo only picture sleeve
POTF	Power of the Force (Star Wars)

continues

Table 8.1   **Continued**

Acronym	Definition
PP	Parcel Post
PP	PayPal
PPD	Post paid
PR	Poor condition Proof (coins)
PROOF	Proof coin
PS	Power supply Picture sleeve (records)
R	Reprint
RBC	Right side of back cover
RC	Reader copy (books—a copy of a book in good condition but with no true investment value)
RET	Retired
RETRD	Retired
RFC	Right side of front cover
RFDO	Removed for display only
RI	Reissue (records)
RMA	Return merchandise authorization number
ROM	Romantic (books)
RP	Real photo postcard
RPPC	Real photo postcard
RR	Re-release
RRH	Remade/repainted/haired (dolls)
RS	Rhinestones Rubber stamped on label (records)
RSP	Rhodium sterling plate
RT	Right
S	Small Stereo (records) San Francisco mint (coins)
S/H	Shipping and handling
S/H/I	Shipping/handling/ insurance
S/O	Sold out

Acronym	Definition
S/P	Salt and pepper (shakers)
	Silverplate (flatware or hollowware)
S/S	Still sealed
	Single sheet (stamps)
SA	Silver Age
SB	Soft bound or soft back (referring to soft large bound books)
SC	Slight crease (hang tags, books, magazines)
	Sawcut (slice cut off record album jacket)
	Soft cover (book)
SCI	Science (books)
SCR	Scratch
SCU	Scuff (records)
SD	Shaded dog (RCA record labels)
SF	Science fiction
SFBC	Science Fiction Book Club (sometimes the true first edition)
SH	Shipping and handling
SHI	Shipping/handling/insurance
SIG	Signature
SLD	Sealed
SLT	Slight
SLW	Straight Leg Walker (dolls)
SO	Sold out
SOL	Sticker on label (records)
SP	Sticker pull (books—discoloration or actual removal of cover color caused by pulling off a sticker price)
	Silverplate (flatware or hollowware)
SR	Slight ring wear
	Shrink wrapped
SS	Stainless steel
	Still sealed
	Store stamp (books—these are stamps which give the name/address of a store that appear on endpapers or edges or books)
ST	Soundtrack (records, CDs)
	Star Trek
	Sterling
STCCG	Star Trek collectable card game

continues

Table 8.1   **Continued**

Acronym	Definition
STER	Sterling
STNG	Star Trek the Next Generation
SUSP	Suspended Suspense (books)
SW	Slight wear Star Wars Shrink wrapped
SWCCG	Star Wars collectable card game
SWCS	Star Wars collector series (toys)
TBB	Teenie Beanie Babies
TC	True crime (books)
TE	Trade edition (books—standard edition of a book often smaller than the first edition)
TM	Trademark
TMOL	Tape mark on label (records)
TNG	The Next Generation (Star Trek)
TOBC	Top of back cover
TOFC	Top of front cover
TOL	Tear on label (records)
TOONS	Cartoon art (paperbacks)
TOS	Tape on spine Terms of service The Original Series (Star Trek)
TOUGH	Tough guy genre (paperbacks)
TRPQ	Tall, round, pyroglaze quart (milk bottles)
U	Used (stamps)
UB	Undivided back (postcards)
UDV	Undivided back (postcards)
ULBC	Upper left (corner) back cover (books, magazines)
ULRC	Upper right (corner) back cover (books, magazines)
UNC	Uncirculated (coins)
URFC	Upper right (corner) front cover (books, magazines)
V/M/D	Visa/MasterCard/Discover
VERM	Vermeil (gold plating on sterling silver, bronze, or copper)

Acronym	Definition
VF	Very fine condition
VFD	Vacuum flourescent display
VFU	Very fine, used (stamps)
VG	Very good condition
VHTF	Very hard to find
W	West Point mint/depository (coins)
W/C	Watercolor (paintings, maps)
WB	White border (post cards)
WC	Watercolor (paintings, maps)
WD	White dog (RCA record labels)
WLP	White label promo
WOB	Writing on back
WOC	Writing on cover
WOF	Writing on front
WOR	Writing on record
WRP	Warp (records)
WS	Widescreen (same as letterbox)
WSOL	Water stain on label (records)
XL	Extra large

Trick #237: "Borrow" Successful Wording

trapperjohn2000

stores.ebay.com/Molehill-Group-Store

Member since 1998, Feedback: Purple star

If writing a hard-hitting title from scratch is too daunting for you, there's no need to reinvent the title. There's no harm in checking out auctions for similar items and "borrowing" their wording. (Just don't copy it exactly!)

Writing a More Effective Description

The item title draws buyers to your auction; the item description does the actual selling. Think of your item description as the copy in a catalog listing, and learn how the eBay Masters do it!

Trick #238: **Provide an Accurate—and Detailed—Description**

trapperjohn2000

stores.ebay.com/Molehill-Group-Store

Member since 1998, Feedback: Purple star

Here's the thing about your item description—it needs to be factual. It should be an accurate description of what you're selling, as detailed as you can make it. Bare minimum, here's what you need to include:

- Name (or title)
- Condition
- Identifying marks and unusual or unique characteristics
- Age
- Original use (what you used it for)
- Value (if you know it)
- Measurements or size (for clothing items)
- Any included accessories (including the original instruction manual, if you have it)
- Any known defects or damage

Remember, your bidders cannot pick up and look at your item; they're depending on you to tell them all about it.

Trick #239: **There's Lots of Space—Use It!**

griffin_trader

stores.ebay.com/Naturally-In-New-Orleans-Mardi-Gras

PowerSeller

Member since 1999, Feedback: Green star

Unlike in the item title, there are no space restrictions on your item description. You don't have to scrimp on words or leave anything out, so you can say as much as you need to say. If you can describe your item adequately in a sentence, great; if it takes three paragraphs, that's okay too.

Trick #240: **Prioritize the Information**

> **satnrose**
>
> PowerSeller
>
> Member since 1998, Feedback: Green star

When you do have a lot to say, prioritize it. You should put the most important and motivating information in your initial paragraph, because a lot of folks won't read any farther than that. Think of your first paragraph like a lead paragraph in a newspaper story: Grab 'em with something catchy, give them the gist of the story, and lead them into reading the next paragraph and the one after that. Even better, break pertinent information into a bulleted list, which many people find easier to digest.

As **satnrose** advises:

> *Too much information is blinding. There's a scene in* Moscow on the Hudson *where Robin Williams, as a recent Russian defector, is sent to the grocery store by his American host family to pick up some coffee. When confronted by rows and rows of a hundred varieties of java, he has a nervous breakdown. Choose the most important information to go at the top of the item description, and save the elaborations for the bottom, where they can be skipped over if the customer so chooses.*

You can make your information easier to digest by formatting it in a clear and logical manner. Use multiple short paragraphs instead of a single long one, break up a long text list into a bulleted list, and so on. When you have a lot of information to impart, make it easy to find the most important bits!

Trick #241: **Write with Authority**

> **satnrose**
>
> PowerSeller
>
> Member since 1998, Feedback: Green star

The more authoritative you can make your description, the better. Browsers are more likely to become bidders if they think you know what you're talking about. Again, **satnrose** has some great advice:

> *Dazzle 'em with your brilliance. Bidders are more willing to trust you if they think you know what you're talking about.*

Trick #242: **Be Unique**

> **flyinggirlart**
> stores.ebay.com/FlyingGirl-Images
> Member since 2003, Feedback: Purple star

To maximize your sales, you somehow need to make your auctions unique. It helps if you have something unique to sell, but if your items aren't that unique, try to describe them in a unique way. And If you can't find a way to write a unique item description, then advertise a unique sale or include a unique gift with the item's purchase. As **flyinggirlart** advises:

> *There are a gazillion sellers out there, and customers are looking for a reason to buy from you rather than from the other guys.*

The last thing you want to be is just one of a hundred sellers offering the same box of number-nine widgets. Find some way to make *your* box of widgets unique—or resign yourself to selling at the market price—if your widgets sell at all.

Trick #243: **Stress Benefits, Not Features**

> **trapperjohn2000**
> stores.ebay.com/Molehill-Group-Store
> Member since 1998, Feedback: Purple star

Although you need to be descriptive, it doesn't hurt to employ a little marketing savvy and salesmanship. Yes, you should talk about the features of your item, but it's even better if you can talk about your product's *benefits* to the potential buyer.

Let's say you're selling a used cordless phone, and the phone has a 50-number memory. Saying "50-number memory" is stating a feature; saying instead that the phone "lets you recall your 50 most-called phone numbers at the press of a button" is describing a benefit. Remember, a feature is something your item has; a benefit is something your item does for the user.

Trick #244: **Describe Every Flaw**

> **bushellcollectibles**
> stores.ebay.com/Bushells-Collectibles
> Member since 1999, Feedback: Red star

Because other users will be bidding on your item sight unseen, you have to be an accurate reporter of the item's condition. If the item has a scratch or blemish, note it. If the paint is peeling, note it. If it includes a few non-original parts, note it. Bidders don't have the item to hold in their hands and examine in person, so you have to be their eyes and ears.

That's right; you need to describe the item in painful detail, and be completely honest about what you're selling. If you're *not* honest in your description, it will come back to haunt you—in the form of an unhappy and complaining buyer. As **bushellcollectibles** notes:

I always describe every flaw and do so in detail. And when people get the item, they thank me for being so descriptive and usually tell me the item was better than described.

Buyers appreciate detailed, honest descriptions. When they see a description that notes a defect or damage, it instills confidence that you, the seller, are honest, and that the rest of the description is accurate.

Trick #245: *Don't* **Describe Every Flaw**

satnrose

PowerSeller

Member since 1998, Feedback: Green star

You don't have to be so painfully honest in your description that you drive buyers away. It's okay to be a little vague in your description, as long as you don't willfully mislead the buyer. Here's what **satnrose** says about it:

I firmly believe that, in most cases, if you describe in detail every single minor flaw in the item you stand the chance of killing the sale. Too much information. I prefer to make a simple statement, like: "slightly worn and soiled" and let the image tell the story. Of course, major faults should always be noted.

Trick #246: **Don't Exaggerate the Condition**

quadaxel83

stores.ebay.com/Buttons-And-Beads

Member since 2001, Feedback: Red star

Your honest description of an item's condition should be honest. It's okay to try to put a positive spin on things, but don't lie. It's definitely not cool to describe an item as "mint" when it's not!

Trick #247: **Keep It Professional**

New Trick

samby
Member since 2001, Feedback: Turquoise star

Your item listing should be a professional description of the item you have for sale, not a personal diary. While it's okay to personalize the listing a little (it adds a nice human touch that the big boys can't provide), avoid sob stories or irrelevant background information about why your widget has to be sold. Buyers aren't interested in your personal problems; they want to find out about the item that's for sale, and that's that.

Trick #248: **Be Positive, Not Negative**

New Trick

quiltworks
Member since 1999, Feedback: Turquoise star

You'll sell more items if your descriptions use positive language rather than equivalent negatives. It's a simple matter of looking at the glass as half full rather than half empty. For example, **quiltworks** suggests:

> *Do not state any auction terms in negatives, rather state the same thing in positive. Rather than saying "do not bid if you don't intend to pay," say "payment requested in five days."*

You see how it works? Take something that could be a negative ("don't do this") and spin it in the positive ("do this instead").

Trick #249: **Include Alternative Spellings—and Misspellings**

berties_house_of_horrors
stores.ebay.com/Berties-Emporium
PowerSeller
Member since 1999, Feedback: Red star

Here's a neat little trick, once again picking up the fact that most buyers are using eBay's search feature. You see, not every person uses the same words to describe things. If you're selling a plastic model kit, for example, some users will search for model, others for kit, still others for statue or figure or styrene. Although you can't put all these variations into the item title, you *can* throw them in somewhere in the description—or, if all else fails, at the bottom of the item description. (Remember, they'll be picked up by eBay's search engine if they're *anywhere* in the description area.)

While you're at it, throw in any alternative spellings you can think of. For example, you might spell `Spider-Man` with a hyphen in the middle, while other users might search for the unhyphenated `Spiderman`. And don't forget differences between American and British spellings, especially if you're selling to an international audience. Whichever variation you use in your title, throw the other one in at the bottom of the description.

Finally, don't forget that some buyers can't spell well. Some sellers benefit by including deliberate misspellings (in addition to the correct spellings, of course), just so poor-spelling searchers will find your item when searching eBay's listings.

Trick #250: **DON'T WRITE IN ALL CAPS!**

regans*closet

stores.ebay.com/Regans-Closet

PowerSeller

Member since 2001, Feedback: Red star

I'd like to think that this one is obvious, but I've seen enough bad auction descriptions to know otherwise. Never, I repeat NEVER, write your description in all capital letters! As **regans*closet** humorously advises:

THIS IS NOT A RULE OR A REGULATION BUT IT DRIVES ME BATTY AND WILL CAUSE ME TO LEAVE YOUR AUCTION IMMEDIATELY BECAUSE TRYING TO READ IT IRRITATES ME. WHEN WRITING YOUR DESCRIPTION TURN YOUR CAPS LOCK OFF. PERIOD. THANK YOU. AN OCCASIONAL BREAK BETWEEN PARAGRAPHS IS NICE TOO IF YOUR DESCRIPTION IS VERY LONG.

Trick #251: **Provide Accurate Measurements**

berties_house_of_horrors

stores.ebay.com/Berties-Emporium

PowerSeller

Member since 1999, Feedback: Red star

When selling clothes or other size-sensitive items, be sure to include accurate measurements or sizing information in your description. It'll save everyone a lot of trouble.

Trick #252: **Spell Check and Proofread**

> **sparrowsnestbooks**
>
> Member since 1998, Feedback: Red star

Nothing diminishes buyer confidence more than a description replete with spelling and grammatical errors. Take the extra minute to proofread your listings, and to run a spell check. As **sparrowsnestbooks** notes:

> *Maybe this is one of those understood admonitions, but too often—and I am to blame as well—unintended errors can either cause readers to question your expertise or be confused about what you are trying to say!*

Trick #253: **Check the Pre-Filled Information**

> **derekcraven**
>
> Member since 2001, Feedback: Red star

Many eBay categories now let you enter a UPC or ISBN number, and eBay will automatically fill in the pertinent item information. Here's the thing, though—this information isn't always correct. Make sure you look over any of this pre-filled info to make sure it's accurate, that it applies to the item you're selling, and that you agree with it. Here's a cautionary tale from seller **derekcraven**:

> *I listed some books with the ISBN#/filled auctions and I picked the extra info, only to find that the reviewer did not care for the book.*

Yikes! Fortunately, if the pre-filled information isn't to your liking, you can edit or delete it—but only if you check it first!

Details, Details, Details…

Experienced eBay sellers know to include what they call the terms of service (TOS) in all their auction listings. What is the TOS, and why do you need it? Read on to find out.

Trick #254: **Include Your Terms of Service**

> **mikeology**
>
> Member since 2002, Feedback: Purple star

Your terms of service are the rules that you apply to your auctions, the do's and don'ts of how you do business. Think of the TOS as the "fine print" that you want potential buyers to be aware of before they make a bid.

Here is a short list of some of the items you might want to include in your TOS:

- Bidding restrictions, such as "No bidders with negative feedback," "Bidders with positive feedback of at least 10 only," or "U.S. buyers only."
- Payment restrictions, such as "U.S. funds only," "No personal checks," or "Personal checks take two weeks to clear."
- Shipping/handling charges (if you know them) and restrictions, such as "Buyer pays shipping/handling" or "Shipping via USPS Priority Mail only."

As a real-world example, here's the very detailed TOS that eBay seller **mikeology** uses; you may want to adapt it for your own use.

Please Read Terms Below Before Placing Bid:

Important Reminder: This is an online auction, please email me with any questions before bidding. Items are generally sold "as is". The seller reserves the right to block bidders with excessive negative feedback. Winning item(s) carefully micro-photographed and cataloged before shipping. Be advised also, I am not responsible for any lost or damaged items once shipped. I use top grade packing/shipping materials and take extra care when packaging to provide the optimum protection I can once the item or items ship. Please feel free to contact me if you have any questions or if additional photos are needed. No problem at all! Winner pays shipping and insurance (optional).

Trick #255: **Make the TOS Distinct**

> **bushellcollectibles**
>
> stores.ebay.com/Bushells-Collectibles
>
> Member since 1999, Feedback: Red star

While it's important to include a TOS in your item description, you don't want it to take precedence over the more important part of the description. To that end, I recommend putting the TOS at the very bottom of the description, perhaps separated from the main text by a horizontal rule or several blank lines. It's not a bad idea to put the TOS in a small typeface, perhaps even in a different color. Make it stand out from the rest of the description, but not overwhelmingly so.

Trick #256: **Don't Scare Buyers Away**

satnrose

PowerSeller

Member since 1998, Feedback: Green star

Remember that your TOS is really just the fine print. If it's too long or too restrictive, you might scare off prospective buyers—which you don't want to do. I've seen many auctions where the TOS looked like a long list of negatives: NO this, DON'T this, NONE of that. It's like walking into a retail store and finding the owner behind the counter holding a shotgun. It's okay to see the eBay equivalent of "no shirt, no shoes, no service," but if there are too many warning signs, buyers will take their business elsewhere. As **satnrose** so succinctly puts it:

If your TOS is too scary, people will be afraid to buy.

Don't scare them away—keep your TOS short and simple!

9

How to Enhance Your Product Listings with HTML

You can tell an eBay pro by how their listings looks. Serious eBay sellers have great-looking listings, with lots of color and fancy typefaces and interesting layouts—much better looking than the standard black text on white background that eBay generates by default.

How do you make your item listings look more professional? You do what the eBay Masters do—enhance your listings with HTML.

Simple Steps to Better-Looking Listings

Before we get into the somewhat-scary world of using HTML in your item listings, there are some simple steps you can take that don't require you to learn any HTML coding at all. These are cool little tricks that *anyone* can use, no learning curve necessary.

Trick #257: **Do Simple Formatting without HTML**

> **kcanddi**
>
> stores.ebay.com/k-ds-auction-templates-and-more
>
> www.kdwebpagedesign.com
>
> PowerSeller
>
> Member since 2003, Feedback: Purple star

If all you want to do is add some bold or color text to your listing, you don't have to learn HTML or use fancy listing-creation tools. eBay's standard text editor, shown in Figure 9.1, is available when you create your item listing. It lets you add HTML effects in a WYSIWYG environment, much the same way you add boldface and italics in your word processor. Just highlight the text you want to format and then click the appropriate formatting button—no manual coding necessary.

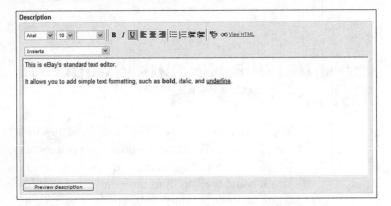

FIGURE 9.1

Enter simple formatting with eBay's standard text editor.

If you do want to enter your own HTML, click the View HTML link in the Description section. This displays eBay's HTML editor, shown in Figure 9.2. (You can return to the standard text editor by clicking Back to Design View.)

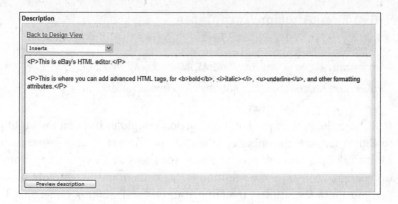

FIGURE 9.2
Enter HTML codes in eBay's HTML editor.

Trick #258: **Use eBay's Listing Designer**

> **trapperjohn2000**
>
> stores.ebay.com/Molehill-Group-Store
>
> Member since 1998, Feedback: Purple star

Another easy way to create a listing that goes beyond plain text is with eBay's Listing Designer. This feature is available to all users, right from the Describe Your Item page, at a cost of $0.10 a listing. Listing Designer provides over a hundred pre-designed templates, which eBay calls *themes*. You choose a theme from the Theme list, as shown in Figure 9.3, and then choose a layout for your pictures from the Picture Layout list. eBay does all the work for you, and you never have to see the HTML code itself.

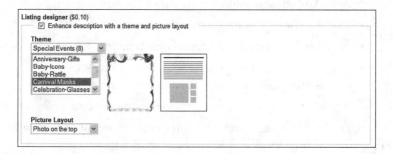

FIGURE 9.3
Choose a theme from eBay's Listing Designer.

Trick #259: **Use Free Auction Templates**

bobal

www.bulls2.com/indexb/bobstips2.html

Member since 1998, Feedback: Turquoise star

If you like the idea of predesigned auction templates but don't want to pay a dime to eBay, there are a number of other sites on the web that offer templates for free. Most work by asking for specific input, then let you choose from a number of colors and designs; you copy the resulting HTML code from the template site into eBay's Sell Your Item form (using the Enter Your Own HTML tab). Other sites have pre-designed template code you can download to your own computer. The results are similar.

Here are some of the most popular of these free auction template sites:

- Antique-Central eZ Auction Template (www.antique-central.com/tips1.html)
- Auction Riches Free Auction Ad Creator (www.auctionriches.com/freead/create.pl)
- AuctionSpice.com Auction Template Creator (www.auctionspice.com)
- AuctionSupplies.com Free Auction Templates (auctionsupplies.com/templates/)
- Auctiva Free Templates (www.auctiva.com)
- Bay Dream Design (www.bay-dream.com)
- DeSa C.S. Auction Templates (www.desacs.com)
- K&D Web Page Design Auction Templates (www.kdwebpagedesign.com/auction_templates.asp)
- K&D Web Page Design Custom Auction Creator (www.kdwebpagedesign.com/tutorials/tut_template.asp)
- ListTailor (www.listtailor.com/quickstart.html)
- RobsHelp.com FreeForm Auction and Template Builder (www.robshelp.com)
- Wizard's Free Auction Template Creation Form (www.ambassadorboard.net/hosting/free-form.php)
- Xample.net Auction Templates (www.xample.net/templates.htm)
- Zoicks.com Nested Tables Design Center (www.zoicks.com/nestedtables.htm)

Trick #260: **Use Listing-Creation Tools**

trapperjohn2000

stores.ebay.com/Molehill-Group-Store

Member since 1998, Feedback: Purple star

The free sites just mentioned aren't the only options you have for creating fancy eBay item listings. There are many software programs and web-based services that let you create great-looking listings without having to enter a line of HTML code. Most of these programs and services let you choose a design and fill in some blanks, and then they automatically write the HTML code necessary to create the listing. These programs and services are easy to use and provide a lot more options than you get with the free site—although they do come at a cost.

Most of these tools work in a similar fashion. You go to a particular web page or program screen, select a template from a list, choose available layout options, and then enter your normal listing title and description. You'll see a preview of what your listing will look like; if you like the way it looks, click a button to post the listing on the eBay site and start your auction.

Here are some of the most popular of these third-party listing-creation tools:

- Ándale Lister (www.andale.com)
- Adomatic Professional (www.slconsultancy.co.uk/adomatic/)
- Auction Hawk (www.auctionhawk.com)
- Auction Lizard (www.auction-lizard.com)
- Auction Orbit Dominant Ad Creator (www.auctionorbit.com)
- Auctiva (www.auctiva.com)
- eBay Blackthorne (pages.ebay.com/blackthorne/)
- eBay Turbo Lister (pages.ebay.com/turbo_lister/)
- Marketworks (www.marketworks.com)
- SpareDollar (www.sparedollar.com)
- Vendio (www.vendio.com)

Using HTML in Your Listings

Predesigned templates and listing-creation software are easy ways to great-looking listings, but they don't provide complete flexibility. If you want to create a truly custom item listing—at zero additional cost—then you need to design your own listings from scratch, using HTML.

This sounds like a lot of work, and it is, kind of. The key thing is that you have to teach yourself how HTML codes work, which is something you can learn from the Masters.

Trick #261: **Learn How HTML Works**

lora_and_steve

stores.ebay.com/Our-Hutch/

www.ourhutch.com/examples/

Member since 1999, Feedback: Red star

HTML stands for *hypertext markup language*, and though the concept of HTML coding might sound difficult, it's really pretty easy—something you can do yourself. (It's not nearly as complicated as a fancy computer programming language, such as BASIC or C++—trust me.) HTML is really nothing more than a series of hidden codes. These codes tell a web browser how to display different types of text and graphics. The codes are embedded in a document, so you can't see them; they're visible only to your web browser.

The first thing you need to know is that HTML is nothing more than text surrounded by instructions, in the form of simple codes. Codes are distinguished from normal text by the fact that they're enclosed within angle brackets. Each particular code turns on or off a particular attribute, such as boldface or italic text. Most codes are in sets of "on/off" pairs; you turn "on" the code before the text you want to affect and then turn "off" the code after the text.

HTML codes—or "tags," as they're sometimes called—look something like this:

```
<tagname>
<tagname attribute>
<tagname attribute="parameter">
```

There is always a tag name, it is always a single word, and it always comes first in the tag, at the very left, right after the opening bracket. Some HTML tags only have the tag name part. Others have one or more *attributes*; still others let you define one or more *parameters*.

Just remember that almost all tags work in pairs, with an opening and closing tag. The effect of the tag pairs is applied to the area or text between them. For example, the code <u><i></u> is used to italicize text; <u></i></u> turns off the italics. As you can see, an "off" code is merely the "on" code with a slash before it.

Trick #262: **Learn the Basic HTML Tags**

> **lora_and_steve**
>
> stores.ebay.com/Our-Hutch/
>
> www.ourhutch.com/examples/
>
> Member since 1999, Feedback: Red star

This book isn't meant to be a comprehensive HTML primer, but it is important that you know which HTML tags you can use in your eBay auction listings. To that end, Table 9.1 shows the most common HTML codes:

Table 9.1   **Common eBay HTML Tags**

HTML Tag	Used For
`<!> </!>`	Adds invisible comments to your document
`<a> </a>`	Anchor or link
`<b> </b>`	Activates bold text
`<blockquote> </blockquote>`	Sets off long quotation
` `	Forces line break
`<center> </center>`	Centers content
`<em> </em>`	Designates emphasis in text, by displaying the text as italic
`<font> </font>`	Designated text characteristics
`<h1> </h1>`	Heading level one
`<h2> </h2>`	Heading level two
`<h3> </h3>`	Heading level three
`<h4> </h4>`	Heading level four
`<h5> </h5>`	Heading level five
`<h6> </h6>`	Heading level six
`<hr>`	Inserts horizontal rule or line
`<i> </i>`	Renders text as italicized
`<img>`	Designates placement of an image file
`<li> </li>`	Designates a list item
`<marquee> </marquee>`	Scrolling text or graphics
`<p> </p>`	Designates a paragraph
`<pre> </pre>`	Preformatted text—displays as entered
`<small> </small>`	Renders text one size smaller

continues

Table 9.1 **Continued**

HTML Tag	Used For
<strong> </strong>	Designates text with strong importance, by displaying the text as bold
	Renders text as subscript
	Renders text as superscript
<table> </table>	Container for tabular content
<td> </td>	Defines table data cell
<th> </th>	Header titles for table cells
<tr> </tr>	Designates table row of data cells
<tt> </tt>	Renders text as monospaced "teletype"
<u> </u>	Renders text underlined

Trick #263: **Learn Which HTML Tags *Not* to Use**

> **kcanddi**
>
> stores.ebay.com/k-ds-auction-templates-and-more
>
> www.kdwebpagedesign.com
>
> PowerSeller
>
> Member since 2003, Feedback: Purple star

Note that there are many other HTML tags, but they're either not capable of being used in eBay item listings or they're not frequently used for such. Just to keep you out of trouble, here's a short list of HTML tags that eBay expressly forbids you to use. Add one of these to your listings, and you'll get an error message!

Here are the HTML tags to avoid: <base>, <basefont>, <body>, <head>, <html>, <link>, <meta>, <style>, and <title>. Note that these are all valid HTML tags used when creating full web pages—but not when creating eBay listings.

Trick #264: **Learn How eBay HTML Differs from Regular HTML**

> **lora_and_steve**
>
> stores.ebay.com/Our-Hutch/
>
> www.ourhutch.com/examples/
>
> Member since 1999, Feedback: Red star

Expanding on that list of HTML tags that aren't used in eBay listings, it's also important to know that HTML coding for your auction listings is different from creating the HTML code for a complete web page. When you create a web page in HTML, there are actually two sections of the page—the *head* and the *body*. When you create HTML code for an eBay listing, eBay has already created the head and body sections; your code is simply inserted into the existing body. As such, you don't need (and can't) use the <head> and <body> tags in your eBay code.

In addition, you can't use any tags that normally insert into the head section of the web page. For example, all <meta> tags, all embedded style sheets, and most JavaScript code work within the head section of the page, and thus can't be used in an eBay listing.

Remember, the code you create for your eBay page will be inserted between the <body> and </body> tags of eBay's existing page code. Make sure the code you use works within the body of the page.

Making Fancy Listings with HTML

Okay, assuming you're somewhat familiar and comfortable with basic HTML coding, let's look at how the eBay Masters use HTML to create fancy eBay item listings.

Trick #265: **Add a Link to Another Web Page**

> **bobal**
>
> www.bulls2.com/indexb/bobstips2.html
>
> Member since 1998, Feedback: Turquoise star

One of the most common uses of HTML is to create hyperlinks to other web pages. This is accomplished with a single piece of code that looks like this:
<a href="*URL*">This is the link</a>

The text between the on and off codes will appear onscreen as a typical underlined hyperlink; when users click that text, they'll be linked to the URL you specified in the code. Note that the URL is enclosed in quotation marks and that you have to include the http:// part of the address.

Know, however, that eBay only allows links to pages that provide additional information about the item listed, additional photos of the item, and your other eBay auctions. eBay prohibits links to pages that attempt to sell merchandise outside of eBay. Link at your own risk.

Trick #266: **Add an Email Link**

> **lora_and_steve**
>
> stores.ebay.com/Our-Hutch/
>
> www.ourhutch.com/examples/
>
> Member since 1999, Feedback: Red star

You can also add links that potential buyers can click to send you email messages. Know, however, that eBay discourages direct email communication between users, preferring that messages get sent through eBay's official email system; it's your call.

This trick is really simple. Just enter the following piece of HTML code:

<a href="mailto:*yourname@domain.com*">Click here to email me</a>

Replace *yourname@domain.com* with your own email address, of course.

Trick #267: **Jump to Another Section of Your Listing**

> **lora_and_steve**
>
> stores.ebay.com/Our-Hutch/
>
> www.ourhutch.com/examples/
>
> Member since 1999, Feedback: Red star

If you have a really long item description, you might want to put a link at the top of the listing that lets visitors jump to another spot somewhere down the page. To do this you have to create a bookmark at the point where you want to jump and then a link to the bookmark elsewhere on the page.

The code you use to designate the bookmark looks like this:

<a name="#*jumphere*">

You insert this code within the text precisely where you want visitors to jump. Replace *jumphere* with the name for the bookmark.

To create a hyperlink to the bookmark, enter this code:

<a href="#*jumphere*">Click to jump</a>

Replace *jumphere* with the name of the bookmark, and *click to jump* with your own text. When visitors click on this link, their browser will automatically scroll down to the bookmarked section of your page.

Trick #268: **Change Font Type and Size**

ghsproducts

stores.ebay.com/GHSProducts

Member since 1998, Feedback: Purple star

One common use of HTML is to change the font type and size in your listings. You can change the font of all the text in your listing (by placing the start tag at the very beginning and the end tag at the very end), or just for selected text. This way you can specify a larger font for the title text and a smaller font for the fine print in your terms of service.

To change the font type or size, you use the `<font>` code. Put the `<font>` opening code just before the text you want to change and the `</font>` closing code just after the selected text.

To specify a font type for selected text, use the `<font>` code with the `face` attribute, like this:

<font face="*xxxx*">*text*</font>

Replace the *xxxx* with the specific font, such as Arial or Times Roman—in quotation marks. It's best to use one of the "safe" fonts that most people will have installed on their PCs— Arial, Comic Sans MS, Roman, Times New Roman, and Helvetica.

To change the size of selected text, use the `size` attribute in the `<font>` tag. The code looks like this:

<font size="*xx*">*text*</font>

Replace the *xx* with the size you want, from 1 to 7, with 1 being the smallest and 7 being the biggest. You get "normal" sized text by leaving this attribute blank.

Of course, you can change both font face and size within a single `<font>` selection. Just "gang" the attributes together, one after another. For example, here's the code that specifies extra-large Arial text:

<font face="Arial" size="7">*text*</font>

Trick #269: **Add Colored Text**

trapperjohn2000

stores.ebay.com/Molehill-Group-Store

Member since 1998, Feedback: Purple star

Another easy thing to do with HTML is add color to your text. This is another trick that uses the `<font>` code, but with the color attribute. The code looks like this:

`<font color="#xxxxxx">text</font>`

Replace the six xs with the code for a specific color. Table 9.2 lists some basic color codes.

Table 9.2   **Common HTML Color Codes**

Color	Code
White	FFFFFF
Red	FF0000
Lime green	00FF00
Green	008000
Blue	0000FF
Fuchsia	FF00FF
Teal	00FFFF
Yellow	FFFF00
Black	000000
Silver	C0C0C0
Light gray	D3D3D3

You can also use the color name in your code. So if, for example, you wanted to code a font as red, you could use this code:

`<font color="red">text</font>`

Trick #270: **Highlight Text in a Sentence**

bobal

www.bulls2.com/indexb/bobstips2.html

Member since 1998, Feedback: Turquoise star

Here's a neat little trick. Instead of adding colored text, add a colored highlight instead. The effect is similar to using a yellow magic marker to highlight text on a printed page. Here's the code:

`<span style="background-color:FFFF00">highlighted text</span>`

Trick #271: **Add a Colored Background to Your Listings**

lesley_feeney

stores.ebay.com/Lesleys-Auction-Template-Designs

www.zoicks.com

PowerSeller

Member since 2000, Feedback: Purple star

One of the most popular HTML tricks used by eBay Masters is to change the background color of the auction listing. When every other listing is simple black text on a white background, giving your listing a colored background really makes it stand out.

To create a colored background, however, you have to enter your entire auction description into a table. Again, we'll cover tables in more detail a little later on, but for now, just enter the code exactly as written:

```
<table width="100%" cellpadding="15" cellspacing="0" bgcolor="#XXXXXX"><tr><td>
```
Type your auction content here
```
</td></tr></table>
```

Replace the *xxxxxx* with the desired color code, as listed in Table 9.2, then insert your entire auction description between the two lines of code.

Trick #272: **Use a Picture as a Listing Background**

lora_and_steve

stores.ebay.com/Our-Hutch/

www.ourhutch.com/examples/

Member since 1999, Feedback: Red star

You can use a similar technique to use a picture as the background for your item listing. As with adding a background color, this trick requires you to put your item text within a table (tables again!); you then add a picture as the table's background. The code looks like this:

```
<table width="100%" cellpadding="20" cellspacing="0" background="URL">
<tr><td>
```
Type your auction content here
```
</td></tr></table>
```

As before, enter your entire item description between the opening and closing table tags, and replace *URL* with the full URL (including http://) and filename of your picture file. Figure 9.4 shows a short listing with a brick-type picture background.

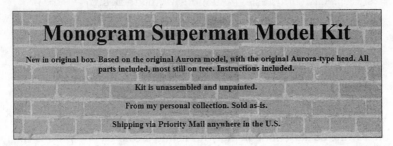

FIGURE 9.4

Add a background picture to your listing.

Trick #273: **Add a Sound Bite to Your Listing**

rufusduff

PowerSeller

Member since 1999, Feedback: Turquoise star

I'll advise you later in this chapter that using too many HTML tricks in your listings is a bad idea. I stand by that advice, except in certain circumstances. For example, adding a sound file to your listing normally turns off buyers, except when you're selling an item with a sound component—such as vintage records, model trains with whistles, music boxes, cuckoo clocks, and the like. For these items, providing a sound console with a short sound bite from the item is a very effective sales tool.

Here's the HTML code you use to add a sound console to your page:

```
<embed src="filename" type="audio/x-pn-realaudio-plugin" align="top"
border="0" width="140" height="50" autostart="false"
console="clip3" loop="true">
```

Naturally, replace *filename* with the full URL and filename of the audio file you want to play. Also, replace the type descriptor with the particular type of audio file; this example is for a RealAudio file.

Using Tables

Finally—tables! As you've probably already gathered, tables are key to creating some of the more interesting auction listing effects. You create a table, and then format the cells within the table however you like, and put whatever you like within each cell. Learn to create HTML tables, and you have a powerful tool at your disposal.

Trick #274: **Learn How to Create Tables**

lora_and_steve

stores.ebay.com/Our-Hutch/

www.ourhutch.com/examples/

Member since 1999, Feedback: Red star

Okay, so tables sound boring—and complicated. In reality, however, they let you break up your auction listing into two or more columns and (as we've previously seen) add color backgrounds and pictures behind your text. And they're not *that* hard to do.

You start by enclosing your table with <table> and </table> codes. Then you enclose each individual row in the table with <tr> and </tr> codes and each cell in each row with <td> and </td> codes.

A basic table with two rows and two columns (four cells total) is coded like this:

```
<table>

<tr>
<td>row 1 cell 1</td>
<td>row 1 cell 2</td>
</tr>

<tr>
<td>row 2 cell 1</td>
<td>row 2 cell 2</td>
</tr>

</table>
```

I put extra lines between each of the table rows to better show the breakdown; the blank lines aren't necessary. Figure 9.5 shows what this simple table looks like with borders. (More on table borders in just a minute.)

| row 1 cell 1 | row 1 cell 2 |
| row 2 cell 1 | row 2 cell 2 |

FIGURE 9.5

A simple two column, two row table.

Within any individual cell in your table, you can insert any type of item—plain text, formatted text, bulleted lists, background shading, and even graphics. One neat effect is to use a simple two-column, one-row table to create the effect of two columns on your page. You can even shade the background of one of the cells or columns to set it off; it's a nice way to include more detailed information about your item.

You can also use some HTML parameters codes to format both the table as a whole and the cells within a table, to some degree:

- To dictate the width of the table border, use the `<table border="xx">` code, where *xx* is in pixels. (A border value of "1" is common.)

- To specify the border color, use the `<table bordercolor="xxxxxx">` code, where *xxxxxx* is the color hex code.

- To shade the background of an individual cell, use the `<td bgcolor="#xxxxxx">` code, where *xxxxxx* is the color hex code.

- To dictate the width of a cell, use the `<td width="xx%">` code, where *xx* is a percentage of the total table width; for example, `<td width="50%">` specifies a cell that is 50 percent of the total table width. You can also specify an exact width, in pixels, like this: `<td width=xxx`, where *xxx* is the number of pixels wide.

These codes gang together with the standard `<table>` and `<td>` codes in the table, as you'll see in some of the following tricks.

Trick #275: **Add a Border to a Picture**

kcanddi

stores.ebay.com/k-ds-auction-templates-and-more

www.kdwebpagedesign.com

PowerSeller

Member since 2003, Feedback: Purple star

We'll start with a relatively simple effect, putting a wide border around a picture, as shown in Figure 9.6. This works by inserting the picture into a single-celled table and specifying a thick border for the table. Here's the code:

```
<table border="25" cellpadding="10" cellspacing="0"
align="center" bgcolor="white bordercolor="blue" >
<tr>
<td>
<img src="URL">
</td>
</tr>
</table>
```

Naturally, replace *URL* with the URL and filename of your picture file. This code creates a gray border; you can change the border color by inserting a different value into the `bordercolor` parameter.

FIGURE 9.6

Add a big border around a picture.

Trick #276: **Add a Left Border to Your Listing**

kcanddi

stores.ebay.com/k-ds-auction-templates-and-more

www.kdwebpagedesign.com

PowerSeller

Member since 2003, Feedback: Purple star

Next up, we'll add a border to the left side of your entire item listing, as shown in Figure 9.7. Here's the code:

```
<table width="100%" cellspacing="0" cellpadding="0" border="0"
style="width: 100%">
<tr>
<td style="background-image: url('URL1'); width: 100px;"></td>
<td style="padding-left: 12px;">
Auction goes here.
</td>
</tr>
</table>
```

Replace URL1 (the one inside the parentheses, *not* the first url in the code) with the full URL and filename of the graphic you want to use for the border. You can set the table width to any percentage you wish (100% will fill the page). The width parameter in the third line specifies how wide the border will be; the default width is 100 pixels, but you can change this to match the width of the graphic you'll be using.

FIGURE 9.7

Add a border to the left edge of your item listing.

Trick #277: **Create a Two-Column Listing**

trapperjohn2000

stores.ebay.com/Molehill-Group-Store

Member since 1998, Feedback: Purple star

Now let's look at how you can use tables to format the layout of your auction listing. This first trick creates a two-column, one-row table. As you can see in Figure 9.8, you put your picture in the left column and your text in the right. As coded, the table background is all blue, with white type. The whole thing is preceded by a large colored headline above the table.

```
<h1><center><font color="#FF0000">Headline Text
<br>
On Two Lines, In Color!</font></center></h1>
<p>
<center>
<table bgcolor="#0000FF">
<tr>
<td>
<img src="URL">
</td>
<td>
<center><h2><font color="#FFFFFF">
Item text, as long as you need.
</font></center></h2>
</td>
</tr>
</table></center>
```

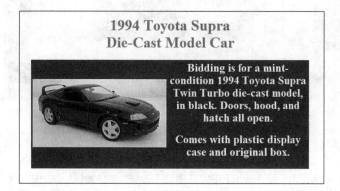

FIGURE 9.8

A table-based listing, with the picture on the left and the description on the right.

Can it get any simpler than that? You can put as much text as you want in the right-hand cell. You can also add text to the left cell, either before or after the graphic. You can even add more regular text *after* the table—a good place, in fact, to display your TOS.

Trick #278: **Use Nested Tables**

New Trick

trapperjohn2000

stores.ebay.com/Molehill-Group-Store

Member since 1998, Feedback: Purple star

If one table is fun, two are more so—especially when you nest one within the other. Nested tables let you create some neat visual effects, by nesting a table that contains text inside a table that contains a graphic. The effect is that of a fancy border around the text table, as shown in Figure 9.9.

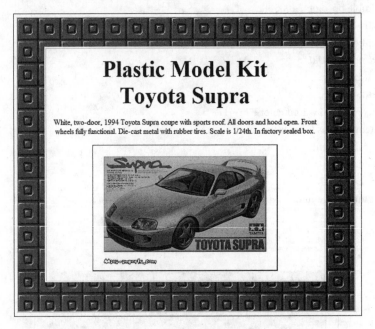

FIGURE 9.9

Create a fancy border effect with nested tables.

To nest a graphics table around a text table, you start by writing the code for the inner, or nested, table. This table can have as many cells as you'd like; for this example, we'll create a single-cell table that you fill with text. We'll configure this table to have a white background; the code should look something like this:

```
<table width="100%" border=1 cellpadding=15 bgcolor="white">
<tr>
<td width="100%">
Your Page Content Goes Here
</td></tr></table>
```

Now surround that table code with the code for the outside table. This table is also a single-cell table, but it will fill 90% of the page width and contain a graphic image.

```
<center>
<table width="90%" cellpadding=60 cellspacing=0 border=1 background="url">
<tr>
<td width="100%">

<table width="100%" border=1 cellpadding=15 bgcolor="white">
<tr>
<td width="100%">
Your auction listing content goes here
</td></tr></table>

</td></tr></table>
</center>
```

Obviously, you replace *URL* with the address and filename of the graphic you want to use in the outside table. You can vary the size of the "border" by changing the percentage of the inside table width.

HTML Editors and Tools

If you think all this HTML stuff is pretty cool, you're probably wondering the best way to create your own HTML code. Well, there are lots of options, from entering it by hand into eBay's Sell Your Item form to using a sophisticated (and expensive) HTML editor program. Read on to see what the eBay Masters recommend—and to learn about other useful HTML-related tools.

Trick #279: **Use a Simple Text Editor**

> **lora_and_steve**
>
> stores.ebay.com/Our-Hutch/
>
> www.ourhutch.com/examples/
>
> Member since 1999, Feedback: Red star

Many HTML-savvy eBayers recommend that you take the simple route and edit your HTML code manually. The best way to do this is to use a simple text-editing program, like Windows Notepad. You can copy your code directly from Notepad into eBay's Sell Your Item page, easy as pie.

Notepad is also a relatively fool-proof solution and much easier to use than some of the more expensive programs. As **lora_and_steve** (aka "The Wiz") notes:

Don't bother with big fancy HTML programs like FrontPage and Dreamweaver. They are too complex (and too expensive!) for creating auction listings. Not only are they totally unnecessary, they will probably cause you more grief than they will save!

Trick #280: **Use a Simple (and Free!) HTML Editor**

> **tradervic4u**
>
> stores.ebay.com/LeeWardBooks
>
> Member since 2002, Feedback: Red star

Still other sellers swear by a variety of simple—and free—HTML editing programs that do a really good job with the kind of simple HTML code you'll be using in your eBay listings. Favorites include 1st Page 2000 (www.evrsoft.com) and AceHTML (software.visicommedia.com/en/products/acehtmlfreeware/).

Trick #281: **Use an Online Color Chart**

> **bobal**
>
> www.bulls2.com/indexb/bobstips2.html
>
> Member since 1998, Feedback: Turquoise star

Remember earlier in the chapter when we talked about adding color text and backgrounds to your item listings? Well, if you want to know the proper HTML codes for all available colors, check out one of the following online color charts:

- ColorMaker (www.bagism.com/colormaker/)
- Doug's Color Picker (www.hypersolutions.org/pages/colorSel.html)
- e-pixs.com Color Chart (www.e-pixs.com/colors.html)
- Gotomy.com Color Chart (www.gotomy.com/color.html)
- Zoicks.com Color Chart (www.zoicks.com/colorchart.htm)

Trick #282: **Find Free Graphics for Your Listings**

> **bobal**
>
> www.bulls2.com/indexb/bobstips2.html
>
> Member since 1998, Feedback: Turquoise star

When you're looking for additional icons and graphics to use in your item listings, here's a list of places to look:

- 3D text banners: www.3dtextmaker.com
- Free backgrounds and clipart: www.coolarchive.com
- Free backgrounds: www.grsites.com/textures/
- More free backgrounds: www.free-backgrounds.com
- Free web page graphics and animations: www.flamingtext.com
- Free stars, GIFs, and backgrounds: www.angelfire.com/ca3/starsgifs/
- Free animated GIFs: www.gifs.net/animate/animate.htm
- More free animated GIFs: www.gifanimations.com
- Free smiley icons: www.bulls2.com/indexb/smileys.html

In addition, HTML expert **kcanddi** recommends doing a Google search for "free graphics" or "free backgrounds." And a quick caution: Don't ever link directly to an image on someone else's server. Instead, when you find an image you like, download it to your computer, and then upload it to your own host or server. Otherwise you could overload the bandwidth of the original server, solely for your own benefit!

Trick #283: **Test Your Code with a Practice Board**

lesley_feeney

stores.ebay.com/Lesleys-Auction-Template-Designs

www.zoicks.com

PowerSeller

Member since 2000, Feedback: Purple star

When you want to test your HTML before you post your auction listing, use a *practice board*. This is a website that lets you enter (or paste) your HTML code and then displays the resulting web page. Some of the most popular free practice boards include:

- auctionSupplies.com Practice Board (auctionsupplies.com/practice/ebay.shtml)
- Practice Board (www.practiceboard.com), shown in Figure 9.10
- Zoicks HTML Practice Board (www.zoicks.com/practice.htm)

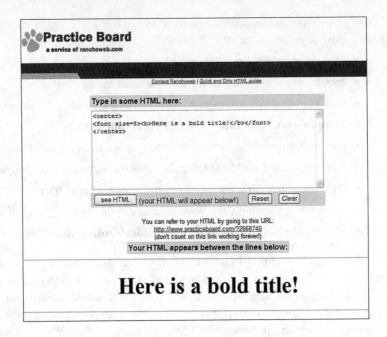

FIGURE 9.10
Test your code on the Practice Board.

What Not to Do

We'll end this chapter on HTML tricks by conveying some advice from the eBay Masters about what *not* to do in your auction listings.

Trick #284: **Avoid HTML Overkill**

New Trick

> **rosachs**
>
> stores.ebay.com/My-Discount-Shoe-Store
>
> home.midsouth.rr.com/rosachs/RKS/
>
> PowerSeller
>
> Member since 1997, Feedback: Red star

Using HTML lets you create really fancy layouts for your item listings. Get too fancy, however, and you could end up inadvertently "hiding" the key information about the item you're selling. Even worse, you could present the wrong image for your items and for your eBay business. Loud colors, large fonts, too many graphics, and a busy layout make your listing look cheap and tacky—and will send potential buyers looking for another seller.

I could give you my specific advice on what to and not to do, but I think PowerSeller **rosachs** puts it quite well:

1. *Keep your background simple and faint. You want buyers looking at your product images and reading your text, not looking to see if you have any other cute puppies or kitties further down the page.*

2. *Stay away from loud colors and massive numbers of colors. Use two or three colors for your fonts and tops, and one of these should be the old classic black. There's a reason most books are black type on white pages—it's easiest to read.*

3. *Keep your images reasonable in size. Every image has to be downloaded to the bidder's PC, even if you are only displaying a thumbnail sized image. If it takes more than just a few seconds for your images to start displaying, chances are the viewer is going to go elsewhere.*

4. *Keep your main item image right up top. If you look at the format of an auction page, the first screen of data is mostly eBay stuff, the next page down starts your stuff. Put your first and best image right there at the top of your part of the listing. Images are worth a thousand words, and if the buyer likes what they see, odds are good they will wait for the rest of the page to load.*

Along the same lines, use restraint when choosing from all the potential HTML goodies available. HTML lets you add all sorts of tricks and effects to your auction listings. That doesn't mean you need to, or should, use these kinds of effects. First of all, they turn off a lot of users. (Do you really like opening an auction listing and being barraged with flashing lights and sound effects?) Second, they make your listing look cheap, not classy. And third, they draw attention away from the item you're selling—which is not really what you want to do.

Trick #285: **Avoid Centered Type**

> ***samby***
> Member since 2001, Feedback: Turquoise star

Here we're talking about readability. Although centered type looks good at first glance, it's very hard to read when you have a long text description. Our eyes are accustomed to reading flush-left or justified type; it's what's used in this book and what you see in most newspapers and magazines, and there's a reason for that. While it's okay to have your title centered, centering the main text makes it difficult for the human eye to read. You want to encourage buyers to read your listing, not drive them away.

Trick #286: **Link with Restraint**

> **rosachs**
>
> stores.ebay.com/My-Discount-Shoe-Store
>
> home.midsouth.rr.com/rosachs/RKS/
>
> PowerSeller
>
> Member since 1997, Feedback: Red star

Although you can include a lot of web page links in your auction listing, that doesn't mean that you should. Any link you include drives potential buyers away from your auction to another web page. Once they leave your listing, they might not come back. You don't see storekeepers in the real world actively driving their customers out the front door, do you?

That said, there are some types of links that it makes sense to include. Here's what **rosachs** suggests:

> *I'd recommend at least one link to your About Me page (and everyone should have one of those), one link to your eBay Store (if you have one), and links to your related items for sale. eBay can help with the related items—be sure to activate this feature. And your About Me page is the only place you can refer buyers to your off-eBay items you might be selling, so that's important.*

Also, remember that any link you add needs to be within eBay's guidelines. A pulled auction never sold anything!

How to Display Better Product Photos

Nothing increases the effectiveness of an auction listing like the use of a good photograph. Auctions without photos have noticeably lower close rates; potential bidders want to see what they're buying before they commit to a bid.

That said, I've seen a lot of really lousy photos in various eBay auctions; a listing with a bad (too dark, too small, out of focus) photo might do worse than one with no photo at all. To that end, here is an entire chapter full of photo tricks from the eBay Masters, all designed to help you shoot and display the best possible product photos.

General Photo Tips

If a picture is worth a thousand words, what are a thousand pictures worth? While you're pondering that imponderable, let's examine some general tips about using photos in your auction listings.

Trick #287: **Include More Than One Photo**

lady-frog-vintage-jewelry

stores.ebay.com/SOMETHING-TO-RIBBIT-ABOUT

www.ladyfrog-vintage-jewelry.com

Member since 2000, Feedback: Red star

Yeah, I know that it costs extra to use more than one photo in an item listing. (Unless you insert the photo via HTML, that is, which we'll discuss in Trick #322.) But, depending on what you're selling, multiple photos might be worth the expense.

Let's be clear what we're talking about there. If you're selling a book, a photo of the front cover is probably enough. If you're selling a motor home, however, there are lots of things to see—the inside, the outside, the back, the front, and so on. The more visually complex the item is that you're selling, the more the buyer wants and needs to see varying views.

Think about the last item you purchased from a catalog. Unless it was a DVD or a CD or something like that, you wanted to see that item from all different angles. After all, you can't examine the item in person, so you need multiple photographs to help you better get a feel for the item. As member **lady-frog-vintage-jewelry** puts it:

> Many sellers seem to think that one picture will do the trick, but as a buyer, I want to see pictures of the front, the back, a close-up of the detail, and so on. I don't think one picture does the trick in letting me know what the item truly looks like.

As eBay becomes more of a buyer's market than a seller's market, the best way to get the most value out of the items you have for sale is with the pictures you post. The more and better pictures that buyers can browse, the more likely it is that you'll get the buyer's money.

Trick #288: **Accessorize Your Photos**

trickie636

Member since 2000, Feedback: Purple star

Add some seasonal interest to your product photos by adding appropriate props and accessories to the picture. During the Christmas season, shoot your items next to a small Christmas tree or fake snowman. At Halloween, use a jack 'o' lantern as a prop. During the hot summer months, have a bikini model pose with your item. (Okay, maybe that last suggestion is a bit overboard…unless you're selling swimwear, that is.) In any case, use props to make your photos stand out, and (during the season) suggest that your item would make a great Christmas gift.

Trick #289: **Use a Tripod**

> **camerajim**
>
> stores.ebay.com/CameraJim
>
> PowerSeller
>
> Member since 1999, Feedback: Red star

It doesn't matter what type of digital camera you use, you need good solid support in order to take shake-free pictures. This means investing a few bucks in a tripod. As **camerajim** points out:

> *A slightly shaky camera is the most common cause of blurry photos.*

Trick #290: **Take More Than One Shot**

> **trapperjohn2000**
>
> stores.ebay.com/Molehill-Group-Store
>
> Member since 1998, Feedback: Purple star

Don't snap off a quick picture and assume you've done your job. Shoot your item from several different angles and distances—and remember to get a close-up of any important area of the item, such as a serial number or a damaged area. You might want to include multiple photos in your listing, or just have a good selection of photos to choose from for that one best picture. The more pictures you shoot, the more likely you are to find one that looks really great.

Setting Up Your Shot

Once you have the right equipment at hand, it's time to start setting up your photo shoot. Grab the items you're ready to sell and listen to what the eBay Masters recommend.

Trick #291: **Put a Neutral Background Behind Your Item**

> **camerajim**
>
> stores.ebay.com/CameraJim
>
> PowerSeller
>
> Member since 1999, Feedback: Red star

You don't want the background of your photo competing with the item you have for sale. One solution is to take your photo against a plain white wall. If you want to get fancier, you can use seamless photography paper, curved up behind your subject. This type of professional seamless paper is surprisingly inexpensive; you can buy a 54-inch × 12-yard roll online for about $20. Or, if you're shooting smaller objects, use a large sheet of poster board. You can use white, gray, or black backgrounds, depending on the color of your subject. Here's what **camerajim** recommends:

> *White is good for most objects. Black works well for jewelry and sometimes glass. I personally like a neutral gray, because you can use it as a reference when balancing your colors in Photoshop.*

Trick #292: **Angle Your Subject**

> **camerajim**
>
> stores.ebay.com/CameraJim
>
> PowerSeller
>
> Member since 1999, Feedback: Red star

Don't shoot your item head-on. Most objects look best when placed at an angle to the camera. Try positioning your light at a 45-degree angle and then facing the item into the light. This type of three-quarter view is quite flattering.

Trick #293: **Get Close Enough to See the Detail**

> **terrisbooks**
>
> stores.ebay.com/Terris-Books
>
> www.terrisbeads.com
>
> PowerSeller
>
> Member since 2002, Feedback: Red star

To take effective photographs, you have to learn proper composition. That means centering the item in the center of the photo and getting close enough to the object so that it fills up the entire picture. Don't stand halfway across the room and shoot a very small object; get close up and make it *big!* Here's what member **terrisbooks** recommends:

> *People want to see clearly what they are buying. I usually take a close-up shot so that everyone can see the detail in the handmade beads I offer. With things like my lampwork bead necklaces, I almost always take a photo of the whole necklace, plus another one of a close up of the center bead or pendant.*

Here's an example. Figure 10.1 shows an item that's photographed from too far away, and off-center besides. Figure 10.2 shows better composition, with the item up close and center. The second photo makes it much easier for potential buyers to see what they're bidding on.

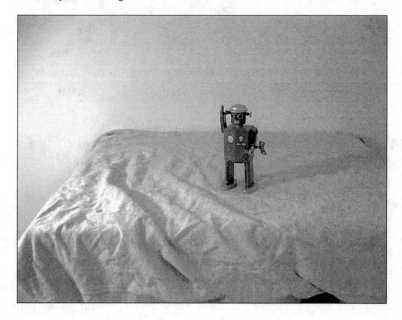

FIGURE 10.1
An item shot from too far away.

FIGURE 10.2

A photograph with proper composition—and close enough to see the detail.

Trick #294: **Use Your Camera's White Balance Control**

camerajim

stores.ebay.com/CameraJim

PowerSeller

Member since 1999, Feedback: Red star

If you find your pictures coming out with unusual tints, you need to adjust your camera's white balance mode. Most cameras let you preset the white balance control to the type of light you're using. For example, if your photos come out with a yellow hue, you're probably shooting under incandescent lighting. When you set the white balance for incandescent light, the yellows will come out a more natural-looking white.

(By the way, white balance is something you can also fix after the shot with image editing software, which we'll discuss later in this chapter.)

Trick #295: **Use eBay's Stock Photos**

> **trapperjohn2000**
>
> stores.ebay.com/Molehill-Group-Store
>
> Member since 1998, Feedback: Purple star

If you're selling a book, audio book, audio cassette, CD, DVD, videogame, or similar item, you might not need to take any photos at all. That's because eBay automatically inserts a stock product photo when you use the pre-filled item description option to create your item listing. If the item you're selling is listed in eBay's product database—and you like the photo they provide—save yourself the trouble and let eBay insert the picture for you.

Trick #296: *Don't* **Use eBay's Stock Photos**

> **hortonsbks**
>
> stores.ebay.com/Hortonsbks
>
> PowerSeller
>
> Member since 2000, Feedback: Red star

Although the previous trick recommends it, a lot of eBay sellers don't like relying on eBay's stock photos. The stock photo won't always match the particular item you have for sale (different editions sometimes have different packaging), nor will it always represent the condition of your item. Here's what member **hortonsbks** thinks about it:

> *I want to know what the book I'm buying actually looks like. I will not bid on stock photos. Let's say they had a stock photo of the first edition of* Confederacy of Dunces *with a white background, when their cover has a dark background. I don't think so!*

So use a stock photo if it matches closely to what you're selling, but not if your item is significantly different.

Lighting Your Shot

The difference between an average photo and a great one is often the lighting. Brightly lit photos show more detail than dark ones; in fact, an overly dark photo might result in few or no bids. Learn how to properly light your photos, and you'll increase your sales.

Trick #297: **Shoot Outdoors**

camerajim

stores.ebay.com/CameraJim

PowerSeller

Member since 1999, Feedback: Red star

One of the worst photographic offenses is to shoot under standard indoor room light. A simple solution is to take your photos outdoors, where there is lots of natural lighting. Shooting on an overcast or hazy day is easiest, because you don't have to worry about direct sunlight washing out your pictures. On a sunny day, shoot in open shade, like that on the side of a building.

If you want a really special shot, shoot during that time of day when the light is just right, as **camerajim** recommends:

Photographers usually refer to the "magic hour" as the first hour after sunrise or the last hour before sunset. It's not so much the warmth of the sun that is prized, but the low angle, providing strong side lighting.

Trick #298: **Shoot Next to a Window**

camerajim

stores.ebay.com/CameraJim

PowerSeller

Member since 1999, Feedback: Red star

If you don't want to shoot outside, shoot indoors next to an open window. Try to avoid direct sunlight coming in; choose a time of day when the sun has shifted, or position a thin white drapery over the window to diffuse the light.

Trick #299: **Don't Use Your Camera's Flash**

camerajim

stores.ebay.com/CameraJim

PowerSeller

Member since 1999, Feedback: Red star

Whatever you do, don't use your camera's built-in flash. That's what many amateur photographers do, and it's not a good thing. Direct flash makes your objects look two-dimensional and also creates a glare from shiny surfaces. Avoid the temptation! It's better to use natural lighting, bounce lighting, a speedlight, or external lights—which we'll discuss next.

Trick #300: **Use External Lights**

camerajim

stores.ebay.com/CameraJim

PowerSeller

Member since 1999, Feedback: Red star

A better approach for indoor photography is to use an external lighting kit. I like the low-priced kits from Smith-Victor, but you can also make your own lights with regular tungsten bulbs in clamp-on reflectors, which you can get from Home Depot or any similar store. Two 150-watt lights are enough for most digital cameras. Position the lights at 45-degree angles to the subject (on either side of your camera, as shown in Figure 10.3), and you're good to go.

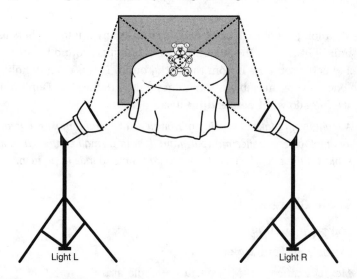

Light L   Light R

FIGURE 10.3

Position auxiliary lights on either side of your digital camera.

Trick #301: **Use a Reflector**

> **camerajim**
>
> stores.ebay.com/CameraJim
>
> PowerSeller
>
> Member since 1999, Feedback: Red star

For a more professional lighting effect, supplement your external lights with a reflector. A reflector on the opposite side of the subject from the light source will reflect some of the main light back, cutting the shadow intensity. A piece of white poster board is a good reflector. If the shadows are still too dark, cover the poster board with crinkled aluminum foil.

Trick #302: **Add "Hair Lighting"**

> **camerajim**
>
> stores.ebay.com/CameraJim
>
> PowerSeller
>
> Member since 1999, Feedback: Red star

Here's another cool trick from **camerajim**. Many photographers use what they call a "hair light" *behind* the subject to add highlights around the edge of the subject and to better separate it from the background. This is a small light placed high on the back side of the subject, sometimes a little to the side. Don't have an extra light? Then do what **camerajim** does:

> *A magnifying makeup/shaving mirror on a table stand makes a great "hair light" for small objects, reflecting your main light in a small controlled spot back at the subject. I use one whenever I want to add some sparkle to an item.*

Trick #303: **Avoid Glare**

> **trapperjohn2000**
>
> stores.ebay.com/Molehill-Group-Store
>
> Member since 1998, Feedback: Purple star

If you're photographing a glass or plastic item, or an item still in plastic wrap or packaging, or just an item that's naturally shiny, you have to work hard to avoid glare from whatever lighting source you're using. This is one reason why I typically don't recommend using a single-point flash—without any fill lighting, it produces too much glare. You avoid glare by not using a flash, adding fill lighting (to the sides of the object), diffusing the lighting source (by bouncing the light off a reflector of some sort), or just turning the item until the glare goes away. A simpler solution is to shoot in an area with strong natural light—like outside on a nice day. Just beware of the glare problem, and somehow compensate for it.

Trick #304: **Use a Light Box or Light Tent**

> **newstartoday**
>
> PowerSeller
>
> Member since 2000, Feedback: Red star

When you're photographing small items, a very effective way to provide soft lighting is to place the item inside a light box or light tent. This is an enclosure with white sides, some of which are translucent, into which you insert the item to be shot. A light shines from outside the box or tent through the translucent wall(s), just providing diffused lighting inside the enclosure. (Your camera typically shoots through an open side or through a hole in one of the sides.)

You can make your own light box/tent out of a plain white milk jug, or a white plastic bowl, or a white sheet. Anything white and translucent will work. If you're using a milk jug, cut the bottom off and place the jug over your subject. Illuminate from the sides and shoot through the open spout of the jug.

You can make a larger light tent just by draping a sheet or other white material over and around a table. Another option is to glue sheets of styrofoam together into a cube form, with the bottom left open—and then shoot through the open end.

Or, if you don't want to go through all that trouble, you can buy a preassembled light box, such as Photo Studio in a Box (www.americanrecorder.com). As you can see in Figure 10.4, this particular device is a compact 16" × 16" × 16" cube that has two halogen lights and white photo material on the side, along with a blue or gray background. It includes two high-output Tungsten lamps and a short camera stand. The whole thing folds up like a portfolio for easy travel or storage. Seller **newstartoday** swears by it:

> *The new pictures I take inside this box are incredible! No more bright spots, as the light is nicely diffused, and the camera stand eliminates any jiggling. My photos are 150% clearer and more professional looking.*

FIGURE 10.4

Photo Studio in a Box—great for photographing small objects.

Other light boxes and light tents are available from EZcube (www.ezcube.com), Light-Tent.com (www.light-tent.com), MK Digital Direct (www.mkdigitaldirect.com), Ortery (www.ortery.com), and Plume (www.plumeltd.com).

Shooting Different Types of Items

Now for a few really useful tricks for shooting different types of items. Learn from the Masters!

Trick #305: **Shooting Clear or Translucent Glass**

camerajim

stores.ebay.com/CameraJim

PowerSeller

Member since 1999, Feedback: Red star

You want to illuminate glass items from the rear and sides, or from the top. Clear or translucent glass often requires more than one light to look best. You can use either a light or dark background, depending on the characteristics of the glass. Faceted or cut glass usually looks best against a dark background.

Trick #306: **Shooting Opaque Glass and Jewelry**

camerajim

stores.ebay.com/CameraJim

PowerSeller

Member since 1999, Feedback: Red star

Shooting opaque glass, jewelry, and silver items is somewhat difficult because of all the potential reflections. To avoid reflections and harsh highlights, you want a very broad, diffused light. The easiest way to get this is to use a translucent light tent or light box around your subject. You then leave a hole for your camera lens to poke through and illuminate the tent evenly from at least two sides.

Trick #307: **Shooting Clothing**

camerajim

stores.ebay.com/CameraJim

PowerSeller

Member since 1999, Feedback: Red star

Shooting clothing requires a lot of light. Photography expert **camerajim** recommends using two lights, one at a 45-degree angle to the subject, with a supplementary light or a large reflector on the other side. If you can, diffuse the lights to soften any shadows. Never use the built-in flash!

Trick #308: **Shooting Colored Fabrics**

camerajim

stores.ebay.com/CameraJim

PowerSeller

Member since 1999, Feedback: Red star

One potential problem with shooting colored fabrics is that most digital cameras are very sensitive to otherwise-invisible infrared light—and fabrics, especially synthetic ones, reflect a lot of infrared. As **camerajim** notes:

You can see if this is the case by shooting similarly-colored natural and synthetic fabrics together. If the natural fabric looks, well, natural, and the synthetic fabric's color shifts, the problem is infrared.

The only real solution to this problem is to correct the colors after the shoot, using image-editing software.

Trick #309: **Shooting Patterned Fabrics**

camerajim

stores.ebay.com/CameraJim

PowerSeller

Member since 1999, Feedback: Red star

Fabrics with strong lines or checks present another problem, in the form of moiré patterns. This is caused when two interfering patterns overlap—in this case, the pattern of the fabric versus the pattern of pixels in your digital image. You may be able to lessen or eliminate the moiré effect by shooting at a different distance or with the camera at a slight angle to the subject.

Trick #310: **Shooting Black Fabric**

camerajim

stores.ebay.com/CameraJim

PowerSeller

Member since 1999, Feedback: Red star

The challenge when shooting black fabric and clothing is pulling detail out of the darkness. You have to step up the lighting to create shadows and highlights on the fabric. You can try shooting next to a window or aiming a supplementary light across the clothing at a fairly close angle. And follow **camerajim**'s advice:

You'll still need close-ups to show much detail, but good lighting will at least show the shape better. Whatever you do, don't use the built-in flash on your camera. Its flat lighting will wipe out any features or shape.

Trick #311: **Displaying Clothing in a Photo**

powershopper

Member since 1998, Feedback: Purple star

Props make your items look more realistic, and the best prop for clothing is a mannequin or clothing form. Hanging the clothing on a mannequin lets potential buyers see what the item looks like in real life. Here's what **powershopper** recommends:

Most clothing looks best when displayed on a mannequin or form. If you don't own one, at least show a view of the items laid flat. Include close-up photos of attractive item details.

Trick #312: **Shooting Wood Furniture**

camerajim

stores.ebay.com/CameraJim

PowerSeller

Member since 1999, Feedback: Red star

The challenge with shooting high-gloss wood furniture is glare. The first thing to do is to *not* use your camera's flash; this will cause the furniture to glare back at you from every highlight, and it won't show the shape of the item well. Better to use diffused daylight coming in from a window, perhaps with large pieces of poster board as deflectors, to get enough light onto the woodgrain.

If it's not too much trouble, move the item outside to shoot. Position it on the shady side of a building; you don't want direct sunlight, for the same reason you don't want direct flash.

And, however you light it, make sure you shoot the item at an angle. Straight-on shots are both boring and graceless.

Trick #313: **Take Pictures of Flat Items with a Scanner**

tradervic4u

stores.ebay.com/LeeWardBooks

Member since 2002, Feedback: Red star

If you're selling relatively flat items (books, CDs, currency, paintings, and so on), you might be better off with a scanner than a camera. (And remember that boxes have flat sides that can be scanned.) Just lay the object on a flatbed scanner and scan the item into a file on your computer. It's actually easier to scan something like a book or a DVD case than it is to take a good steady picture of it!

Oh, and if you're scanning a compact disc, take the CD booklet out of the jewel case to scan. Don't shoot through the plastic if you don't have to.

Trick #314: **Take Pictures of Small Items with a Scanner**

> **milehiauctionaction**
>
> Member since 2000, Feedback: Turquoise star

The scanner trick isn't just for flat items. It can also work, in a pinch, for small items, such as jewelry. In fact, some sellers swear by scanning jewelry— **milehiauctionaction** claims that the "detail is much sharper" with a scanner than with a typical digital camera!

Optimizing Your Images for eBay

After you've taken your photograph, you need to transfer it to your computer and do a little clean up work before you load it into your eBay auction listing. There's all sorts of editing tasks you might need to do—lighten photos shot in low light, correct the color, crop the picture, resize the image, and decrease the resolution to produce smaller-sized files. That's the great thing about digital photography—you can fix a lot of "mistakes" after the fact!

Trick #315: **Use Image-Editing Software**

> **rosachs**
>
> stores.ebay.com/My-Discount-Shoe-Store
>
> home.midsouth.rr.com/rosachs/RKS/
>
> PowerSeller
>
> Member since 1997, Feedback: Red star

How do you perform all this image editing? With image-editing software, of course! The right program will let you do everything you need to do, with a few clicks of the mouse. Although hard-core picture fanatics swear by the extremely full-featured (and very expensive) Adobe Photoshop CS, there are several lower-cost programs that perform just as well for the type of editing you'll be doing. These programs include the following:

- Adobe Photoshop Elements (www.adobe.com)
- IrfanView (www.irfanview.com)
- Paint Shop Pro (www.corel.com)
- Microsoft Digital Image (www.microsoft.com/products/imaging/)
- Roxio PhotoSuite (www.roxio.com)

Most of these programs cost under $100 and have similar features. Or, if you'd rather not muck around with this sort of picture editing, you can always have somebody else do it for you; FedEx Kinko's is a good place to start.

Trick #316: **Crop to the Most Important Part of Your Image**

nktower

Member since 1999, Feedback: Turquoise star

If you didn't frame your image properly to begin with, use your image editing software to crop the unnecessary edges off your image. The goal is to focus attention on the main part of your item, so crop off everything else that doesn't matter.

Trick #317: **Resize Your Photos to Match eBay's Dimensions**

camerajim

stores.ebay.com/CameraJim

PowerSeller

Member since 1999, Feedback: Red star

Cropping isn't the only thing you have to do to fit your photo to eBay's image parameters. You also need to resize your photo to best fit within your eBay listing. Most pictures you take with a digital camera will come out too big to fit on a web page without scrolling, which means resizing the photo to fit within the confines of a normal web page.

eBay recommends that you size your image to no more than 300 pixels high by 400 pixels wide. This is particularly important if you use eBay Picture Services, which will compress pictures to these dimensions. The results of this compression are yucky-looking pictures, so either resize to fit, or use a different picture-hosting service—which we'll discuss in Trick #321.

Trick #318: **Shrink the File Size**

griffin_trader

stores.ebay.com/Naturally-In-New-Orleans-Mardi-Gras

Member since 1999, Feedback: Green star

You also need to optimize your image file so that it doesn't take forever for people to download. This is especially important for your potential buyers who are using older computers, or are on a slower dial-up Internet connection. My recommendation is to keep your file size below 50KB, which results in reasonable downloads for most users.

There are three ways to reduce the size of an image file. You can reduce the resolution (in dots per inch or pixels per inch); you can resize the width and height; or you can reduce the number of colors used. Depending on your pictures, you may need to use some or all of these techniques to get the file down to a workable size. Most image editing software lets you perform all three of these operations.

Trick #319: **How *Not* to Name Your Photos**

> **bobal**
>
> www.bulls2.com/indexb/bobstips2.html
>
> Member since 1998, Feedback: Turquoise star

When you name your image files, know that the filename you use can affect how (or even *if*) the image is displayed in certain web browsers. You definitely want to save your images as either JPG or GIF files, *not* BMP files, as many browsers won't display BMP images. You also want to keep your filename short, and use all lower-case letters.

As to what *not* to do, don't use any characters like # $ % ^ & * @ because these characters in a filename can cause problems. Also, don't use spaces in your filenames, as many browsers will not recognize your files as picture files. If you really need to use two words in your filename, use a dash or an underscore.

Choosing an Image Host

When you have your photos all edited and optimized, you need to upload them to the web so you can use them in your eBay auctions. You actually have a choice here. You can use eBay Picture Services or a third-party picture host. Let's see what the eBay Masters recommend.

Trick #320: **Use eBay Picture Services**

> **trapperjohn2002250**
>
> stores.ebay.com/Molehill-Group-Store
>
> Member since 1998, Feedback: Purple star

If you let eBay host your photos, the process is relatively easy. All you have to do is enter the names of the image files when you're listing your item for sale, as shown in Figure 10.5, and eBay does all the uploading and hosting for you. This is definitely the method of choice for newbie and occasional sellers, although not necessarily the choice of most eBay Masters. That's because eBay charges for this service, above and beyond your first (free) photo. Basically, you pay $0.15 for each picture past the first, which can add up.

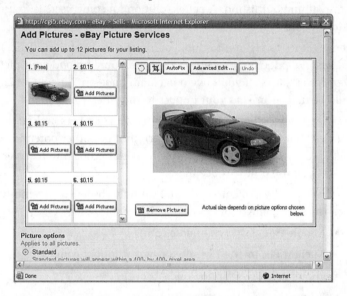

FIGURE 10.5

Use eBay Picture Services to upload your photos.

One plus to using eBay Picture Services is that you get a free picture of your item in the title bar of your item listing page. You don't get this if you host your pictures on another website.

eBay also offers a subscription-based picture hosting service, dubbed eBay Picture Manager. Picture Manager works a lot like a third-party picture host; you can store up to 50MB of image files for $9.99 per month, 125MB for $19.99 per month, or 300MB for $39.99 per month. (Prices are slightly less if you have an eBay Store.) The service itself is fine, but you need to compare eBay's prices with those of the various third-party services—which we'll look at next.

Trick #321: **Use a Third-Party Picture Host**

nktower

Member since 1999, Feedback: Turquoise star

Many sellers are less than thrilled with eBay's picture hosting service, which can be both expensive and limited, especially in terms of how and where you can place photos within your listing. A better solution for some users is to use another web hosting service to host their files.

When it comes to picture hosting, you have a lot of options. First, if you have your own personal page on the web, you can probably upload your pictures to that web server. For example, if you have a personal page on Yahoo! GeoCities or Tripod, you should be able to upload your images to that site.

If you don't have a personal page but *could* have a personal page (via America Online or your Internet service provider), that's another potential place for you to upload picture files. If the company you work for has a web server, there's a chance it will let you use a little space there.

Then there are the dedicated picture hosting websites, which many eBay Masters prefer. Here are some of the most popular of these sites:

- Ándale Images (www.andale.com)
- Auction Pix Image Hosting (www.auctionpix.com)
- Photobucket (www.photobucket.com)
- PictureTrail (www.picturetrail.com)
- Vendio Image Hosting (www.vendio.com)

Most of these sites offer a variety of picture hosting services, typically for a small fee—along the lines of $5 or so per month for 10MB or more of storage. This would let you store 200 images at a time, for less than half of what eBay would charge. Photobucket goes a step further and offers a free service, which many sellers recommend. (Free is always good!)

Adding Pictures to Your Listings

As you learned in Chapter 9, "How to Enhance Your Product Listings with HTML," one of the great things about creating your own listings with HTML is that you can insert photos anywhere in your item listing, not just where eBay says you can put them. And, since you're linking to pictures stored on your own server (or other hosting service), you don't have to pay eBay for the privilege! Insert as many pictures as you like, wherever you like, for free. (Just remember that too many pictures can slow down the load time for your listing—and irritate potential bidders with dial-up connections.) Read on to learn how the eBay Masters add great-looking pictures to their auction listings.

Trick #322: **Insert a Picture with HTML**

> **lora_and_steve**
> stores.ebay.com/Our-Hutch/
> www.ourhutch.com/examples/
> Member since 1999, Feedback: Red star

The code for inserting a picture is incredibly simple. Here's all there is to it:
`<img src="URL">`

Just make sure you include the *complete* URL of the picture file, including the http:// and the filename, and make sure the URL is enclosed within quotation marks.

Trick #323: **Link to a Larger Picture**

> **omeganut**
> Member since 2002, Feedback: Blue star

Some potential buyers are on high-speed broadband connections and have no problems downloading large, high-resolution images. Other potential buyers are on slow dial-up connections that take forever to download large images. This is why, in general, you want to include only smaller images in your listings, so that your page loads acceptably for all potential buyers.

That doesn't mean, however, that having larger, higher-resolution photos available isn't a good idea. You just don't want to burden all potential buyers with those slow-to-download image files. A better solution is to display a standard low-resolution photo in the listing itself, but then link to a higher-resolution photo, hosted on another website. (Another good reason to use a non-eBay photo host, of course.)

One way to do this is to provide a text link to the high-res photo, like this:
`<a href="URL">Click here to view a larger photo.</a>`

Naturally, you should replace URL with the full URL and filename of the larger photo file.

An alternative method is to let the user click on the low-res photo to display the high-res one. Here's how that code works:

```
<a href="URL1"> <img src="URL2"></a>
```

In this code, replace *URL1* with the address for the high-resolution photo, and *URL2* with the address for the low-resolution photo.

Trick #324: **Insert Two Pictures Side-by-Side**

lora_and_steve

stores.ebay.com/Our-Hutch/

www.ourhutch.com/examples/

Member since 1999, Feedback: Red star

Now the fun really starts. Want to include two pictures side-by-side? Then include two image links on the same line, like this:

```
<img src="URL1"><img src="URL2">
```

The result is shown in Figure 10.6.

FIGURE 10.6
Two pictures side-by-side.

Trick #325: **Insert Four Pictures in Two Rows**

lora_and_steve

stores.ebay.com/Our-Hutch/

www.ourhutch.com/examples/

Member since 1999, Feedback: Red star

Now let's get a little fancier and display four pictures in a two-by-two grid, as shown in Figure 10.7. The code looks like this:

```
<img src="URL1"><img src="URL2">
<br>
<img src="URL3"><img src="URL4">
```

FIGURE 10.7
Four pictures in a grid.

Pretty simple. Note, however, that you need to watch that your picture files aren't too wide for the space. If they're too big, they'll push your page out of shape or not line up properly. HTML expert **lora_and_steve** (also known as "The Wiz") recommends the following:

> *A maximum width of 500 pixels for a single picture and 250 pixels for each of two pictures side-by-side is about right on a full page.*

Trick #326: **Add One Big Picture That Changes When You Click a Button**

bobal

www.bulls2.com/indexb/bobstips2.html

Member since 1998, Feedback: Turquoise star

Now we'll get really fancy. This trick displays a single large picture, with a row of buttons underneath, as shown in Figure 10.8. Click a button, and the picture changes. It's a great way to display multiple photos in a limited space.

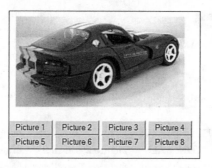

FIGURE 10.8
Click a button to see another picture.

The code for this trick is a trifle complex, but it works. The code as-written creates eight buttons (for eight photos), but if you don't have that many you can cut the excess lines of code.

Start by putting the following code at the very beginning of your listing:

```
<SCRIPT LANGUAGE="JavaScript">
var CachedImages
CachedImages = new Array(8)
CachedImages[0] = new Image
CachedImages[0]="URL1"
CachedImages[1] = new Image
CachedImages[1]="URL2"
CachedImages[2] = new Image
CachedImages[2]="URL3"
CachedImages[3] = new Image
CachedImages[3]="URL4"
CachedImages[4] = new Image
CachedImages[4]="URL5"
CachedImages[5] = new Image
CachedImages[5]="URL6"
CachedImages[6] = new Image
CachedImages[6]="URL7"
CachedImages[7] = new Image
CachedImages[7] ="URL8"
function ChangeImage(n)
{
document.SpaceImage.src=CachedImages[n]
}
</script>
```

Now put the second bit of code next, wherever you want the picture to appear in your listing:

```
<CENTER>
<IMG SRC="URL1" NAME="SpaceImage">
</CENTER>
<P>
<FORM NAME="ImageSelector">
<CENTER>
<INPUT TYPE="BUTTON" VALUE="Picture 1" onClick="ChangeImage(0)">
<INPUT TYPE="BUTTON" VALUE="Picture 2" onClick="ChangeImage(1)">
<INPUT TYPE="BUTTON" VALUE="Picture 3" onClick="ChangeImage(2)">
```

```
<INPUT TYPE="BUTTON" VALUE="Picture 4" onClick="ChangeImage(3)"><br>
<INPUT TYPE="BUTTON" VALUE="Picture 5" onClick="ChangeImage(4)">
<INPUT TYPE="BUTTON" VALUE="Picture 6" onClick="ChangeImage(5)">
<INPUT TYPE="BUTTON" VALUE="Picture 7" onClick="ChangeImage(6)">
<INPUT TYPE="BUTTON" VALUE="Picture 8" onClick="ChangeImage(7)">
</CENTER>
</FORM>
```

That's it. It's a neat touch for a fancy item listing!

(Note that if you try to test this code with pictures stored locally on your hard disk, it won't work; for some reason, it only works with pictures actually uploaded to a web server.)

Trick #327: **Add a "Click to Enlarge" Picture with Thumbnails**

bobal

www.bulls2.com/indexb/bobstips2.html

Member since 1998, Feedback: Turquoise star

This next trick creates a similar picture effect, this time with thumbnails of the additional pictures below the main picture, as shown in Figure 10.9. Click a thumbnail, and the big picture changes to display the new picture.

Click On Thumbnails To Enlarge

FIGURE 10.9

Click a thumbnail to enlarge a picture.

This code requires you to create a table to hold the thumbnails, so enter the code carefully as written.

```
<table align=center cellspacing=20 height="400">
<tr><td><center>
```

```
<img src="URL1" height=300 alt name="the_pic">
<br>
<A href="#"; onClick="document.the_pic.src='URL1';return false;">
<IMG src="URL1" width=75 border=0 alt="Pic1"></a>
<A href="#"; onClick="document.the_pic.src='URL2';return false;">
<IMG src="URL2" width=75 border=0 alt="Pic2"></a>
<A href="#"; onClick="document.the_pic.src='URL3';return false;">
<IMG src="URL3" width=75 border=0 alt="Pic3"></a>
<A href="#"; onClick="document.the_pic.src='URL4';return false;">
<IMG src="URL4" width=75 border=0 alt="Pic4"></a>
<A href="#"; onClick="document.the_pic.src='URL5';return false;">
<IMG src="URL5" width=75 border=0 alt="Pic5"></a>
<A href="#"; onClick="document.the_pic.src='URL6';return false;">
<IMG src="URL6" width=75 border=0 alt="Pic6"></a>
</center>
<center><font color=red> Click On Thumbnails To Enlarge </center>
</font></tr></table>
```

Note that there are other approaches to this effect, although they require you creating two versions of each image—one regular-sized and one thumbnail-sized. The code presented here only requires a single version of each picture, so it's a bit simpler.

Keeping Your Photos from Being Copied

One problem that some sellers face is other users reusing their photographs. That is, you post a photo for an auction, then later find out another seller is selling a similar item but using your photo in their item description. This type of image theft is against eBay's rules and is a particular problem for eBay's many artist/sellers. You can report the offenders, of course, but what can you do to keep the problem from occurring in the first place?

Trick #328: **Add a Watermark**

> **kyrn**
>
> stores.ebay.com/The-Art-of-Meredith-Dillman/
>
> www.meredithdillman.com
>
> Member since 1998, Feedback: Turquoise star

The most common solution to the problem of image theft is to add your name across the front of all your images in the form of a watermark. As you can see in Figure 10.10, this would tend to discourage others from reusing your photos, although it also makes your images a little less legible. You can add this type of watermark with just about any image editing program, simply by adding text over the top of the main image.

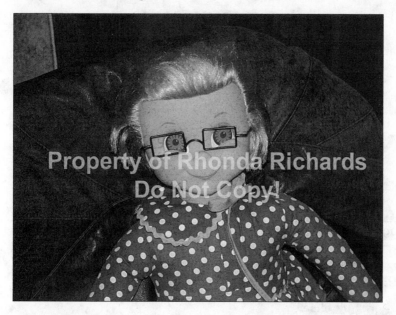

FIGURE 10.10

A photo with a watermark signature.

How do you add a watermark to your photos? While you can use any Photoshop or any similar graphics editing program to perform this task, I like the online water-marker at Birddogs Garage (www.birddogsgarage.com/bdg_2/modules.php?name=bdgwatermark). As you can see in Figure 10.11, all you have to do is select the pictures on your hard drive you want to watermark, indicate whether you want a text watermark or logo watermark, and then click a button. The water-marker automatically creates a new image file, complete with watermark, which you can then download back to your hard disk. Pretty neat!

FIGURE 10.11
Birddogs Garage's online watermarker.

Trick #329: **Shoot with a Plastic "Sample" Sign**

art_by_eileen

Member since 2002, Feedback: Blue star

A low-tech version of the previous trick is to add your watermark while you're photographing the picture. Just take a clear piece of plastic laminate and write "Sample" or some such word or phrase across it. Then lay this across your item before shooting the picture, and you have your watermark. This method is particularly well-suited for paintings and other types of flat artwork, especially when you're scanning the piece into a digital file.

Trick #330: **Overlay a Transparent Gif**

lora_and_steve

stores.ebay.com/Our-Hutch/

www.ourhutch.com/examples/

Member since 1999, Feedback: Red star

If you're comfortable with HTML, there's a way to use tables and transparent GIF files to make it extremely difficult for anyone to steal your images via the right-click-save method. You have to create a clear GIF file, the same dimensions as your regular image file, and then use the following code:

```
<table border="0" cellpadding="0" cellspacing="0" align="center">
<tr><td background="URL">
<img src="transparent.gif" border="0">
</td></tr></table>
```

Essentially, this technique inserts your main image as the background layer in a table, then places a transparent image on top of it. Anyone right-clicking on what appears to be a single image is actually right-clicking on the transparent image, not your main image, so it's the "empty" image that gets copied. Pretty nifty arrangement. Make sure to replace URL with the location and filename of your main image; replace transparent.gif with the image and filename of your transparent image.

Trick #331: **Use a No-Click Script**

> **lora_and_steve**
>
> stores.ebay.com/Our-Hutch/
>
> www.ourhutch.com/examples/
>
> Member since 1999, Feedback: Red star

An even more effective anti-theft method is to employ a no-click script to your HTML code, using JavaScript. This script prevents any users from right-clicking on your image.

This is a bit complicated, so don't attempt it if you're not comfortable with the code. Here's how it works:

```
<script language="javascript">
var message="Function Disabled!";
function clickIE4(){
if (event.button==2){
alert(message);
return false;
}
}
function clickNS4(e){
```

```
if
document.layers||document.getElementById&&!document.all){
if (e.which==2||e.which==3){
alert(message);
return false;
}
}
}
if (document.layers){
document.captureEvents(Event.MOUSEDOWN);
document.onmousedown=clickNS4;
}
else if (document.all&&!document.getElementById){
document.onmousedown=clickIE4;
}
document.oncontextmenu=new Function("alert(message);return false;")
</script>
```

Insert this code immediately before the image on your page. Don't insert the code below the image or at the very top of the document, or it won't work.

11

How to Better Manage Your Auctions

Managing your eBay auctions is a lot of work! You have to keep track of everything you've listed, watch over all the auctions in process, and then—when the auctions are over—send emails to the winning bidders, manage all the auction payments, and track what's been shipped and what hasn't.

The true sign of an eBay Master is the ability to manage all this activity without sweating hard. Read on to learn how they do it.

Managing Your Workflow

The first step to managing your auction activity is to set up a workflow. The eBay Masters have it down to a science; it all flows step-by-step just like clockwork.

Trick #332: **Develop a Routine**

> **trapperjohn2000**
>
> stores.ebay.com/Molehill-Group-Store
>
> Member since 1998, Feedback: Purple star

You can't let your eBay auctions rule your life. You have to take charge, set up a workable routine, and fit your auctions to your schedule.

Some eBay sellers work on a daily schedule, where mornings (for example) are for listing and afternoons for packing and shipping. Others work on a weekly schedule, where they list one day a week, and pack and ship just one or two days a week. The key point is to set up a routine and then stick to it. You don't want to be jumping all over the place just because you receive a check in the mail!

Trick #333: **Automate the Process**

> **rosachs**
>
> stores.ebay.com/My-Discount-Shoe-Store
>
> home.midsouth.rr.com/rosachs/RKS/
>
> PowerSeller
>
> Member since 1997, Feedback: Red star

The more auctions you list, the more you'll find yourself doing the same things over and over. You create item listings, you send winning bidder notifications, you process payments, you pack boxes, you ship boxes. It's a routine—a profitable routine, mind you—but a routine, nonetheless.

The best way to handle routine activities is to automate them. The less things you have to do manually, the more time you'll have for yourself—and to do those non-automatic activities. As high-volume seller **rosachs** notes:

> The best thing my automation ever did for me was give me back time to do things I want to do, instead of having to do what I need to do. I have auctions posting every night at 8:00 p.m. I don't even have to be in the house for that to happen! I missed too much of my kids growing up, chasing the almighty dollar; I'm not planning to repeat that mistake with my grandkids.

How do you automate your eBay-related activities? That's what the rest of this chapter is all about!

Trick #334: **Hire an Assistant**

quadaxel83

stores.ebay.com/Buttons-And-Beads

Member since 2001, Feedback: Red star

Of course, if your eBay business keeps on growing, it may get too big for you to handle by yourself. Many high-volume sellers have an assistant (or two) to help them with various tasks—ideally with those tasks you like to do the least. Don't like standing in line at the post office? Then hire someone to do it for you!

Trick #335: **Don't Rely on eBay's Notification Emails**

funfindsfromsuz

PowerSeller

Member since 2001, Feedback: Red star

One part of the auction management process is notifying the winning bidder at the end of the auction. Of course, eBay sends out official notification emails, but the best eBay sellers supplement these notices with emails of their own. eBay Master **funfindsfromsuz** explains why:

> *Winning bidder notices automatically go out from eBay, but I never rely on that. Send an end-of-auction email yourself; it's more personal, and you know it went out in a timely fashion.*

And sending your own emails doesn't have to be a lot of work. You can automate the process by creating pre-written emails for every imaginable situation. Instead of writing a message from scratch, just pull out the appropriate pre-written message, fill in the necessary information about the current buyer, and let it fly. A real time-saver!

Trick #336: **Store All Your Emails**

craftiques

Member since 2000, Feedback: Red star

It's good form to save all the emails—sent and received—relating to each of your eBay transactions, just in case. Here's how **craftiques** does it, using the flagging feature found in Microsoft Outlook and Outlook Express:

I do not get rid of any emails until a transaction is complete. When payments come in, I place a flag in front of that email. When the package is ready to ship, I email the bidder to let them know the date it is shipping. Having the flag on the email makes it faster to find. It also shows me at a glance who has not paid or responded to any email. Those emails then go to the send file and stay there until the bidder emails me that they have received their package.

The simple way to do this is to have your auction management program copy you on all emails sent. This way you have copies of all your messages, which you can then filter in your email program to a special "eBay messages" folder. You never know when you might need to refer to past correspondence!

Using Auction Management Tools

If you're a high-volume seller, trying to manage each and every auction individually gets real tedious real fast. That's why many eBay Masters use third-party auction management programs and services. These programs and services not only track the progress of in-process auctions, but also manage all manner of post-auction activity.

Trick #337: **Use an Excel Spreadsheet**

pcgeektobe
Member since 2001, Feedback: Turquoise star

An approach that many do-it-yourself sellers use is to keep all the information pertaining to your auctions in an Excel spreadsheet—which is a lot cheaper than using a pay-as-you-go auction management service. As **pcgeektobe** points out, you can keep track of all your sales this way:

Format the columns a bit wider [than normal] and have column headings for Product, Product Cost, Product Sold, Form of Ship, Weight, and Handling Fee (if you charge one). At the end of the month, add each column (not the Form of Ship or Weight, of course) to get your bottom line.

Figure 11.1 shows what this spreadsheet should look like.

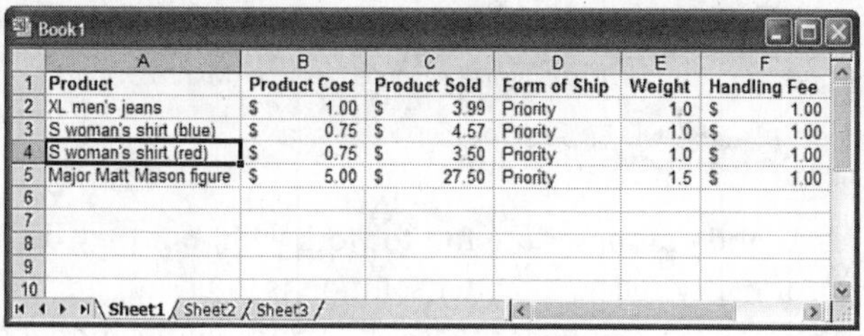

	A	B	C	D	E	F
1	Product	Product Cost	Product Sold	Form of Ship	Weight	Handling Fee
2	XL men's jeans	$ 1.00	$ 3.99	Priority	1.0	$ 1.00
3	S woman's shirt (blue)	$ 0.75	$ 4.57	Priority	1.0	$ 1.00
4	S woman's shirt (red)	$ 0.75	$ 3.50	Priority	1.0	$ 1.00
5	Major Matt Mason figure	$ 5.00	$ 27.50	Priority	1.5	$ 1.00
6						
7						
8						
9						
10						

FIGURE 11.1

An Excel spreadsheet to track your auction activity.

Trick #338: **Use Plane Cents' eBay Auction Tracker Spreadsheet**

plane_cents

www.plane-cents.com

PowerSeller

Member since 2001, Feedback: Turquoise star

If you don't want to create your own Excel spreadsheet, check out the predesigned eBay Auction Tracker spreadsheet solution from eBay member **plane_cents**. This spreadsheet is all set up in advance for the most common auction activities, and fully automated with a variety of macros and such. Buy it for $9.95 at www.plane-cents.com.

Trick #339: **Use an Access Database**

scottwhitt

Member since 2004, Feedback: Blue star

Another good way to track your auctions is with a Microsoft Access database. Databases are actually better than spreadsheets in managing large amounts of information; if you're at all familiar with Access, it's easy to set up a database to handle your inventory and track all your auctions.

Trick #340: **Use eBay Selling Manager**

> **nonie6966**
>
> stores.ebay.com/Nonies-Nook-Jerseys-and-More
>
> Member since 2001, Feedback: Red star

Spreadsheets and databases are fun to work with, but they do require a bit of effort to set up. For many sellers, a better solution is to use an auction management tool, such as eBay Selling Manager (pages.ebay.com/selling_manager/). Selling Manager is eBay's official auction management tool, and it lets you keep track of current and pending auctions, as well as all your closed auctions. You can use Selling Manager to send emails to winning bidders, print invoices and shipping labels, and even leave feedback. It costs $4.99 per month, and has a 30-day free trial. (The subscription is free if you have an eBay Store.)

Everything you need to do is accessed over the web, on the eBay site, through your normal web browser. When you subscribe to Selling Manager, the My Selling tab of your My eBay page is transformed into a Selling Manager page, as shown in Figure 11.2. From here, Selling Manager lets you manage all your post-auction activity.

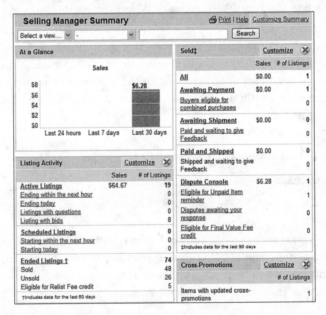

FIGURE 11.2

Viewing eBay Selling Manager from My eBay.

I find eBay Selling Manager an extremely useful tool if I have a moderate number of auctions running simultaneously. The flat monthly fee is prohibitive if you're only running a few auctions, and the automated tools really aren't powerful enough for high-volume sellers. Like I said, it's probably best for medium-level sellers—a half-dozen or so auctions a week, maybe a little more. As **nonie6966** notes:

> Use Selling Manager. For five bucks a month, it's a real life saver.

Know, however, that Selling Manager isn't perfect. One of its biggest problems is that you pretty much have to manage one auction at a time—it lacks features that let you manage multiple auctions in bulk. If you're a high-volume seller, a better solution is eBay's higher-end Selling Manager Pro (pages.ebay.com/selling_manager_pro/), which offers bulk management features. For $15.99 per month, Selling Manager Pro does everything the basic Selling Manager does, plus it offers bulk email messaging, inventory management (with restock alerts), and monthly reporting. It also incorporates the bulk listing features of Turbo Lister. Cost is $15.99 per month (with a 30-day free trial), which makes it an option only if you're running a hundred or so auctions a month.

Trick #341: **Use Ándale Checkout**

trapperjohn2000

stores.ebay.com/Molehill-Group-Store

Member since 1998, Feedback: Purple star

Let's move beyond eBay's tools into third-party auction management services. One of the most popular of these services is Ándale Checkout (www.andale.com). Ándale provides a post-sale checkout option similar to eBay's Checkout feature, as well as automated post-auction tools similar to those of Selling Manager Pro. At the close of an auction, Ándale automatically sends the high bidder an email with a link to an Ándale Checkout page. (Buyers can also check out by responding to the end-of-auction email.) You can view the entire post-auction process for all your auctions from Ándale's sales console; you can also use this page to generate invoices and shipping labels.

The nice thing about Ándale Checkout is that its fees are scalable based on the number of auctions you run in a given month. If you only run a handful of auctions, you pay a low fee—20 cents an auction, roughly. You're not forced into a high fixed monthly cost, which can translate into high per-auction costs. It's a good choice for low-volume sellers, or sellers whose volume varies from month to month.

Trick #342: **Use Marketworks**

> **internestauctions**
>
> stores.ebay.com/Internest-Auctions
>
> Member since 1999, Feedback: Red star

Similar to Ándale is Marketworks (www.marketworks.com), one of the oldest and most established third-party auction management services. Marketworks (formerly known as Auctionworks) offers a variety of professional auction tools, including inventory management, a bulk listing creator, traffic counters, image hosting, automatic end-of-auction emails, the proprietary Clickout checkout system, reciprocal feedback posting, web-based storefronts, and customizable reports.

Marketworks charges a flat $14.95 per month charge, plus a 2.2% fee on each successful transaction. Many high-volume sellers like what they get for their money, as noted in the following testimonial from **internestauctions**:

> *I have used many auction management programs and left dissatisfied, but after more than a year with Marketworks (Auctionworks) I can't imagine changing. I like the inventory-based listing, tracking devices, store options, upselling, report options, and hosting. I get far more for my dollar than I have anywhere else (I've tried several over the years), and the customer support is timely and helpful.*

Trick #343: **Use Vendio**

> **abc-books**
>
> stores.ebay.com/ABC-Books-by-Ann
>
> www.abcbooksbyann.com
>
> PowerSeller
>
> Member since 1999, Feedback: Red star

Here's another auction management service, similar to both Ándale and Marketworks. Vendio (www.vendio.com) offers bulk listing services, listing templates, post-auction checkout, and the whole nine yards. Their pricing plans are many and diverse (and not a bit complicated), so you're bound to find a plan to your liking.

Here's what PowerSeller **abcbooksbyann** likes about Vendio:

> *This is the bulk lister I use to allow me to work on my eBay auctions at any time while I'm offline. I upload them all at the same time to start whenever I want. They also send emails at auction ending, and when I receive payment and ship the item.*

I wouldn't sell on eBay without using Vendio! They currently have a free two-week trial and a pay-as-you-go plan if you want to start off slow. The reason I use Vendio instead of one of the eBay products is because Vendio includes scheduled listings and templates as part of the standard package.

Trick #344: **Use SpareDollar**

chunkypunkys

stores.ebay.com/chunky-punkys-gifts-and-crafts

Member since 1998, Feedback: Red star

SpareDollar (www.sparedollar.com) is a very affordable auction service that many cost-conscious sellers swear by. As you can see in Figure 11.3, SpareDollar offers a variety of auction-management services (including a bulk lister, post-auction tracking and emails, and image hosting) for a flat $4.95 per month. You certainly can't beat the price, although its services might be too limited for really high-volume sellers. That said, a lot of sellers swear by Sparedollar; give it a try to see if it fits your particular eBay business.

FIGURE 11.3

A selection of selling tools from SpareDollar.

Trick #345: **Use Auctiva**

New Trick

Every eBay Master has his or her own favorite auction listing and management
tool, and there's something good (and sometimes something not so good) to be said
about all of them. Of late, Auctiva (www.auctiva.com) has been garnering a lot of
converts, especially since they started offering most of their tools for free. (They used
to charge for them, like most of the other sites.) As you can see in Figure 11.4,
Auctiva offers a lot of useful auction management tools—and free is good!

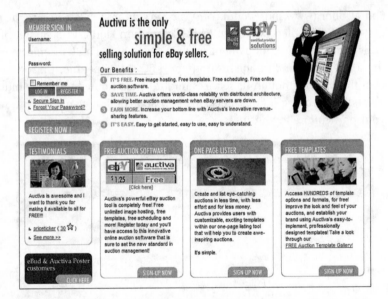

FIGURE 11.4

The free auction management tools offered by Auctiva.

So, other than that free thing, what else do eBay sellers like about Auctiva? Here's
some praise from a savvy seller **mississippi*mercantile**:

> I have recently started using a free software program that is completely idiot-proof
> and totally eBay compatible—Auctiva. Auctiva is easy, a no-brainer for people who
> want to spice up their listings. It's a great enhancement to the low-tech listers, with
> free templates to decorate your listing with and clickable HTML tools like font and

color and paragraph structure. It even provides a scrolling picture gallery of all of your listed auctions on every listing. I love it!

And did I mention that these Auctiva tools are *free*? I thought I might have...

Trick #346: **Use Zoovy**

ghsproducts

stores.ebay.com/GHSProducts

Member since 1998, Feedback: Purple star

At the opposite end of the scale from Sparedollar and Auctiva is Zoovy (www.zoovy.com), a high-end auction management service that integrates your eBay auctions with a web-based storefront. Zoovy is targeted toward high-end sellers and retailers, so it's something to think about if you're running an eBay Store or your own separate online storefront.

Trick #347: **Use Auction Wizard 2000**

New Trick

lady-frog-vintage-jewelry

stores.ebay.com/SOMETHING-TO-RIBBIT-ABOUT

Member since 2000, Feedback: Red star

Another option is to invest in a software program to manage your post-auction activity. To that end, seller **lady-frog-vintage-jewelry** recommends the Auction Wizard 2000 program, which you can download from www.auctionwizard2000. com. AW2000 includes everything but the kitchen sink, managing both the front-end and back-end of the auction process. Here's what **lady-frog-vintage-jewelry** says about it:

I have used this program for the past four years. It is by far one of the easiest programs to use. It not only helps to create nice listings with great templates, but you can do all of the work of listing on one page. The other, most wonderful thing I like about it is that it has a program that tracks your inventory, takes care of the bookkeeping, allows you to give feedback with the click of a button, and downloads the information from eBay with the stroke of one key. It also will automatically send out emails, including invoices, reminder notices, etc. I have not had a problem with this program!

Trick #348: **Use eBay Blackthorne Software**

New Trick

rosachs

stores.ebay.com/My-Discount-Shoe-Store

home.midsouth.rr.com/rosachs/RKS/

PowerSeller

Member since 1997, Feedback: Red star

Seller **rosachs** swears by the eBay Blackthorne software, shown in Figure 11.5. This software used to be called eBay Seller's Assistant, but now goes by its original Blackthorne name, even though it's still owned and distributed by eBay. There are two flavors of the Blackthorne software, Basic and Pro; **rosachs** recommends the Pro version, especially for high-volume sellers. Both versions let you create listings in bulk, track your live auctions, and manage post-auction activity (including emails and feedback). Pro adds the ability to manage your inventory and create a variety of sales reports. You'll pay $9.99 per month for Blackthorne Basic, or $24.99 per month for Blackthorne Pro. Learn more at pages.ebay.com/blackthorne/.

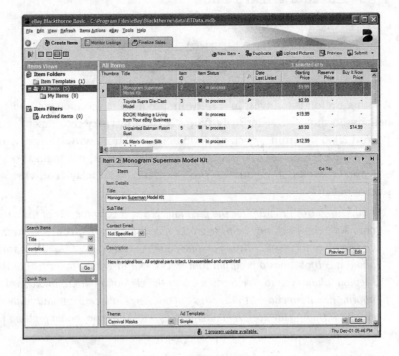

FIGURE 11.5

Manage your auction activity with eBay Blackthorne software.

Trick #349: **Use Other Auction Management Tools**

> **shopofvalues**
>
> PowerSeller
>
> Member since 2001, Feedback: Turquoise star

The auction management tools previously discussed are just a small sampling of what's available on the web. (Apparently there's a big business in helping eBay sellers manage their auctions!) While you're shopping for services, here are a few more sites to consider:

- Auction Hawk (www.auctionhawk.com)
- AuctionHelper (www.auctionhelper.com)
- HammerTap (www.hammertap.com)
- inkFrog (www.inkfrog.com)
- ManageAuctions (www.manageauctions.com)
- Trak Auctions (www.trakauction.com)
- Vrane: Amherst Robots (www.vrane.com)

Trick #350: **Write Your Own Custom Auction Management Program**

> ***retropolis***
>
> www.retropolis.com
>
> Member since 1999, Feedback: Red star

One final option for really high-volume sellers is to write your own custom auction-management software. If your eBay business is extremely complex (or impossibly idiosyncratic), this may be the only way to get everything just to your liking. For example, here's how eBay seller ***retropolis*** describes their custom inventory management system:

> *When an item is added to inventory a record is created in a MySQL table and it is assigned an inventory ID number. The "record edit" page allows us to enter the following: Title, Subtitle, Manufacturer, Designer, Decade, Keywords, Description, Notes, Cost, Quantity, Price, Location Purchased from, Current Location, Channel, Description Template, Start Bid, Reserve, Duration, eBay Category, Retropolis Category, Boxed Weight, and Boxed Dimensions.*

Sound complicated? Well, that's the whole point; if your business is complex, you need a sophisticated auction/inventory management solution—and the only way to get it is to write it yourself!

How to Handle Customer Payments

Trust me—the best part of the entire auction process is getting paid. Unless, of course, the check bounces. Or the payment never arrives. Or something else goes wrong.

Fortunately, most eBay auctions work as advertised, meaning you get your money within a reasonable period and then you ship out the item. Determining how you get paid, however, is another issue—as is figuring out what to do if you get stiffed. Read on for some advice from the eBay Masters, who've seen it all.

Payment Methods

Determining which payment methods you'll accept is something you need to do upfront, before you post your first auction listing. That's because you need to display your payment preferences in your TOS at the bottom of your listing. (You don't want to surprise any buyers after they've made their high bid!) Which methods are best? Let's see what the eBay Masters recommend.

Trick #351: **Don't Accept Personal Checks**

kattinsanity

Member since 2000, Feedback: Red star

One of the most common—and, for sellers, most detested—forms of payment is the personal check. Buyers like paying by check because it's convenient, and because checks can be tracked (or even cancelled) if problems arise with the seller. Sellers, however, uniformly dislike receiving checks in the mail. That's because a personal check isn't instant money. When you deposit a check in your bank, you're not depositing cash. That $100 check doesn't turn into $100 cash until it tracks back through the financial system, from your bank back to the buyer's bank, and the funds are both verified and transferred. That can take some time, typically 10 business days or so.

All of which can lead to problems. The buyer can write a check that he doesn't have the funds for or stop payment on a check that's been mailed. Plus you have to wait for the check to arrive in the mail and then wait another X number of days after you deposit a check before you can ship the item, all of which extends the already lengthy auction process and makes it harder to manage.

Bottom line is that many experienced sellers simply refuse to accept payment via check—and state so upfront in their auction listings.

Trick #352: **Only Accept Personal Checks from Returning Customers**

amrell

stores.ebay.com/The-Hot-Mannequin

Member since 2002, Feedback: Turquoise star

Other sellers *will* accept payment by personal check, but only from returning customers. The thinking here is that returning customers are more trustworthy, which is probably true. Something to consider.

Trick #353: **Hold Personal Checks for at Least 10 Business Days**

amrell

stores.ebay.com/The-Hot-Mannequin

Member since 2002, Feedback: Turquoise star

Still other sellers have no problem accepting personal checks and realize that it's the preferred method of payment for many buyers. Refusing to take checks could reduce your pool of potential buyers.

If you decide to accept personal checks, make sure that the check clears your bank before you ship the item to the buyer. Most sellers hold the item for 10 business days before they ship the item; if the check bounces, you should find out within that time frame. As **amrell** notes:

> My bank claims that checks usually clear in 3 business days. I hold for 10 business days just to be sure.

It's also a good idea to notify the buyer (via email) when you receive the check in the mail, and then estimate a ship date for the purchase. Otherwise you'll have some buyers emailing you after a few days wanting to know how come they haven't received their merchandise yet!

Trick #354: **Call the Bank Before You Deposit a Check**

mombottoo
Member since 2001, Feedback: Purple star

Another thing you do if you receive payment via check is call the bank before you deposit it, to see if the buyer's checking account has enough funds in it to cover the check. As **mombottoo** relates:

> If I receive a questionable check I call the bank before I deposit it into my account. Banks won't tell you the exact amount of money in the account, but they will tell you if there is enough money to cash the check you have.

Note, however, that not all banks provide this information. Still, it's worth a shot.

Trick #355: **Accept Money Orders and Cashier's Checks**

mgr1969
Member since 2001, Feedback: Purple star

One of my favorite methods of payment is the money order. Money orders—and cashier's checks, too—are, to sellers, almost as good as cash. You can cash a money order immediately, without waiting for funds to clear, and have cash in your hand. When you receive a money order or cashier's check, deposit it and then ship the auction item. There's no need to hold the item. (And you don't have to pay any fees to anybody as you do with credit card payments.)

Here's what **mgr1969** says:

> *I always have the money order option for people who don't like PayPal. As long as I'm not hurting for money, I actually prefer it so I can save some fees.*

Trick #356: **Accept PayPal**

berties_house_of_horrors

stores.ebay.com/Berties-Emporium

PowerSeller

Member since 1999, Feedback: Red star

The most popular method of payment for eBay auctions is the credit card, facilitated via PayPal. As you're probably aware, PayPal (www.paypal.com) serves as the middleman for your credit card transactions. The buyer pays PayPal via credit card, PayPal handles all the credit card paperwork, and then PayPal sends a check to you (or deposits funds in your checking account). As you can see in Figure 12.1, PayPal lets you accept payment by American Express, Discover, MasterCard, and Visa.

FIGURE 12.1

Attract more buyers by accepting credit cards via PayPal.

As recently as a year or two ago, most buyers still paid via personal check. Today, PayPal accounts for almost 90% of my personal auction payments. Bottom line, you have to accept PayPal, or you'll lose business, as noted by **berties_house_of_horrors**:

> *Love it or hate it, accepting PayPal is a must, in my opinion. The drawbacks (potential chargeback, fees on merchant account) are outweighed by the 200% increase in hits, higher purchase prices, better feedback (because I can ship faster), and so on.*

Trick #357: **Clean Out Your PayPal Account Daily**

trapperjohn2000

stores.ebay.com/Molehill-Group-Store

Member since 1998, Feedback: Purple star

When a buyer pays via credit card, the funds for that transaction are automatically deposited in your PayPal account, where the money stays until you request a transfer to your personal bank account. It's a good practice to clear out your PayPal account daily, for a couple of reasons. First, you get your money sooner. Second, if your PayPal account is empty, there won't be any funds for PayPal to freeze if something gets charged back to your account.

Some sellers have a different opinion, as is their right. One seller I know keeps a small balance in her PayPal account at all times, in order to cover any refunds she might need to make. It's certainly a reasonable approach, if you don't mind running the risk of frozen funds in the light of any complaints.

Trick #358: **Get a PayPal Credit/Debit Card**

artchick48

stores.ebay.com/Lee-Smith-Art

www.leesmithart.com

Member since 2001, Feedback: Turquoise star

Here's another neat trick. You can use your PayPal account like a banking account, and withdraw funds with an official PayPal-issued MasterCard, Visa, or debit card. And there's more, as **artchick48** notes:

> You get a small rebate for every purchase using the PayPal debit card; you can even use it to pay your eBay fees.

Trick #359: **Sign Up for a PayPal Personal Account—Not a Business Account**

jakki01

Member since 2000, Feedback: Purple star

Many sellers dislike paying fees to PayPal, and that's fair. One way to avoid fees is with a PayPal Personal account. As opposed to the Business account, the Personal account comes with zero fees. The drawback, however, is that you can only accept auction payments via electronic check or transfer, not via credit card. While this might be okay with many buyers, this negates the real reason to accept PayPal payments, which is to let your buyers pay via credit card. If you decide to go this route (and it's not necessarily my personal recommendation, mind you), make sure you remove the PayPal credit card logo from your auction listings.

Trick #360: **Accept BidPay**

maxtechtronics

Member since 2003, Feedback: Turquoise star

Another form of payment that many sellers are now accepting is BidPay, formerly known as Western Union Auction Payments. BidPay (www.bidpay.com), shown in Figure 12.2, is an alternative to PayPal that lets buyers pay via credit card; you get paid via a Western Union money order, at no charge to you. Not a bad deal.

FIGURE 12.2
An alternative to PayPal—BidPay, by Western Union.

By the way, don't confuse BidPay's Western Union Auction Payments with a Western Union wire transfer, as discussed in Trick #94 in Chapter 4, "How to Be a

Smarter—and Safer—Buyer." Most buyers will (or at least should) shy away from wire transfers, as this payment method is frequently (mis)used by scam sellers. I know you're not a scammer, so it's best to just avoid wire transfers completely.

Trick #361: **Establish a Merchant Credit Card Account**

ghsproducts

stores.ebay.com/GHSProducts

Member since 1998, Feedback: Purple star

There's little downside to using PayPal for your credit card transactions, except for the cost. If you're a real high-volume seller, you may be able to get a lower per-transaction rate by signing up for a merchant credit card account with a separate banking or financial institution.

However, there are a few downsides to establishing a traditional merchant credit card account. First, it's more hassle than signing up for PayPal; you may have to submit various business documentation and possibly have your own credit checked. Second, getting everything up and running may also be more involved than simply plugging into the PayPal system. And finally, there may be upfront or monthly fees involved. Here's what eBay seller **ghsproducts** discovered:

> It does take a lot to justify your own merchant account. From my initial calculations, I could not justify it until I was doing about $1500/month in sales. That is about the point where the fees are covered.

If you want to investigate merchant accounts, here are some services to start with:

- Cardservice International (www.expandyourbusiness.com)
- Chase Paymentech Solutions (www.paymentech.com)
- Charge.com (www.charge.com)
- CreditCardProcessor.com (www.creditcardprocessor.com)
- Fast Merchant Account (www.fast-merchant-account.com)
- Merchant Accounts Express (www.merchantexpress.com)
- Monster Merchant Account (www.monstermerchantaccount.com)
- ProPay (www.propay.com)
- Total Merchant Services (www.merchant-account-4u.com)

For what it's worth, **ghsproducts'** favorite of these services is Chase Paymentech Solutions. She says that this service is very reasonable, fee-wise, compared to the others.

Trick #362: **Get a Merchant Account via Your Wholesale Club**

trapperjohn2000

stores.ebay.com/Molehill-Group-Store

Member since 1998, Feedback: Purple star

If you're interested in merchant credit card accounts, there's one more avenue to check out—your local wholesale club. That's right, both Costco and Sam's Club offer merchant credit card processing to business members, at very affordable rates.

For example, Costco offers credit card accounts through Nova Information Systems. Costco waives the $25 setup fee and offers a discount rate just over 2%. (Of course, the Executive membership itself costs $100, so you'll need to factor that in, as well.) See the Costco website (www.costco.com) or call 888-474-0500 for more details.

Oh, and when you inquire, ask about *all* applicable fees. In particular, check on software integration fees, monthly virtual terminal fees, and the like. You may also have to hit monthly minimums or pay an additional fee. Bottom line—sounds like a good deal, but check the fine print before you sign up!

Dealing with Problem Payers

Ninety-nine-point-nine percent of your transactions will go smoothly. But every now and then you'll get a buyer who doesn't follow your payment instructions, or doesn't send a check, or sends you a bad check. How do you handle these deadbeat bidders? Here's some advice from the eBay Masters.

Trick #363: **How to Handle Customers Who Pay via an Unacceptable Method**

gothgirlscloset

PowerSeller

Member since 1999, Feedback: Red star

One of the most frustrating things is to clearly state in your auction listing that you don't accept payment via personal check and then have some buyer send you a check in the mail. If this happens to you, what do you do?

First, know that you're not obligated to accept any payment method that wasn't offered. Then send the buyer a polite email informing him that you don't accept personal checks, and that he's welcome to pay via PayPal or send you a money order. You should also return the check, of course—unless you want to cut the guy a break. If the buyer refuses to pay via your accepted methods, file a non-paying bidder alert and relist. As **gothgirlscloset** says:

> *Stick to your guns and be polite. I hate bidders who assume you'll do whatever they want without even asking first.*

Trick #364: **How to Deal with Slow Payers**

trapperjohn2000

stores.ebay.com/Molehill-Group-Store

Member since 1998, Feedback: Purple star

More common is the buyer who doesn't send payment. Most often these guys are just slow, for one reason or another. (I can't tell you how many buyers I've had who've "forgotten" about the auction they've won!) The most important thing you can do here is to politely remind the buyer that you're still awaiting payment. That means sending out one or more emails. More often than not, a few pointed prompts will get the payment on its way. If you still haven't received payment after a reasonable period of time, then you're okay to open an unpaid item dispute and relist.

How long should you wait? If a buyer is responsive to my emails, I'll give him up to three weeks or so to get the payment to me. If the buyer disappears off the face of the earth, it's 10 days max and then I file a for non-paying buyer credit and relist the item.

In other words, if the buyer responds to your emails, he's probably honest. (Just a tad irresponsible.) If you don't get any response, you probably have a deadbeat on your hands. And that 10-day period seems to be fairly common among experienced eBay sellers; several sellers have emailed me with the exact same payment due terms.

Trick #365: **How to Handle Bad Checks**

trollslayer

Member since 1999, Feedback: Red star

The most onerous form of deadbeat bidder is the one who sends you a bad check. Fortunately, if you're on the bad end of a bounced check, all hope is not lost.

The first thing to do is get in touch with your bank and ask them to resubmit the check in question. Maybe the buyer was just temporarily out of funds. Maybe the bank made a mistake. Whatever. In at least half the cases I've encountered, bounced checks unbounce when they're resubmitted.

Whether you resubmit the check or not, you should definitely email the buyer and let him know what happened. At the very least, you'll want the buyer to reimburse you for any bad check fees your bank charged you. The buyer might also be able to provide another form of payment to get things moving again. (Credit cards are nice—as are money orders.)

As with slow payers, most check bouncers aren't deliberately dishonest. Some people just have more trouble than others in balancing their bank accounts. That's why I like **trollslayer**'s advice:

> *Before getting nasty and threatening, give him a chance to make good. Ask him if he intends to make good on it, including any service fees. After the first email you should get an idea of his intentions. After that, explain exactly what you will do, no threats, just facts.*

As with all customer correspondence, it pays to keep your cool and be polite—even when dealing with deadbeats!

13

How to Pack and Ship More Efficiently

If you're like me, the whole packing and shipping thing is the hardest part of the entire auction process. I admit it; I'm not a good packer. (Or at least not a natural one.) So when it comes to packing and shipping, I can definitely use some tips from the pros!

Setting Shipping/Handling Charges

The first thing you have to deal with is how much you charge your customers for shipping and handling. You want to cover your costs, of course, but you also don't want to overcharge if you can help it. How do you set the right shipping/handling charges before you create your item listing?

Trick #366: **Use eBay's Shipping Calculator**

> **qhnut**
>
> stores.ebay.com/Country-Horse-Gifts
>
> PowerSeller
>
> Member since 1998, Feedback: Red star

The most successful eBay sellers spell out everything upfront in their auction listings. This includes the shipping/handling charge. Leave out the shipping/handling specifics, and you'll either lose potential buyers or run the risk of ticking off your winning bidder after the fact. Bidders want to know the total price upfront; they don't want to have to guess how much shipping they'll have to pay.

Of course, figuring out the shipping cost before you know where the item is shipping to is sometimes difficult. One solution to this problem is to use eBay's built-in Shipping Calculator, shown in Figure 13.1. The Shipping Calculator lets buyers enter their ZIP code on the auction listing page and then calculates the actual shipping cost based on the shipping service you selected. (You can also choose to have the Shipping Calculator add a predetermined handling charge for each shipment, which we'll discuss in a minute.) When buyers check out at the end of an auction, they can also use the Shipping Calculator to automatically add shipping and handling fees to their total.

FIGURE 13.1

The Shipping Calculator in an eBay listing.

Trick #367: **Charge a Flat Shipping/Handling Charge**

> **titan_deals_2**
>
> Member since 2003, Feedback: Purple star

Another option is to charge a flat shipping/handling charge on your item. You can either calculate an average shipping cost (and eat the difference if the actual shipping comes in on the high side of average) or charge the highest possible shipping rate. If you do the latter, just calculate the rate based on the shipping zone farthest from your location.

In any case, a flat shipping/handling charge makes it easy for buyers. Here's how **titan_deals_2** does it:

> I always charge a flat $5.00 anywhere in the U.S. for Priority Mail. If it goes over, oh well; I eat the difference, just for customer satisfaction. If I'm under, I get enough to re-fill the old coffee mug.

Some eBay Masters have found that buyers tend to shy away from listings that use the Shipping Calculator, or that don't have the shipping charge stated upfront in the auction listing. Going with a flat shipping charge eliminates a lot of potential confusion, and gives potential buyers a firm idea of what their total cost will be before they bid. You don't want wary bidders, you want confident ones, and going with a flat fee helps to accomplish this.

Trick #368: **Add a Handling Fee to Your Shipping Costs**

griffin_trader

stores.ebay.com/Naturally-In-New-Orleans-Mardi-Gras

Member since 1999, Feedback: Green star

Note that so far in this chapter I've been talking about shipping and handling costs—not just shipping costs. That's because many eBay sellers tack on a little extra to cover their "handling." What's a handling cost? This should cover the costs of your packaging (box, label, peanuts, tape, and so on) as well as compensate you just a bit for your time. Most buyers won't complain if they have to pay an extra buck or two above the actual shipping costs, especially if you state this upfront.

Trick #369: **Don't Gouge on Shipping/Handling**

rufusduff

PowerSeller

Member since 1999, Feedback: Turquoise star

If you do tack on an additional handling charge, don't overdo it. You shouldn't regard the shipping/handling fee as a profit center. Charge a reasonable overage, but no more. As **rufusduff** advises:

Never try to generate hidden profits through inflated shipping charges. This will mark you as an eBay hustler—buyers are becoming hipper to actual tariffs. I charge a flat 7 1/2% of the selling price for packaging overhead above actual tariffs and state this up front on my Terms of Sale.

Here's another reason not to overcharge on shipping/handling—eBay prohibits it. Charge too much, and you risk someone complaining to eBay and eBay yanking your account. Keep it reasonable!

Trick #370: **Use Stealth Postage**

bartonknifeco

Member since 2002, Feedback: Purple star

One way to make a handling charge more palatable is to hide it from the customer. The way to do this is to use "stealth" postage—that is, to hide the shipping costs on the label. If you print your own prepaid postage labels, you often have the option of printing or hiding the postage cost on the label. Choose the stealth option, and the buyer won't know that you're charging $3.00 for $2.00 worth of postage—that is, you effectively hide your extra handling charge. As **bartonknifeco** notes:

I ship through PayPal and always hide the postage. It makes for happier customers if they don't know what it really costs. Never had a problem with a payment question. There is a 3D barcode at the top that shows the postage amount, and the post office has the equipment to read it if they want to.

Trick #371: **Offer a Combined Rate for Multiple Items**

jakki01

Member since 2000, Feedback: Purple star

However you calculate your shipping/handling charges, it's good business to offer some sort of discount or combined rate if a buyer wins more than one item. This makes for happier customers, more accurately reflects the actual shipping costs (you can ship two items in a single package), and you might even encourage additional sales. Here's what **jakki01** found:

State your combined shipping terms on the page. I end up buying several items from someone when I only would have bought one because "I offer $1 (or whatever) combined shipping on all additional items" always causes me to check out their other auctions, when I might otherwise not.

Choosing a Shipping Service

Who you choose to ship your items is a very important decision. There are a lot of choices, but there's no real consensus—even among the eBay Masters—as to where you'll get the best service and pricing. There's a lot of conflicting advice here, so read on to learn all the pros and cons.

Trick #372: **Use Priority Mail**

> **trapperjohn2000**
>
> stores.ebay.com/Molehill-Group-Store
>
> Member since 1998, Feedback: Purple star

Without a doubt, U.S. Postal Service Priority Mail (www.usps.com) is the most-used shipping method for eBay auctions and the preferred service for many experienced sellers. It's relatively simple (all you have to do is visit your local post office), relatively fast, and relatively low cost. You also get the benefit of free Priority Mail boxes, which can save you a ton of money over buying boxes elsewhere. I personally use Priority Mail for most of the small items I ship.

Trick #373: **Use Priority Mail Flat-Rate Boxes and Envelopes**

 New Trick

> **kyderbyfan**
>
> PowerSeller
>
> Member since 1999, Feedback: Red star

If you're a fan of Priority Mail, your best bet, shipping-wise, may be the Postal Service's flat-rate Priority Mail boxes and envelopes—depending on the type of items you ship, that is. Anything you can stuff into one of those flat-rate envelopes will cost only $4.05 to ship anywhere in the continental United States; the Postal Service offers several different-sized flat-rate boxes, with equally low flat shipping rates. These flat-rate boxes are great when you're shipping small, heavy objects, where the weight would normally kill you in shipping fees.

An added benefit to using these flat-rate envelopes and boxes is that it lets you quote a single flat shipping/handling charge in your auction listings. It doesn't matter where the eventual buyer lives; it's the same flat rate to ship anywhere in the country. That's what **kyderbyfan** likes:

> *I try to use USPS Priority Mail flat-rate boxes whenever possible, to lower shipping costs. This also takes away the guesswork in calculating shipping costs for buyers*

and sellers. USPS flat-rate Priority Mail boxes cost $8.10 to send regardless of weight or destination ZIP code, as long as it is a domestic package. Rates are the same for APO and FPO military addresses as well. Savings can be substantial with these boxes, especially when packages weigh 3 pounds or more.

Trick #374: **Use Media Mail**

scifi4me2004

stores.ebay.com/Needle-In-a-Haystack-Treasures

Member since 2003, Feedback: Turquoise star

One of the Postal Service's best-kept secrets is Media Mail shipping. What USPS used to call "book rate," Media Mail can be used to ship books, DVDs, videotapes, compact discs, and other printed and prerecorded "media." The rates are much cheaper than those for Priority Mail, although delivery is typically in the Parcel Post range—seven to nine days. Still, this is a good, low-cost way to ship many popular items; the cost for shipping a book like this one across the country is less than two bucks, compared to $4.05 for Priority Mail.

Note, however, that Media Mail is reserved for publications without advertising—so you can't use it to ship magazines, newspapers, or comic books.

Trick #375: **Use Bound Printed Matter**

New Trick

scifi4me2004

stores.ebay.com/Needle-In-a-Haystack-Treasures

Member since 2003, Feedback: Turquoise star

Because you can't ship magazines via Media Mail, is there any way to cut your shipping costs for these surprisingly heavy items? Yes, there is; it's called Bound Printed Matter. This USPS service, which costs a little more than Media Mail but less than Parcel Post, is designed for shipping thick envelopes and large and small packages containing magazines, newspapers, catalogs, phone directories, and the like.

Trick #376: **Use First Class Mail**

scifi4me2004

stores.ebay.com/Needle-In-a-Haystack-Treasures

Member since 2003, Feedback: Turquoise star

First Class mail is an option if your item fits into an envelope or if you have a small package that weighs under 13 ounces. The nice thing about First Class mail is that you can ship directly from your mailbox, without making a trip to the post office, assuming that you can figure out the correct postage on your own. Delivery time is similar to Priority Mail, typically three days or less—often for a slightly lower rate.

Member **scifi4me2004** especially recommends First Class for items less than 9 ounces, where the cost is quite affordable—lower than Media Mail for CDs and DVDs, actually. She uses it to ship DVDs, collectibles, clothing, and some small paperback books.

Trick #377: **Use UPS (United Parcel Service)**

geo20299

Member since 2002, Feedback: Turquoise star

Moving away from the post office, UPS (www.ups.com) is a good option for shipping larger or heavier packages, although they can be a little costly for smaller items. UPS offers various shipping options, including standard UPS Ground, Next Day Air, Next Day Air Saver, and 2nd Day Air.

Know, however, that UPS charges a premium for delivering to residential addresses. Don't forget to factor this charge into your shipping costs.

Trick #378: **Use FedEx Ground**

sumaut

Member since 2002, Feedback: Turquoise star

Some sellers swear by FedEX (www.fedex.com), especially the FedEx Ground service. You can drop off your package at a variety of approved locations, including most Kinkos stores (now called FedEx Kinkos). They're also fairly easy to work with, as **sumaut** relates:

> I recommend FedEx Ground because you can get insurance and tracking cheaper than USPS. (Usually.) And if I send it with a tracking number, as soon as I get home I send an email [to the buyer] with the number, telling them how they can track it via the Internet.

I particularly like using FedEx Ground for heavy items. Even though I use Priority Mail for the majority of my shipping, when I have something big or heavy to ship (such as a piece of audio/video equipment), I always make the trip to my local

FedEx Kinko's store. They're considerably lower priced than the Postal Service on heavier items; for example, shipping a five-pound item from coast-to-coast costs almost five dollars less with FedEx Ground than with Priority Mail. Check out their rates before you ship!

Trick #379: **Use DHL**

california_artisan

Member since 1999, Feedback: Yellow star

Here's a shipping service that sellers don't always consider. DHL Worldwide Express (www.dhl.com) is actively courting the online auction business and will set up a house account for anyone at no charge. Their rates are comparable to UPS and FedEx. (They're also great for international shipments.)

Trick #380: **Ship Bulky Items via Ride-Share Services**

New Trick

rufusduff

PowerSeller

Member since 1999, Feedback: Turquoise star

Now here's a trick you probably haven't heard before. I bet you didn't know that you can ship bulky items long distance by letting them share the ride with someone (or something) else. The way it works is that you make an informal contract between you (the seller) and a casual carrier who is going in the direction that you want and has excess capacity. This might be students renting trucks for the back-to-school move, military personnel making a transfer, coast-to-coast 18-wheelers with deadhead space on their return, or just regular folks making a move who want to defray some of their moving expenses.

Where can you find these ride-share services? Here are just a few:

- U-Haul's College/Military Connection Messageboards (boards.uhaul.com/connection/)
- CraigsLists (www.craigslist.org—check both the origin and destination sites)
- U-Ship (www.uship.com)

Charges are negotiable. For what it's worth, seller **rufusduff** typically pays half on loading, and has the buyer pay the other half upon delivery. It's a good deal for all.

Trick #381: **Be Nice to Your Shipping Carriers and Clerks**

New Trick

> **swlakat**
> stores.ebay.com/Books-Along-The-Bayou
> Member since 2003, Feedback: Purple star

Whichever shipping service you use, it pays to make friends with the folks who are doing your shipping. That means being extra nice to your postal carrier, the UPS or FedEx delivery guy, the clerks behind the shipping counter, and so on. Treat them well, have a nice word for them, even give them cards and gifts over the holidays if that's your style. (And it's a good style to have.) The nicer you are to them, the better care they'll take of you—and your packages.

Confirmation and Insurance

Another important point—and point of contention among sellers—is whether or not to offer delivery confirmation and insurance for the items you ship. Read on to join the debate.

Trick #382: **Use Delivery Confirmation on Everything**

> **dave*watts**
> http://stores.ebay.com/Longhorn-Sports-Cards
> Member since 2000, Feedback: Purple star

Many experienced sellers use delivery confirmation on every item they ship via the U.S. Postal Service. They find it invaluable for those times when the buyer says he hasn't received an item; all you have to do is punch in the number at the USPS.com website to see if the item has been delivered or not. In addition, delivery confirmation is necessary to cover PayPal's requirement for online shipping tracking.

And if you decide to use delivery confirmation on the items you ship, make sure you factor in the cost. Many sellers simply add the 50-cent DC charge (for Priority Mail) to their shipping/handling charge. Simple enough to do.

Trick #383: **Get Free Delivery Confirmation When You Buy Postage Online**

> **amrell**
> stores.ebay.com/The-Hot-Mannequin
> Member since 2002, Feedback: Turquoise star

Here's another good reason to buy your postage online (which we'll cover later in this chapter). When you print out your own prepaid Priority Mail shipping labels/postage, delivery confirmation is thrown in for free.

Trick #384: **Email the Tracking Number to the Buyer**

> **dfrazier18**
>
> stores.ebay.com/Fraziers-Finds
>
> Member since 2000, Feedback: Red star

If you purchase delivery confirmation, you might as well make something of it. Email the delivery confirmation number to the buyer as part of your normal end-of-auction correspondence. It provides a bit of peace of mind for the buyer.

Trick #385: **Delivery Confirmation Isn't Delivery Tracking**

> **carlmarxx**
>
> stores.ebay.com/Karls-Ye-Olde-Hobbies
>
> Member since 2001, Feedback: Red star

Okay, you know that the Postal Service's delivery confirmation can be a valuable business tool. But don't rely on it too much. That's because the Postal Service's delivery confirmation doesn't actually track the shipment, nor does it actually confirm that the item was actually received by the recipient. All it does is tell you when the item was delivered—that is, when the postal carrier stuck the package in the mailbox. It's not an official receipt, and there's no way to track the package mid-shipment. As **carlmarxx** notes:

> USPS tracking is a delivery confirmation number only! It isn't the same as UPS, FedEx, or DHL, where you can track it from point A to point B. USPS' number is put into the system when it gets to the buyer's address.

If you want true confirmation of receipt, you'll have to pay extra to get a signature confirmation.

Trick #386: **Use Signature Confirmation on High-Priced Items**

> **california_artisan**
>
> Member since 1999, Feedback: Yellow star

Speaking of signature confirmation, it might be a good idea to get a signature receipt when you're shipping out high-priced items—just to be safe. It's always good to know when the buyer has actually received the item, just in case there's a dispute.

Trick #387: **Require Insurance for High-Value Items**

2ndhand4u

Member since 1998, Feedback: Red star

Now let's move on to the issue of insurance. Insurance can protect you if an item is damaged in shipment or if it never arrives at its destination. To that end, many experienced sellers require buyers to purchase insurance when they're selling high-value items. It's a good way of protecting yourself just in case, as **2ndhand4u** notes:

Insure everything of value. Make it a requirement. Otherwise, you'll receive emails from buyers asking for refunds. When you buy insurance, the P.O. or the shipping company pays for damages, and you are off the hook.

Trick #388: **Use a Third-Party Insurance Company**

xweb10

Member since 2000, Feedback: Yellow star

The only problem with insurance—especially from the Postal Service—is that it can be a tad costly. The post office charges $1.35 to insure items up to $50, or $2.30 for items between $50 and $100. You can often find cheaper rates from a third-party insurance provider, such as Discount Shipping Insurance (DSI) (www.dsiinsurance.com). As you can see in Figure 13.2, DSI has several plans geared toward eBay sellers, and works with shipments via USPS, UPS, FedEx, and other carriers. Here's what seller **xweb10** has to say about DSI's services:

They charge a fraction of the cost of the carriers to insure my shipments, and they pay claims in five days. Saves me a bunch of money.

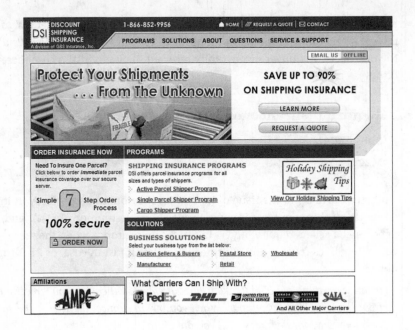

FIGURE 13.2
Shipping insurance programs from Discount Shipping Insurance.

Trick #389: **When You Ship via UPS or FedEx, Insurance Is Included**

New Trick

> **ilene**
>
> stores.ebay.com/Ilenes-Discount-Collectibles
>
> PowerSeller
>
> Member since 1997, Feedback: Green star

One of the drawbacks to shipping via the U.S. Postal Service is that you have to
purchase insurance separately; it's not included in the basic cost of shipping. That's
not the case with UPS and FedEx, both of which include insurance in their shipping
costs. By the time you add insurance to Postal Service shipping, you usually end up
paying more than you would with UPS and FedEx. Even if their rates start out
higher, the fact that insurance is included makes them the better deal.

Trick #390: **Take Care of Your Customers—Even If It's Out of Your Own Pocket**

kotamooncreations

stores.ebay.com/Kotamoon-Creations-Metal-Art

PowerSeller

Member since 1999, Feedback: Red star

Most professional eBay sellers feel an obligation to satisfy the customer, even if they're not responsible for the problem. That means refunding the buyer's money if the item is damaged or not received, even if no insurance was purchased. Yeah, it's money out of your pocket, but that's part of what being a professional seller is all about. After all, it wasn't the buyer's fault the item was lost or damaged. And when you treat the customer right, you'll make big points, as **kotamooncreations** relates:

> I have had one package get severely damaged via USPS—it was a towel rack, and it had to have been run over by a truck! The customer called me crying since she didn't purchase insurance. I sent her a new one anyway, and she has been a great repeat customer. Always treat the customer how you would like to be treated!

Labels, Invoices, and Postage

Now on to the next part of the process—generating a label and purchasing postage.

Trick #391: **Print Prepaid Postage/Shipping Labels from My eBay**

trapperjohn2000

stores.ebay.com/Molehill-Group-Store

Member since 1998, Feedback: Purple star

Here's something I can heartily recommend—printing out your own labels, complete with postage, on your own computer and printer. eBay now makes it easy, with links to print labels from either the closed item listing page or your My eBay page. You can print labels and postage for both U.S. Postal Service and UPS shipping, there's no software to download, and you don't have to use any fancy labels; as you can see in Figure 13.3, the labels print on plain paper, which you then tape to the outside of your package. You pay for the shipping charges via your PayPal account. After you've affixed the label to your package, you can take it to your post office or UPS office for shipping—or just hand the package to your mail person or brown shirt guy for pickup.

FIGURE 13.3
Print USPS postage on your own PC, directly from your eBay item listing.

Trick #392: **Put the Right Date on Your Prepaid Postage**

dan80906

stores.ebay.com/Mostly-Nascar

Member since 2002, Feedback: Turquoise star

When you print your own postage-paid labels, make sure you enter the correct date in the form—that is, the date you'll actually be shipping the item. Sometimes I print labels the night before I ship, and if I enter today's date (instead of tomorrow's), the label is voided, screwing up the entire shipment. Get your dates straight!

Trick #393: **Skip the Post Office**

New Trick

mrsdocy2k1

Member since 2000, Feedback: Red star

Here's another nice thing about printing your own prepaid postage labels—you don't have to go to the post office! That's right, if you use prepaid postage, you don't even have to go to the post office; you can hand your postage directly to your postman or postwoman on their daily rounds. This will save you time and money, as **mrsdocy2k1** notes:

> With the increase in gas prices, I am often standing by my mailbox with my boxes to ship out. This is saving me quite a bit on gas to the post office, since I like to ship everyday.

Trick #394: **Put Clear Tape Over the Label Address**

trapperjohn2000

stores.ebay.com/Molehill-Group-Store

Member since 1998, Feedback: Purple star

No matter what kind of label you use, you don't want the ink to get smeared if your package gets delivered on a rainy day. For extra security, put a piece of clear tape over the address on the label. (But don't tape over any bar codes; most bar code readers can't read through the tape!)

Trick #395: **Put a Packing Slip in the Box**

craftiques

Member since 2000, Feedback: Red star

Inexperienced sellers put the item in a box, slap on a label, and think they're done. More experienced sellers prefer to put on a more professional front, which they do by placing a good-looking packing slip in the box. One easy way to do this is to prepare a generic packing slip/invoice ahead of time, and then fill in the blanks specific to the item you're shipping. Here's how seller **craftiques** does it:

> All of my packages have an invoice that I created. All I have to do is fill in the blanks. It has blanks for item, auction number, bid price, shipping & handling cost, and type of payment. If they pay with a personal check I always put on the check number. This packing slip also has my email address just in case the bidder misplaced it.

Boxes and Packing Supplies

Okay, you have your label and your item and you're ready to pack everything up. What's the best kind of box to use—and where do you get it? The eBay Masters have lots of advice when it comes to packing supplies, so read on!

Trick #396: **Buy Packing Materials on eBay**

clact

stores.ebay.com/Once-Upon-A-Bid

PowerSeller

Member since 2002, Feedback: Red star

You could buy your boxes from a brick and mortar office supply store, or from a retail box store—but you'd end up spending a fortune. A better option is to buy your boxes online from fellow eBay sellers. Pick the right seller, and you could save 50% or more from what you'd pay at traditional retail. Just do an eBay search on the term "packing supplies" or "shipping supplies."

Trick #397: **Buy Packing Materials from Another Online Store**

tommytomasian

Member since 1999, Feedback: Purple star

eBay isn't the only place to buy packing materials online. A number of eBay Masters recommended many different online box and packaging stores, including

- Onepak (www.onepak.com)
- Papermart (www.papermart.com)
- Uline (www.uline.com)

Trick #398: **Get Free Priority Mail Boxes**

puglover2000

Member since 2000, Feedback: Red star

If you ship via USPS Priority Mail, you can get a whole variety of shipping boxes, envelopes, and labels for free! (I like free...) Most larger post offices will have a good supply of boxes; otherwise you can order what you need online at supplies.usps. gov—they'll be delivered to your door for free. (And, as you can see in Figure 13.4, you have a larger selection online than you'll find at most post offices.)

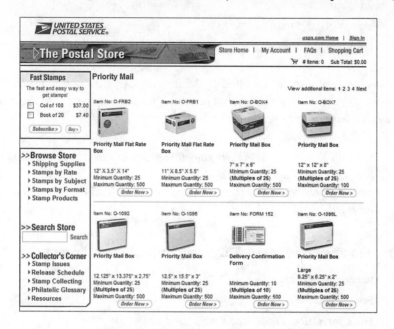

FIGURE 13.4

Get free Priority Mail boxes online at the postal store.

Trick #399: **Don't Try to Use Priority Mail Boxes for Non-Priority Mail**

*janies*jeans-n-things

Member since 2001, Feedback: Red star

Okay, you get these wonderful free Priority Mail boxes from the postal service. What's to stop you from using them for shipping some way other than Priority Mail? Well, you can try turning them inside-out to ship via First Class or Media Mail, but if you get caught (and you *will* get caught), the post office guys will charge you the full-bore Priority Mail rate. Hey, they're doing you a real favor with those free boxes—don't try to abuse the system!

Trick #400: **You Can Squeeze Almost Anything into a Priority Mail Flat-Rate Envelope**

> **ghsproducts**
>
> stores.ebay.com/GHSProducts
>
> Member since 1998, Feedback: Purple star

Speaking of those flat-rate Priority Mail envelopes, they're not just for letters and such; they're good for just about anything you can squeeze into them. As eBay seller **ghsproducts** relates:

> *I used to think that Priority Mail flat-rate envelopes were only for paper-like items, basically things that fit in there smooth and flat. It was a kind mail clerk who first instructed me to put a very odd shaped five-pound package inside a flat rate envelope, so I only had to pay the one-pound rate. I use it all the time now and it saves me a lot!*

Trick #401: **Get Free Recycled Shipping Supplies at Freecycle**

New Trick

> **torreyphilemon**
>
> PowerSeller
>
> Member since 1999, Feedback: Red star

Why pay for shipping supplies when you can get them for free? Seller **torreyphilemon** notes that Freecycle (www.freecycle.org) offers recycled shipping supplies at no charge. The organization is composed of numerous local groups; just locate a group near you and put in your request. It's especially a great way to save money on Styrofoam peanuts!

Trick #402: **Get Boxes from Your Local Retailers**

> **granny.go-go**
>
> stores.ebay.com/Granny-Go-Gos-Shop
>
> Member since 1999, Feedback: Turquoise star

One great source of boxes is the local retailers in your area. They get lots of merchandise shipped to them in boxes, which they then have to dispose of. Many merchants will be glad to let you take some of these boxes off their hands. In other cases, you might have to appropriate the boxes yourself, via that time-honored sport of dumpster diving. (Given my druthers, I'd rather ask for permission first.)

What kinds of boxes and packing materials are we talking about? Well, the eBay Masters have lots of favorites, including the following:

- **craftiques**—From the local grocery store, the boxes that salad dressing comes in.

- **dixiedollie**—From the local furniture store, free bubble wrap, foam wrap, and lots of odd-sized boxes.

- **mgr1969**—Mother Hubbard's Dog Biscuits boxes, as well as empty boxes from the local grocery store. (Hit 'em at 2:00 a.m. when they're restocking.)

- **nonie6966**—From the local auto parts shop, bubble wrap and small, sturdy boxes.

- **puglover2000**—Schwann's ice cream boxes, as well as small and medium-sized boxes from salon supply stores.

- **lady-frog-vintage-jewelry**—From the local health food store, packing peanuts, bubble wrap, foam strips, and air pocket bags.

Get the idea? You won't know what you'll find until you start looking!

Trick #403: **Reuse Packing Materials**

casadejunque

stores.ebay.com/Casadejunque

Member since 2001, Feedback: Red star

Speaking of reusing packing materials, what about all the boxes you receive in the mail from your own online and catalog shopping? I do a lot of shopping on Amazon.com myself, and there's no reason to throw those great boxes away. I have a huge stack of once-used boxes in my garage, and use what I can to pack and ship my own auction items.

Trick #404: **Don't Reuse Packing Materials**

rosachs

stores.ebay.com/My-Discount-Shoe-Store

PowerSeller

Member since 1997, Feedback: Red star

Some eBayers frown on this type of "recycling" of packing boxes. Let's just say it looks a little unprofessional to find a beat-up old grocery store or Amazon box in your mail. As **rosachs** so elegantly puts it:

> No dumpster diving! That box is the first thing of "you" the buyer can see and touch. First impressions…

Trick #405: **How to Recycle Printed Boxes**

powershopper

Member since 1998, Feedback: Purple star

If you do decide to reuse an old box, you want to cover up any existing printing or markings. That means removing old labels, and then using brown mailing tape or a magic marker to cover up the old printing. Some sellers use spray paint to paint over the box; this idea is particularly neat, as it makes your box stand out among the flood of anonymous tan boxes on the mail truck. Just make sure the old box is still structurally sound, and reinforce it with additional tape, if necessary.

Seller **powershopper** passes on another trick for reusing old boxes. Instead of trying to mark out or tape over existing labels and box markings, split the box and refold it inside-out, with the fresh, unprinted side showing. Know, however, that splitting and retaping a box can reduce its integrity; for that reason, the inside-out approach is best when shipping lighter items that won't stress the newly reassembled box.

Trick #406: **Use a Box Sizing Tool to Cut Down Large Boxes**

jsachs

Member since 1998, Feedback: Red star

One size doesn't fit all. If you have a large box and a small item, what do you do? The best solution is to invest in a box or carton sizing tool that lets you quickly and easily cut a corrugated box down to any required height. You can find them at most shipping supplies stores.

Trick #407: **Standardize on Similar-Sized Boxes**

casadejunque

stores.ebay.com/Casadejunque

Member since 2001, Feedback: Red star

Run a lot of eBay auctions, and you'll find yourself stocking large stores of boxes in your garage to ship all those items out. All those boxes can get to be a real pain to keep organized—and they take up a lot of space, besides. When packaging management becomes a major issue, follow the advice of expert seller **casadejunque** and try to limit the types of items you sell—and thus the number of different boxes you need to keep on hand:

> *I have found that it is easier to keep things organized when all of the boxes are the same size. The USPS Priority Mail boxes stack nicely and are compact in a small space. If you have a box from here, another box from there, they are different types, sizes, and dimensions, and you can spend a lot of time going through the boxes just to find the right one.*

Trick #408: **Use Plastic Grocery Bags for Cushioning**

rockinghorsegirl4now

stores.ebay.com/Hollyhock-Cottage-Collectibles

Member since 2002, Feedback: Purple star

Here's a trick I really like, if only because it's better than throwing away those darned grocery bags every week. Seller **rockinghorsegirl4now** recommends reusing your plastic grocery store or retail bags as cushioning materials when you pack your items for shipment. It's a lot cheaper than using peanuts or bubble wrap!

Trick #409: **Get Plastic Baggies for Less**

New Trick

swlakat

stores.ebay.com/Books-Along-The-Bayou

Member since 2000, Feedback: Purple star

Throughout the latter part of this chapter you'll find several references to clear plastic baggies, which have many uses when you're packing your items. Know, however, that buying these bags can get expensive, even if you buy in bulk at the local dollar store. Fortunately, seller **swlakat** has found a low-priced alternative:

> *Go to your local day-old bread store, and check for new bread/roll bags. As they change packaging or discontinue an item, they will sell the unused bags at a very reasonable rate.*

Trick #410: **Self-Pad Your Own Envelopes**

photoforyoustore

stores.ebay.com/Photo-For-You

Member since 2000, Feedback: Purple star

And here's a specific use for those plastic bags. Instead of buying padded envelopes, buy the cheaper non-padded kinds and use the plastic bags as padding. Here's how **photoforyoustore** does it:

I hate spending money on padded envelopes. I buy manila envelopes and wrap my books, CDs, etc. in plastic grocery bags. Usually three. It protects as well as a padded envelope and only costs about 15 cents.

Trick #411: **Use Styrofoam Peanuts**

sellerdropoff

stores.ebay.com/SellerDropoff

PowerSeller

Member since 2004, Feedback: Turquoise star

Probably the single best cushioning material is the Styrofoam peanut. Peanuts not only are very effective at protecting your items during shipping, they're also very lightweight. Compared to packing with crumpled up or shredded newspapers, peanuts can save you several ounces in total weight on a good-size box—and every ounce costs you shipping fees. Packing peanuts are the lightest fill material you can find, hands-down.

Trick #412: **Use Bubble Wrap Instead of Peanuts**

pondfork

Member since 2000, Feedback: Turquoise star

I'm a big fan of those Styrofoam peanuts as cushioning, but a lot of eBay sellers (and buyers) hate the stuff. As an alternative, **pondfork** recommends using lots and lots of bubble wrap:

I also use bubble wrap. It's more expensive, but I've had people write and ask me not to use packing peanuts as they create a mess. I've received packages with the peanuts and they are a mess, and I always feel guilty throwing away all that Styrofoam. (It's bad for the environment.) People can always re-use bubble wrap.

Trick #413: **Big Bubbles Are Better**

sellerdropoff

stores.ebay.com/SellerDropoff

PowerSeller

Member since 2004, Feedback: Turquoise star

We all love bubble wrap. (I particularly like popping the bubbles, myself.) But did you know that there are different sizes of bubble wrap? That's right, some wraps have bigger bubbles than others. When you're shipping anything fragile, especially glass items, go with the bigger 1" bubble wrap. Using the smaller 1/4" bubble wrap is much less effective against vibration during shipment. Here's what **sellerdropoff** experienced:

> *I cannot tell you how many broken glass ornaments we received from novice packers, who packed several loose in a box wrapped up in only 1/4" bubble wrap. They bang against each other from vibration.*

Trick #414: **Use Shredded Paper Instead of Peanuts**

geo20299

Member since 2002, Feedback: Turquoise star

Another alternative to peanuts—shredded paper. This can be shredded computer paper, or even just crumpled newspaper. The upside? Used paper costs you nothing. The downside? Paper is heavier than Styrofoam, so if you use too much of it you can increase the weight of your package and thus increase your shipping costs. Also, the ink from newsprint can rub off and damage some items; take particular care when packing light-colored items in this fashion.

Trick #415: **Bag Your Paper**

quiltworks

Member since 1999, Feedback: Turquoise star

Okay, so shredded paper is a very inexpensive packing material. But it can be a mess for the buyer when he opens up the box—that shredded paper goes *everywhere*. One way around this problem is to put your shredded paper in plastic baggies, instead of stuffing it loosely into the box. This way it still does the job it's supposed to do, but it's a lot easier to handle for the person on the receiving end.

Trick #416: **Use Egg Cartons Instead of Peanuts**

| **mrsdocy2k1** |
| Member since 2000, Feedback: Red star |

We have a lot of alternatives to Styrofoam peanuts. (It's because peanuts cost so much, relative to the alternatives.) Seller **mrsdocy2k1** recommends Styrofoam egg cartons; it's the same Styrofoam as peanuts, but you get the cartons for free when you buy the eggs. As she says:

> I can rely on those wonderful Styrofoam egg cartons to fill up the space in the box and add protection as well, and they weigh practically nothing. They do a great job protecting eggs, so why not our eBay items!

Trick #417: **Use Foam Wedges in the Box**

| **jsachs** |
| Member since 1998, Feedback: Red star |

Let's not forget that packaging is meant to cushion and protect. To that end, you want to hold the item in place in the box so that it doesn't bounce all around during shipping. Seller **jsachs** is a big fan of using foam wedges in the box, as explained here:

> Find a foam store that sells scraps cheaply. Prices very wildly. Some stores charge $2 to $3/square foot, which is outrageous. I found one store that charged me $5 for a 30-gallon garbage bag full of scraps. Foam is most useful for making wedges to hold an item in place, away from the walls of the box. You can cut it with an electric carving knife.

You can find all sorts of foam pieces at most box stores, as well as at hardware and home improvement stores.

General Packing and Shipping Advice

In putting together this chapter, I received *tons* of great tricks from dozens and dozens of eBay Masters. Some of that advice is general in nature, and I present it here in no particular order.

Trick #418: **Ship Promptly**

> **the_southern_yankee**
>
> stores.ebay.com/The-Southern-Yankee-Toys-and-Gifts
>
> Member since 1999, Feedback: Turquoise star

Buyers love getting their stuff as fast as possible. To that end, many eBay sellers pride themselves on their rapid shipping. That means shipping the same day you receive payment, next day at the latest. Buyers like the results, as **the_southern_yankee** attests:

> *I ship same day if I can, and you can see by my feedback that folks like getting their stuff fast.*

Trick #419: **Ship Just a Few Days a Week**

> **trapperjohn2000**
>
> stores.ebay.com/Molehill-Group-Store
>
> Member since 1998, Feedback: Purple star

On the other hand, if you're selling a ton of items every week, you just can't drop everything to race down to the post office every time you receive a PayPal payment. A more efficient approach is to designate one or two days a week when you do all your shipping. Schedule the day before to do all your packing, and then head down to the post office on a regular, predetermined schedule.

One seller told me that he ships on Tuesdays and Fridays, and notes so in his listings' TOS. He says he doesn't get any complaints from customers about slow shipping.

Trick #420: **Email Your Buyer When the Item Ships**

> **pondfork**
>
> Member since 2000, Feedback: Turquoise star

One common characteristic of successful eBay sellers is great communication. I particularly like those sellers who email their buyers when the item is shipped. It's just common courtesy to keep the buyer informed, as **pondfork** notes:

> *I always write and let people know when I've mailed their packages. It gives them an idea of when it will arrive so they can be watching for it, and it lets them know*

if its been overly long and we need to check on it. I keep a list and as soon as I come back from the post office I send everyone an email letting them know their package is on the way, thank them one last time, and remind them that if they're happy with their purchase, positive feedback would be appreciated.

Trick #421: **Weigh Your Item *and* the Packing Box**

sunfarmer

stores.ebay.com/Sunfarmers-Wild-Bird-Seeds

Member since 2002, Feedback: Purple star

One of the biggest mistakes that newbie sellers make is weighing only the item they're selling. Thing is, you not only ship the item, but also the box you pack it in and all the packing materials. Cardboard, Styrofoam, and paper are not without weight. If you don't factor them in, you could end up underestimating your total shipping weight by a pound or so, which costs real money. So when you're figuring shipping weight, weigh *everything*—box and packing materials, too.

Trick #422: **Use Multiple Boxes for Heavy Shipments**

aaana

stores.ebay.com/aaanas-Collectibles-and-Books

Member since 2000, Feedback: Red star

This trick is more practical advice. When you're shipping lots of stuff, try not to ship over 20 pounds in a single box. This has nothing to do with what your shipping service allows; it's more about how much you can lift without straining your back!

Trick #423: **Wrap Multiple Items Separately**

sellerdropoff

stores.ebay.com/SellerDropoff

PowerSeller

Member since 2004, Feedback: Turquoise star

If you're shipping several items in the same box, wrap each one separately (in separate smaller boxes, if you can), and provide enough cushioning to prevent movement and to keep the items from rubbing against or knocking into each other.

Previously, **sellerdropoff** noted how some careless sellers packed several loose ornaments in a box, and the damage that resulted. Here's how he suggests doing it:

> When shipping multiple glass items like ornaments, try to place each individual one in its own little ornament box, then put them in the shipping box with loose fill in between.

Trick #424: **Lightly Tape the Bubble Wrap**

lady-frog-vintage-jewelry

stores.ebay.com/SOMETHING-TO-RIBBIT-ABOUT

www.ladyfrog-vintage-jewelry.com

Member since 2000, Feedback: Red star

Here's more practical advice, this time with the buyer's convenience in mind. When you're fastening bubble wrap, don't use a lot of heavy packing tape. Use Scotch tape instead, and go light with it. Too many eager buyers damage their items by using razors or scissors to remove heavily-taped bubble wrap. A little Scotch tape should hold everything in place and be easy enough for the recipient to remove.

Trick #425: **Ensure Smooth Sliding**

New Trick

scifi4me2004

stores.ebay.com/Needle-In-a-Haystack-Treasures

Member since 2003, Feedback: Turquoise star

Here's a good one you probably haven't thought of. When you're shipping an item in a Kraft envelope or bubble mailer, it's easy for the envelope to snag against the automated shipping machinery. To prevent this, simply place an "X" of clear shipping tape on the back of the envelope or mailer. This should enable the envelope to slide easily along the post office's conveyor belts and surfaces.

Trick #426: **Leave Space Around Your Item**

sellerdropoff

stores.ebay.com/SellerDropoff

PowerSeller

Member since 2004, Feedback: Turquoise star

It's important when you're packing to leave space between the item you're shipping and the box you're shipping it in, to prevent damage if the box is bumped or dropped. That means using some sort of cushioning material (peanuts, popcorn, paper) to separate your item from the corners and sides of the box. Seller **sellerdropoff** recommends putting at least 2 inches of packing around all sides of the item you're shipping, which I second. This leaves just enough room to avoid any damage to your item in case the outside box gets crushed or dinged during shipment.

Trick #427: **Double Box Fragile Items**

> **trapperjohn2000**
>
> stores.ebay.com/Molehill-Group-Store
>
> Member since 1998, Feedback: Purple star

Here's another technique to keep in mind when you're packing fragile items, such as glass or ceramic pieces—double-boxing. That means packing the item tightly in a smaller, form-fitting box, and then placing that box inside a slightly larger, shock-absorbing box—with at least 3 inches of cushioning material between the boxes.

Trick #428: **Ship Fragile Items Faster**

> **sellerdropoff**
>
> stores.ebay.com/SellerDropoff
>
> PowerSeller
>
> Member since 2004, Feedback: Turquoise star

Seller **sellerdropoff** has some additional advice when shipping fragile items, which makes a lot of sense. When you're shipping a fragile item, the longer it takes to ship, the more likely it is to get damaged. Speed up the time in transit, and you reduce the odds of it getting bent, folded, spindled, or mutilated by the shipping carrier. Here's what he recommends:

Try to ship fragile items by second-day Priority Mail, or overnight. The least amount of time it spends in the postal system, the less chance it has to be broken.

Trick #429: **Keep It Dry**

New Trick

> **scifi4me2004**
>
> stores.ebay.com/Needle-In-a-Haystack-Treasures
>
> Member since 2003, Feedback: Turquoise star

When you're shipping books, magazines, CDs, DVDs, clothing, and other items that really need to stay dry, even when it's raining outside, you need to wrap the item in some sort of waterproof packaging. One very effective approach is to seal your item in a plastic gallon freezer bag, then place it in the envelope or box you normally use. This will keep the item from getting wet in transit—which could be a big problem in certain areas at certain times of the year.

Trick #430: **Don't Indicate That You're Shipping Valuables**

> **funkyres**
>
> Member since 2001, Feedback: Turquoise star

It happens. Things get stolen. Valuable things. So don't tempt the people doing the shipping. Avoid putting any notice on the outside of the package that you're shipping something valuable. And that even includes your return address; a note that something is shipped from "Joe's Mail Order Jewelry" is just asking for trouble.

Trick #431: **Before You Ship It, Shake It**

> **trapperjohn2000**
>
> stores.ebay.com/Molehill-Group-Store
>
> Member since 1998, Feedback: Purple star

Here's one last piece of general shipping advice. After you think you're done packing, gently shake the box. If nothing moves, it's ready to be sealed. If you can hear or feel things rattling around inside, however, it's time to add more cushioning material. Remember this: If you can shake it, they can break it!

Packing and Shipping Specific Types of Items

Now let's get down to nuts and bolts and see how the eBay Masters pack and ship specific types of items.

Trick #432: **Packing and Shipping Clothing**

> **berties_house_of_horrors**
>
> stores.ebay.com/Berties-Emporium
>
> PowerSeller
>
> Member since 1999, Feedback: Red star

There are lots of things to keep in mind when you're shipping clothing. One of the most important, especially when shipping socks and other small items, is that you don't have to use a big, bulky box to ship. As **berties_house_of_horrors** advises, small clothing items can actually ship in an envelope, which can save you several bucks in shipping costs over even the smallest-sized box.

> **jakki01**
>
> Member since 2000, Feedback: Purple star

Super-shipper **jakki01** expands on that idea by recommending Priority Mail flat-rate envelopes for all types of clothing. Her trick is to first pack the item in a Ziploc bag, which is great for squishing the air out and getting the contents as small as possible. Here's what she says:

> *Flat rate doesn't mean flat envelope! I've put jackets, jeans, etc. all in there. My P.O. workers sometimes laugh at my lumpy deformed envelopes, but they've never not let me mail one before. You can fit a ton in Priority flat rates with some careful folding and a Ziploc, and it saves a lot of $$$.*

> **lady-frog-vintage-jewelry**
>
> stores.ebay.com/SOMETHING-TO-RIBBIT-ABOUT
>
> www.ladyfrog-vintage-jewelry.com
>
> Member since 2000, Feedback: Red star

Seller **lady-frog-vintage-jewelry** notes that she always prepares a clothing item for shipment by first enclosing it in an envelope of tissue paper. Then she puts a plastic bad—usually a new white garbage bag—over the item, and it's ready to go.

tilcia

stores.ebay.com/Tels-Closet

PowerSeller

Member since 2003, Feedback: Turquoise star

Finally, eBay Master **tilcia** says that she tries to add a little extra touch on the clothing items she ships, especially if the item isn't new, by making sure the clothing is as clean and neat as possible. Here's what she recommends:

I have it cleaned right before the auction ends so that when the recipient gets the item, it is clean, in the dry cleaning bag (which, believe it or not, helps cut down on wrinkling during packing and shipping). If it is a new item, I make sure that there aren't any spots or dirt/dust, markings, etc., by double checking before I pack the items. If there are tags, I try to remember to put a tag sleeve over the tag to keep it from getting torn.

In case you're wondering, a *tag sleeve* is a little plastic sleeve you slip over clothing tags for shipment.

Trick #433: **Packing and Shipping CDs and DVDs**

funkyres

Member since 2001, Feedback: Turquoise star

Shipping CDs is simple enough; just buy some of those CD-sized bubble wrap envelopes. The problem, though, is that these envelopes are a bit on the expensive side, unless you order a massive quantity. However, you can easily make your own bubble wrap envelopes, as **funkyres** instructs:

I went to Staples and bought a box of 100 6" × 9" envelopes and a roll of 12" bubble wrap. I wrap each CD [in bubble wrap] and insert it into the envelope—it's a snug fit, but that's good. This is a cheap solution that works well.

This is a great method for shipping CDs and DVDs domestically. For international shipment, use double bubble.

Trick #434: **Packing and Shipping Small Items**

swlakat

stores.ebay.com/Books-Along-The-Bayou

Member since 2003, Feedback: Purple star

Here's a quick trick for packing small, unbreakable items, such as votive candles. Seller **swlakat** recommends using half-gallon orange juice waxed cartons—thoroughly washed, of course, and cut down to size. Here's how it works:

> With my utility knife I remove the top (at the fold line) and pouring spout, then insert this [top piece] into the bottom, to add more support. Then I slit down the sides as much as needed to snugly fit my items. Fold one flap over the other, cutting off any excess, and round a few times with tape. Small, neat, secure, easy to transport, lighter weight for cheaper shipping—and most of all, free!

Trick #435: **Packing and Shipping Fragile Items**

kaycy

Member since 1998, Feedback: Red star

Shipping fragile, breakable items is particularly vexing. It takes a lot of packing—and a lot of padding—to make sure the item won't break during shipment. Seller **kaycy** has a lot of experience with these kinds of items and has a whole routine worked out:

> If there are any openings in the item I pack it well with newspaper and cover it in bubble wrap. If it is like a handle on a piece of porcelain, I put popcorn in the open area and put bubble wrap around that part, also. Then I take the item and wrap it really well in newspaper and then bubble wrap, then put it in the box and either put crumpled-up newspaper or the popcorn things all around it.

hulagirlmele

www.hulagirlmele.com

Member since 2002, Feedback: Purple star

That's a lot of padding, but you need it. You can, however, use your imagination in terms of what type of cushioning to use, as **hulagirlmele** attests:

> For breakables I use egg cartons to cushion all sides of the box and sometimes, depending on how large the item is, I double box. Lots of bubble wrap and peanuts. Sometimes I use newspaper, but only when I've run out of peanuts, because newspaper adds more weight than peanuts.

Trick #436: **Packing and Shipping Plates and China**

alamode

Member since 1997, Feedback: Turquoise star

Shipping plates and fine china is like shipping any fragile item, with lots of cushioning being the name of the game. Seller **alamode** has a strict routine for packing these types of items:

> Packing a plate or vase or pretty much anything breakable can often be best done using a "compression sleeve" as the inner pack of your cardboard box. Basically, you find the box you're going to use (which should be at least 2" larger than the item on all sides) and measure the exact height of the inside when the flaps are closed. Get a strip of regular-weight corrugated cardboard or B-flute (two or three times longer than the diameter of the item) and cut it to the height you just measured. Lay the item on the strip at one end, with the item halfway between top and bottom. Carefully fold the strip around the item and tape the end closed. You now have the item suspended in a rigid cardboard sleeve. To keep the piece in this position during transport, fill the open ends with Styrofoam chips or other filler, then tape over the open ends to hold the fill (and therefore the plate) in place.

You then insert the sleeved plate into the larger box, filling any excess space with packing peanuts. It's a bit of work, but extremely effective.

geo20299
Member since 2002, Feedback: Turquoise star

If you don't want to go to all this trouble, **geo20299** recommends wrapping each plate in large bubble wrap. (The small bubbles might not work as well.) Line the bottom of your box with peanuts or shredded paper, place the bubble wrapped plate on top of that, and then fill with more paper/peanuts.

brookszilla
Member since 2003, Feedback: Turquoise star

Seller **brookszilla** adds to that advice by wrapping each plate in tissue paper before the bubble wrapping. And there's this advice about not using newspaper:

> Don't use newspaper with old china, as the ink can bleed into the glazing if it's cracked. [The china] can also pick up the smell [of the newspaper].

granny.go-go
stores.ebay.com/Granny-Go-Gos-Shop
Member since 1999, Feedback: Turquoise star

Finally, **granny.go-go** has a unique spin on this same packing technique, putting paper plates between the china plates to prevent scratching. Then you can bubble wrap the whole thing.

Trick #437: **Packing and Shipping Artwork and Paintings**

california_artisan

Member since 1999, Feedback: Yellow star

As most artists know, shipping large paintings and artwork is particularly trouble-some—and particularly expensive. That's because this type of item is charged by size, not by weight. You also have to work with very large (frequently custom) boxes, and lots of wrapping and padding. In short, it's a lot of work to get a paint-ing ready to ship. To that end, **california_artisan** recommends adding a generous handling charge to your item:

> *Time is money. Schlepping to the post office is money. Making boxes is money. Charge enough, gang! Actual costs plus $5 or $10 is not out of hand. A 16" × 20" painting on canvas might be charged as much as $40 for S/H here on eBay with-out the eBay price patrol coming down on them for excessive fees. I have gradually been increasing my S/H fees to a point where I now don't feel any aggravation at having to pay an extra few dollars over what I estimated the shipping was to be or for the extra time a particular piece took to package properly.*

artchick48

stores.ebay.com/Lee-Smith-Art

www.leesmithart.com

Member since 2001, Feedback: Turquoise star

Note that bit about making your own boxes. That's because you can't always find large-enough standard boxes to house large pieces of artwork. In fact, it's some-times tough to find the right-sized box for smaller pieces; you need something big but flat, and that's hard to come by. To that end, **artchick48** recommends making your custom boxes out of existing packaging:

> *You can also sandwich [your artwork] between a flattened (unopened, unassem-bled) Priority Mail box, then insert that into a larger flat Priority Mail box, and tape the ends. I ship my canvas boards and masonite pieces like this, as well.*

Trick #438: **Packing and Shipping Antiques**

lmeads

Member since 2001, Feedback: Turquoise star

Shipping antiques is challenging not only because of the need to protect fragile items, but also because of the sizes involved. The best bet here is to mimic how the furniture stores do it, as **lmeads** advises:

> I usually go to a local furniture store and get the leftover packing material they use. It is a heavy, grayish, plastic covering. They may also have some clear plastic sheets left over from their furniture arrivals. I will take the antique we sell and wrap it in the gray furniture wrap. This makes a ball-type glob, which I then put into the box I'm using for shipping. The box is sometimes twice as big as really needed. I can put the "glob" into the box and fill in any space or tighten up the package using the plastic sheets. Using this method, we could take this to the stairs and throw it down; it wouldn't break.

Trick #439: **Packing and Shipping Books**

lady-frog-vintage-jewelry

stores.ebay.com/SOMETHING-TO-RIBBIT-ABOUT

www.ladyfrog-vintage-jewelry.com

Member since 2000, Feedback: Red star

Books are relatively easy to ship; you don't really have a breakage issue, in most cases. That doesn't mean that you don't have to take care when packing. They can still get bent in shipment, and you have to worry about water damage during the rainy season. That's why **lady-frog-vintage-jewelry** goes to an extra effort when packing her books for shipment:

> I will wrap them in heavy bubble wrap and place them in a manila envelope or put them in a plain brown box. They all get mailed via media mail.

satnrose

PowerSeller

Member since 1998, Feedback: Green star

Seller **satnrose** sells a lot of vintage books, which are more easily damaged than newer books. That argues for a different packing technique, as explained here:

Books have a tendency to break in transit. The text block comes loose, the hinges crack, the covers separate. To counter this, I put large rubber bands over the bubble wrap that I always ship books in. Just don't put the rubber bands directly on the surface of the book.

Trick #440: **Packing and Shipping Magazines and Postcards**

lady-frog-vintage-jewelry

stores.ebay.com/SOMETHING-TO-RIBBIT-ABOUT

www.ladyfrog-vintage-jewelry.com

Member since 2000, Feedback: Red star

Magazine and postcards present a similar problem as books, with the added issue of wanting to ship the item flat, not rolled or folded. Here's how **lady-frog-vintage-jewelry** does it:

If I am wrapping magazines or postcards, my husband cuts cardboard that is about 1/4" larger than the item. I put the item in a plastic Ziplock bag (or a page protector) and then sandwich it between two pieces of the cardboard. I tape the cardboard lightly on all four edges to prevent slippage, then place it in either a padded or manila envelope with the words "do not bend" and "fragile" on the envelope.

Trick #441: **Packing and Shipping Stamps**

rufusduff

PowerSeller

Member since 1999, Feedback: Turquoise star

Shipping stamps seems like a simple thing (they're not big, they're not heavy, and they're not fragile), but you still want to take some simple precautions. Seller **rufusduff** always encases stamps in a thin transparent envelope, against a sheet of black construction paper (which shows off the stamps' perforations). This document envelope then fits inside your larger mailing envelope. And there's an added touch, which is nice:

For my philatelic clients, I always mail their winnings using a mix of current commemorative stamps. Know your audience!

Trick #442: **Packing and Shipping Coins**

Collectible coins ship similarly to stamps, as **brookszilla** notes:

> With coins, the high-end singles go into airtight containers. I use bubble wrap insulated containers and separate everything with tissue paper.

Trick #443: **Packing and Shipping Jewelry**

Packing jewelry items requires adequate padding plus wrapping the item so it won't get scratched in shipment. Here's what **rockinghorsegirl4now** recommends:

> When I sell jewelry items I put each one in a baggy before wrapping in bubble wrap or tissue. That way the buyer already has a baggy to keep their item from being scratched or to keep their earrings together. And the items don't get scratched in shipping, either.

She also has some advice on how *not* to pack jewelry:

> Don't tape jewelry to a piece of paper or cardboard! I've had beaded jewelry break apart trying to get it off the cardboard, and finishes even come off on the tape. Don't put any tape on jewelry!

Trick #444: **Packing and Shipping LPs and LaserDiscs**

If you're into vintage technology, you know the challenges of properly packing and shipping vinyl LPs and LaserDiscs. eBay Master **jimrick1** has it down to a science, as you can see here:

> Materials include pizza box, plastic bag, 2" clear packing tape, 1/2" reinforced filament tape, and anti-static Styrofoam chips. First, the LP and inner sleeve are removed from the cover. The LP (in the inner sleeve) is then set on top of the cover,

and everything is put into the plastic bag, which is then sealed with tape. A single layer of Styrofoam curls is poured into the pizza box, then the LP is placed into the box. The box is topped up with Styrofoam packing curls, sealed with 2" clear packing tape, and crisscrossed all three ways with strong 1/2" fiberglass (filament) tape. LPs packed like this will resist even the most determined attempts to damage them.

Trick #445: **Packing and Shipping Tires**

> **ikwewe**
>
> stores.ebay.com/Good-Things-to-Share
>
> Member since 2001, Feedback: Purple star

People can sell just about anything on eBay, including (via eBay Motors) large auto parts. How, pray tell, does one ship something as big and non-square as a car tire? Here's what **ikwere** recommends:

Check with UPS; we have sent and received tires/rims bare with a label glued on. No wrap is necessary, except to protect the finish on the wheel.

If only packing and shipping everything was as easy as slapping a label on it!

Shipping with an Extra Touch

As noted earlier, your packaging is a form of marketing. How your package looks reflects on you and your business. So it's no surprise that many eBay Masters take special pride in their packaging and the little personal touches they add.

Trick #446: **Include Your Business Card**

> **dixiedollie**
>
> Member since 2001, Feedback: Red star

Here's a good way to get customers to remember you for future purchases. Get some business cards printed up, and include one in each package you ship. Here's what **dixiedollie** does:

I like to have my cards say, "Thank you for your business! Please remember feedback on eBay!" They have my eBay ID on them, and my email address as well, for the customer to contact me if necessary. I like to have them printed like this for a feedback reminder. Customers love it, and my feedback is almost 100%!

You can get business cards printed just about anywhere, although **dixiedollie** offers the additional tip that VistaPrint (www.vistaprint.com) offers an initial 250 business cards for free.

Trick #447: **Include a Handwritten Thank-You Note**

> **boutiqueannemarie**
>
> PowerSeller
>
> Member since 2002, Feedback: Turquoise star

This one's simple but makes a big impression. Instead of (or in addition to) an impersonal packing slip or business card, include a handwritten thank-you note in all your packages. It's a personal touch that your customers will remember, as **boutiqueannemarie** notes:

> *We had professional looking cards printed saying thank you, with our names and email addresses. We write a quick handwritten note on each card and people love it.*

Trick #448: **Include a Special Gift**

> **dixiedollie**
>
> Member since 2001, Feedback: Red star

I was surprised to find so many sellers including little gifts in the packages they ship out. It adds a great personal touch to your eBay transactions and costs next to nothing. It really distinguishes your auctions from everybody else's, as seller **dixiedollie** attests:

> *I love to add that little extra special touch to my shipments! Customers love it, and it really has done wonders for my feedback, as well!*

What kinds of special gifts are we talking about? Here are some ideas from some of my favorite eBay Masters:

- **dixiedollie**—During the spring/summer, a packet of flower seeds. During the holidays, decorative pencils and other holiday gifts. All through the year, an individual wrapped mint.
- **michelelise**—Handmade gift tags.
- **peaches1442**—Greeting cards.
- **pondfork**—Small, colorful stickers (cats, dogs, Winnie the Pooh, Spongebob Squarepants, and so on).

- **slfcollectibles2**—Lipstick-shaped pens, small paper pads, high-heel shoe pencil sharpeners.

- **steveparkfan2001**—Thank-you mints and smiley face mints. Handmade American flag pins. During the Christmas season, candy canes. With cosmetic items, a makeup brush.

- **the_southern_yankee**—Handmade photo buttons with a picture of the merchandise on it and a magnet on the back (to hang on the refrigerator).

- **tilcia**—Cosmetic samples (body lotion, shower gel, perfume, and so on).

As you can see, thoughtful sellers pack all sorts of fun and interesting items with their eBay shipments. You need to be cautious, however, of using scented wrap or perfumes. Seller **dixiedollie** warns that some people are sensitive to smells or have allergic conditions, so whatever you do, do it scent-free!

Trick #449: **Gift Wrap the Item**

> **dixiedollie**
>
> Member since 2001, Feedback: Red star

If you know the item is purchased as a gift (or if it's during the holiday season), just go ahead and gift wrap it—for free! Customers will appreciate the extra effort.

14

How to Sell and Ship Internationally

Even though most U.S. sellers sell to U.S. buyers (and most Irish sellers sell to Irish buyers, and most Japanese sellers sell to Japanese buyers, and so on), eBay is a global marketplace. There's nothing stopping you from offering your goods to bidders in other countries—nor is there anything stopping you from restricting your auctions to your fellow countrymen. Let's see what the eBay Masters have to say about selling internationally and what advice they have for preparing international shipments.

Selling Internationally

Let's start with the big question: Should you sell internationally? The answer to this isn't a simple one. It depends a lot on your tolerance for differences (in money, in language, in routine), and your ability to deal with unusual post-auction activity—especially in regard to payment and shipping. Even the eBay Masters have differing opinions on this one.

Trick #450: **Invite International Bidders**

> **lludwig**
>
> stores.ebay.com/LLudwig-Books
>
> PowerSeller
>
> Member since 1998, Feedback: Green star

Many eBay sellers recognize the increased profit potential of opening up their auctions to buyers outside the U.S. The more potential bidders you have, the more likely you'll be to sell your item—and command a higher price. Besides, it can be a lot of fun to deal with people in different countries and cultures.

If you decide to sell outside the U.S., you'll want to state this in your auction listings. International seller **lludwig** not only recommends selling globally, but also in advertising so in your listings:

> *Include in your template a sentence welcoming international bidders. The inclusion of "International bidders welcome"—in addition to the standard eBay "We ship worldwide"—is a simple goodwill gesture that bidders in other countries appreciate. Although I do not include every language possible and the translations may not be "perfect" French, German, or Spanish, it does get the idea across.*

And what are the magic phrases? Here are the ones **lludwig** uses:

> *International bidders welcome!*
>
> *Internationales Bewerber Willkommen!*
>
> *Bienvenue Internationale De Soumissionnaires!*
>
> *Recepción Internacional De los Licitadores!*

Trick #451: **Include International Shipping Charges in Your Listings**

> **ghsproducts**
>
> stores.ebay.com/GHSProducts
>
> Member since 1998, Feedback: Purple star

Another way to invite bidders from outside the U.S. is to include international shipping charges in your listings. International buyers are easily confused or intimidated; you can make things easier for them by clearly stating upfront how much shipping will be to their country. (And learn more about shipping outside the U.S. in the "Shipping Internationally" section, later in this chapter.)

Trick #452: **Buy Low in One Country, Sell High in Another**

New Trick

> **berties_house_of_horrors**
>
> stores.ebay.com/Berties-Emporium
>
> PowerSeller
>
> Member since 1999, Feedback: Red star

If you're selling internationally, you can buy internationally, too. This lets you utilize the technique of arbitrage, which is where you search for—and take advantage of—price discrepancies from one market to another. You might be able to find bargains in one country that can be resold at a higher price in another. PowerSeller **berties_house_of_horrors** relates his experience:

> *I buy Von Dutch caps in Canada for $10.00 CDN and resell on eBay UK, where Von Dutch sells for four times as much. I do the same with Calvin Klein and Diesel, which sell for three times more in Australia than I what it costs me on the Canada or U.S. eBay sites.*

Trick #453: **There's Money in Repatriation**

> **rufusduff**
>
> PowerSeller
>
> Member since 1999, Feedback: Turquoise star

Here's another trend in international sales—selling back home-grown goods to the seller's country of origin. Seller **rufusduff** calls this "repatriation," and notes that it's becoming a big business:

> *I've noticed that my client base has grown much more international over the last three years, probably up to around 40% now. The most striking thing about this is "repatriation," i.e., the exporting of antiques, glassware, vintage stamps and covers, antiquarian books, you-name-it, back to sellers' countries of origin. Much of this is estate stuff that has been in the U.S. for generations, some family heirlooms, others parts of collections, still others later acquisitions.*

He gives the example of selling vintage 1950s Matrushka dolls to buyers in Moscow, Buffon engravings to buyers in Paris, and a Val St. Lambert chandelier to a buyer in the Netherlands. It's something to consider!

Trick #454: **You Don't Have to Sell to International Buyers**

> **trapperjohn2000**
>
> stores.ebay.com/Molehill-Group-Store
>
> Member since 1998, Feedback: Purple star

On the other hand, selling and (particularly) shipping internationally can be a real hassle. Selling to someone in Europe or Asia isn't quite the same as dealing with someone in California or New Jersey. You can run into difficulties communicating with non-English speaking bidders; you may have to deal with payment in non-U.S. funds, or non-U.S. banks; and the whole shipping thing is a real hassle. You'll have to put extra effort into securely packing your item, investigate different shipping services, deal with unusual shipping costs, and fill out a lot of paperwork. It may not be worth the effort, especially if all the extra (and somewhat confusing) paperwork disrupts your normal shipping routine. Some sellers don't mind the additional work, but some do. It's your choice to make—there's nothing that says you *have* to ship outside your native country.

Trick #455: **Blocking Non-U.S. Bidders**

New Trick

> **selling4-u**
>
> stores.ebay.com/Selling-4-U-Consignment-Store
>
> PowerSeller
>
> Member since 2002, Feedback: Purple star

Saying that you only sell within the U.S. often doesn't stop users from other countries from placing bids. I've had more than a few "U.S.-only" auctions that ended up being won by users well outside the U.S.

A solution to this problem is to tell eBay to block all bidders from countries you don't sell to. Go to your My eBay page, and then go to Seller Preferences > Buyer Requirements. Check the Block Buyers Who Are Registered in Countries to which I Don't Ship option, and you should be all set.

International Payments

One of the issues with selling outside the U.S. is in dealing with foreign payments—often in foreign currency. First, you have to convert it to U.S. dollars. (How many lira to the dollar today?) Then you have to receive it in a form that is both secure and trusted. (Do you trust a personal check drawn on a small Spanish bank?) Then you have to find a way to deposit those funds and convert them to U.S. dollars. (Does your bank accept foreign deposits?) Let's see how the eBay Masters handle it.

Trick #456: **Accept Payment in U.S. Funds Only**

> **trapperjohn2000**
>
> stores.ebay.com/Molehill-Group-Store
>
> Member since 1998, Feedback: Purple star

You can simplify the whole international currency issue by specifying bidding and payment in U.S. funds only. This puts the onus of currency conversion on the buyer, which is a plus for you.

Trick #457: **Accept International PayPal Payments**

> **trapperjohn2000**
>
> stores.ebay.com/Molehill-Group-Store
>
> Member since 1998, Feedback: Purple star

The payment process can be further simplified when the buyer pays by credit card, using PayPal. PayPal is active in dozens of foreign countries and can handle all the payment, conversion, and deposit functions for you.

Trick #458: **Accept BidPay Money Orders**

> **dfrazier18**
>
> stores.ebay.com/Fraziers-Finds
>
> Member since 2000, Feedback: Red star

Another good method of payment for non-U.S. buyers is international money orders—in particular, via BidPay (www.bidpay.com), formerly known as Western Union Auction Payments. The buyers pay BidPay via credit card, and BidPay sends you a U.S. money order. Simplicity itself.

Trick #459: **You Can Cash Canadian Postal Money Orders at Your Local Post Office**

> **selectro_cute**
>
> Member since 2000, Feedback: Turquoise star

If you're selling to Canada, it's okay to accept Canadian Postal money orders issued by Canadian post offices. That's because the U.S. and Canadian postal services have an agreement to cash each other's money orders, no extra fees involved. Just take the Canadian Postal money order to your local post office, and you should be able to cash it, no problem.

Trick #460: **Use an Online Currency Converter**

lesley_feeney

stores.ebay.com/Lesleys-Auction-Template-Designs

PowerSeller

Member since 2000, Feedback: Purple star

When selling internationally, it also helps if you know how much the dollar is worth versus a particular foreign currency. To that end, check out the Universal Currency Converter at www.xe.net/ucc/, shown in Figure 14.1.

FIGURE 14.1
Convert your currency with the Universal Currency Converter.

Shipping Internationally

All that said, I've found that the biggest difficulty in selling to non-U.S. buyers is shipping the item. Not only are longer distances involved (which necessitates more secure packaging and longer shipping times), but you also have to deal with different shipping options and all sorts of new paperwork. As you might expect, however, the eBay Masters have some advice that might prove useful.

Trick #461: **Know What You Can—and Can't—Ship**

trapperjohn2000

stores.ebay.com/Molehill-Group-Store

Member since 1998, Feedback: Purple star

Not surprisingly, there are certain items you can't ship to foreign countries—firearms, live animals and animal products, and so on. (There are also some technology items you can't ship, for security reasons.) You need to check the government's list of import and export restrictions to see what items you're prohibited from shipping outside U.S. borders. Ask your shipping service for a list of restricted items and shipping limits, like the one that the U.S. Postal Service provides at pe.usps.gov/text/Imm/Immctry.html.

Trick #462: **Fill Out the Proper Paperwork**

trapperjohn2000

stores.ebay.com/Molehill-Group-Store

Member since 1998, Feedback: Purple star

All packages shipping outside U.S. borders must clear customs to enter the destination country and require the completion of specific customs forms to make the trip. Depending on the type of item you're shipping and the weight of your package, you'll need either Form 2976 (green) or Form 2976-A (white). Both of these forms should be available at your local post office, or you can print them online at webapps.usps.com/customsforms/.

Trick #463: **Don't Lie on the Customs Forms**

gothgirlscloset

PowerSeller

Member since 1999, Feedback: Red star

One of the lines you have to complete on the customs form is the value of the item. In some countries, the recipient has to pay a tax based on this value. To get around this, some foreign buyers will ask you to mark the item as a "gift" so they can avoid paying import taxes. Don't do it. Lying on a customs form has legal implications and just isn't a good idea. Follow the advice of **gothgirlscloset**:

Make sure to tell international bidders that they are responsible for all taxes and duties. You should put the exact bid price on the customs form, not the "value" or the full total including shipping.

Trick #464: **Ship via the U.S. Postal Service**

dan80906

stores.ebay.com/Mostly-Nascar

Member since 2002, Feedback: Turquoise star

Just about any shipping service can ship outside the U.S., but they're far from equal when it comes to costs. Several eBayers have noted how expensive UPS and FedEx are for shipping internationally, often charging high "brokerage" fees to clear through customs. This is one instance where the U.S. Postal Service has it all over the competition, with lower costs across the board. Check it out for yourself!

Trick #465: **Use Global Priority Flat Rate Envelopes**

chunkypunkys

stores.ebay.com/chunky-punkys-gifts-and-crafts

Member since 1998, Feedback: Red star

While you're using the U.S. Postal Service, check out those flat-rate Global Priority envelopes. They work just like domestic Priority Mail envelopes; anything you can fit in ships at a reasonable flat rate.

Trick #466: **Ship Airmail**

carlmarxx

stores.ebay.com/Karls-Ye-Olde-Hobbies

Member since 2001, Feedback: Red star

Probably the best bet of all the postal service's international shipping services is Airmail. You can ship small items Airmail Letter post, and larger items Airmail Parcel Post. Items get there relatively fast, and the cost isn't totally outrageous.

Trick #467: **Use M-Bag Mail for Media**

> **ghsproducts**
>
> stores.ebay.com/GHSProducts
>
> Member since 1998, Feedback: Purple star

Here's a trick that not a lot of people know about. The post office offers an international version of Media Mail called M-Bag. Seller **ghsproducts** explains how it works:

> *I was selling some baking textbooks and had orders from all over the world. I prepared them for shipping as normal, then took them to the post office and told the clerk that I want to send them "M" class. In most cases the clerk has no idea what I am talking about and has to ask around first. Last time I sent books that way it cost $9 for 11 pounds to ship to Germany. It is slow though, 4-6 week delivery, so if timing is an issue, forget it.*

Trick #468: **Don't Leave Price Tags on the Merchandise**

> **rockinghorsegirl4now**
>
> stores.ebay.com/Hollyhock-Cottage-Collectibles
>
> Member since 2002, Feedback: Red star

Here's a trick you fortunately don't have to learn the hard way. While you're packing an item for international shipment, always remove all the original retail price tags. Leave the price tags on, and customs could charge the buyer a hefty fee based on the retail price—not on the declared price that the buyer actually paid on eBay!

Trick #469: **Always Insure International Shipments**

 New Trick

> **ilene**
>
> stores.ebay.com/Ilenes-Discount-Collectibles
>
> PowerSeller
>
> Member since 1997, Feedback: Green star

Given the increased risk of damage when shipping internationally (the longer a package travels, the more likely it is to be damaged), it pays to always insure your international shipments. Member **ilene** recommends using a private insurance service, such as Discount Shipping Insurance (www.dsiinsurance.com).

Trick #470: **Add an Additional Handling Charge for International Sales**

bartonknifeco

Member since 2002, Feedback: Purple star

Here's one last piece of advice. Because of all the extra effort involved in preparing and shipping international shipments, do yourself a favor and tack on an additional handling charge for all non-U.S. sales. It's a legitimate charge, especially when you note it upfront in your listing's TOS.

How to Deal with Customer Problems—and Problem Customers

Not every eBay transaction goes smoothly. The more items you sell, the more likely you'll run into some sort of problem—a buyer who doesn't pay, a buyer who complains about what he received, or even a buyer who tries to scam you. Dealing with these sort of irritations is part and parcel of selling on eBay, and the eBay Masters know how to handle these types of situations.

Handling Customer Complaints

You list an item for auction. The high bidder wins the auction. You receive payment and ship the item to the buyer. End of story? Not always. Sometimes the buyer isn't happy, and now you have to deal with a complaining customer. Let's see how the eBay Masters deal with these types of complaints.

Trick #471: **Don't Overreact**

brewcity_bob

stores.ebay.com/Brew-City-Limited

PowerSeller

Member since 1998, Feedback: Red star

You'll get complaining customers and deadbeat bidders from time to time. Don't let them bother you. In particular, don't overreact—and definitely don't take the complaint personally. Avoid the temptation to respond with a scathing email and give the customer a piece of your mind. Get up from the computer and go take a walk; blow off some steam.

And whatever you do, don't let that one complaining customer dictate changes in the way you run your eBay auctions. Yeah, you'll have some problems from time to time, but the vast majority of eBay auctions go smoothly. Tailor your business to the smooth majority, not to the pain-in-the-rear minority. Take the advice of experienced seller **brewcity_bob**:

> *I see anything like this as part of doing business. You can try to minimize your risk but only to a point. Once you start restricting buyers you also start restricting sales. So it ends up being a lose-lose situation for the business. Don't let something that went wrong affect the way you do business.*

Trick #472: **Issue a Refund If the Customer Complains**

terrisbooks

stores.ebay.com/Terris-Books

www.terrisbeads.com

PowerSeller

Member since 2002, Feedback: Red star

Happy customers are repeat customers; unhappy customers generate negative word of mouth—and leave negative feedback, too. It's in your best interest to make sure your customers are happy.

If you want to offer the best possible customer service, that means offering a no-questions-asked guarantee. If the customer asks for a refund, for whatever reason, you give it. That might sound extreme, but it's how companies like Nordstrom do business, and it works for them. As the old motto goes, "the customer is always right." This may not be a good policy for all eBay sellers, but it's certainly something to consider.

I like the customer-friendly attitude of seller **terrisbooks**:

I will issue a refund if someone isn't happy. Or, if something gets lost in the mail, I often send another one out at my expense. Granted, it rarely happens, but I want everyone to get their item and be happy with me as a seller.

Coming from a retail background, I follow this advice myself. The customer is always right, even if they're not really. I treat my eBay business as a real business, and real businesses bend over backward to satisfy their customers. Good customer service will earn you good feedback, repeat business, and overall good karma. Just because you don't *have* to give a refund doesn't mean that you *shouldn't*!

Trick #473: **Add a Returns Policy to Your Auction Listings**

berties_house_of_horrors

stores.ebay.com/Berties-Emporium

PowerSeller

Member since 1999, Feedback: Red star

In the world of traditional retail, the customer is always right. Shouldn't it be the same online? If you really believe in what you're selling, you shouldn't have to reluctantly refund a customer's money when they complain; you should proudly offer a money-back guarantee up-front.

Offering a returns policy will gain you more sales, at very little cost. That's because you'll probably never have to take a return; most sellers like the peace of mind a returns policy provides, but seldom (if ever) actually return anything. As **berties_house_of_horrors** notes:

Offer a money-back guarantee on the purchase price, minus the shipping. Your sales will go up. Most people will not do a return anyway. Out of 440 sales, only once did I have a return (for non fit).

eBay now makes it easy to include your returns policy in your auction listings. Just click the appropriate boxes on the Describe Your Item page, and your item will be listed as having a returns policy. It's the way professional sellers operate.

Trick #474: **You Don't Have to Refund Shipping Charges**

New Trick

rosachs

stores.ebay.com/My-Discount-Shoe-Store

home.midsouth.rr.com/rosachs/RKS/

PowerSeller

Member since 1997, Feedback: Red star

Refunding the purchase price of an item is one thing. Refunding the shipping costs is quite another. The key to having a reasonable returns policy is the word "reasonable." Some customers might try to take advantage of an over-lenient policy, and you don't have to go along with that. Here's how experienced seller **rosachs** views it:

> If a buyer has a change of heart or the item doesn't fit or is somehow unusable to them, allowing for returns may actually entice them to purchase again. Just be sure your policy is clear on who pays for return shipping and whether or not the original shipping is returned. Many sellers who allow returns for any reason will not refund original or return shipping—this is the buyer's cost for "trying out" your product. And adding a "restock fees may be imposed for damaged or otherwise unsellable returns" clause is also a good idea; hopefully you will never have to use it, but it's good language to make part of your terms of sale.

Trick #475: **Don't Refund Any Money Until the Item Is Shipped Back to You**

spookimojo

Member since 2002, Feedback: Turquoise star

Just because you're customer-friendly doesn't mean you have to be stupid about it. Every now and then you'll run across a "complaining customer" who's really out to scam you; they're looking to get an item for free, which can happen if you refund their money *and* let them keep the merchandise. You've met these folks. They claim the merchandise was damaged or that they never received it, in the hopes of you sending their money back, no questions asked. If you send a refund, they essentially get free merchandise.

There's nothing in the customer-is-always-right manual that says you have to refund any customer's money, no questions asked. In other words, it's okay to ask a few questions, and specifically to ask for proof of damage or unsuitability, before you send a refund check.

Perhaps a better approach is to ask the buyer to return the item if they're unhappy, and then issue a refund when you receive the merchandise back. (In this situation, the buyer is typically responsible for paying the return postage.) Someone trying to scam you won't send the stuff back, and that's the end of it. And if you get the item back and it's actually in okay shape, you can resell it at a later time.

Dealing with Problem Customers

Complaining customers aren't the only problems you'll run into. Let's see what the eBay Masters have to say about those customers who don't pay—the folks we refer to as deadbeat buyers.

Trick #476: **Contact the Buyer Again—and Again**

> **ilene**
>
> stores.ebay.com/Ilenes-Discount-Collectibles
> PowerSeller
> Member since 1997, Feedback: Green star

Some apparently deadbeat buyers are just forgetful. If you haven't received payment within a reasonable period of time, send a polite reminder email. If another few days go by without payment (or if you don't receive a response to your message), email the buyer again. I typically plan for three separate emails (beyond the original winning bidder notification) before I consider a bidder a true deadbeat. There's no reason to rush things; give the buyer enough time to respond, and don't be in such a rush about it.

Trick #477: **File for an eBay Fee Refund**

> **trapperjohn2000**
>
> stores.ebay.com/Molehill-Group-Store
> Member since 1998, Feedback: Purple star

Of course, you can't be expected to wait forever to be paid. If you haven't heard from the buyer in 7 to 10 days, or haven't received payment in two weeks or so, then it's fair to write the buyer off and move on. Give the buyer one last chance (with a 24-hour time limit); then notify him that you're canceling the auction transaction.

Now comes the extra work. The first thing you want to do is file for a refund of eBay's final value fee. After all, there's no sense paying eBay for something you didn't really sell. To file for a final value fee credit, you have to go through eBay's Unpaid Item Dispute process. Start at feedback.ebay.com/ws/ eBayISAPI.dll?CreateDispute, and follow the onscreen instructions. You typically have to wait until 7 days after the auction has ended, but not more than 45 days. Follow the process as described, and eBay will issue a credit against your account for the final value fee.

You can now relist the item, or offer it to a losing bidder via eBay's Second Chance Offer function. And take the time to put the deadbeat bidder on your blocked bidders list, just in case they show up again in the future. (See Trick #477 for instructions.)

Trick #478: **Cancel Unwanted Bids**

> **amrell**
>
> stores.ebay.com/The-Hot-Mannequin
>
> Member since 2002, Feedback: Turquoise star

When you do identify a potential problem bidder, get rid of them by canceling their bid. eBay makes it fairly easy to cancel a bid. All you have to do is go to the Site Map page and click the Cancel Bids on Your Listing link. When the next page appears, as shown in Figure 15.1, cancel that user's bid. It's as simple as that.

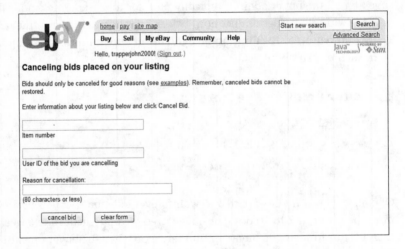

FIGURE 15.1

Canceling bids on your auctions.

One thing, though. When you cancel a person's bid, it's good form to email that bidder and explain why you're canceling. You might not be able to totally avoid ticking off the canceled bidder, but at least you can try.

Trick #479: **Block Deadbeat Bidders**

*janies*jeans-n-things

Member since 2001, Feedback: Red star

Of course, if you cancel a bidder's bid on one auction, you don't want them bidding on any future auctions either. eBay lets you add users to your blocked list so that they won't be able to bid on any of your auctions, now or later.

To add a bidder to your block list, go to the Site Map page and click the Block Bidder/Buyer List link. When the Buyer/Bidder Management page appears, click the Add an eBay User to My Blocked Bidder/Buyer List link. This displays the Blocking a Bidder/Buyer page, shown in Figure 15.2. Add the buyer's user name to the list in the big text box; separate multiple names with commas. Click the Submit button when done, and the bidder is officially blocked and is unable to bid on any of your auctions in the future.

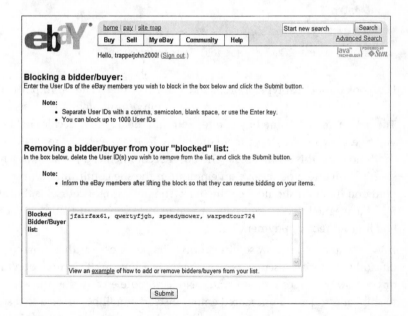

FIGURE 15.2

Adding a buyer to your blocked bidder/buyer list.

Trick #480: **Don't Ship to a Different Address**

New Trick

> **going1nceamc**
>
> stores.ebay.com/GOing1nceAMC
>
> www.going1nce.com
>
> PowerSeller
>
> Member since 1999, Feedback: Red star

Here's a scam to avoid. You're selling an item, the auction ends, and you get an immediate notice of payment (typically via PayPal) with a request to ship to a different address, as a gift to someone else. Unless you can verify the legitimacy of this request, do *not* ship the item—it's likely that someone has hijacked the buyer's account and is trying to get the item shipped to their own address. (And the payment is likely fraudulent, as well.) If you ship the item to the second address, you'll probably lose both the item and the payment. When in doubt, double-check with PayPal, or hold onto the item long enough for the payment to be verified or cleared.

Trick #481: **Avoid Fraudulent Escrow Service Scams**

> **jeffostroff**
>
> www.carbuyingtips.com
>
> Member since 2003, Feedback: Turquoise star

Let's look at one last type of problem customer—the scammer. In particular, the scammer who tries to get your money through a fraudulent escrow service scam. The trick here is that the buyer, after winning the auction, decides he'd rather pay via an escrow service. Now, there are many legitimate escrow services out there, but that's not how this scam works. The buyer recommends a particular escrow site, and shortly thereafter you receive an email from the site confirming that the buyer has paid and that you should ship the item. The problem, of course, is that the site is fraudulent, the buyer hasn't paid anything, and you've just shipped an item that you'll never receive payment for.

How do you avoid escrow service scams? First, deal only with Escrow.com, eBay's officially authorized escrow service, shown in Figure 15.3. Second, don't respond to any escrow messages sent via email. No legitimate escrow site will send "confirmed to ship" messages via unsecured email; instead, you'll be directed to a secure website for all communication. And check out the discussions on eBay's Escrow & Insurance discussion board; it's a great place to learn about all the latest escrow-related scams!

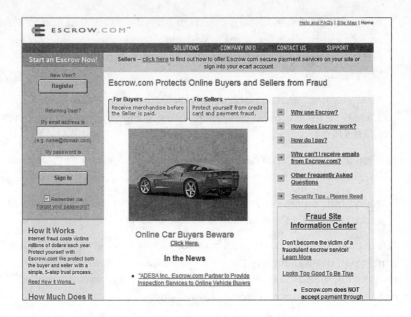

FIGURE 15.3
Escrow.com—a legitimate escrow service.

And, just to be on the safe side, check out the following advice offered by eBay Master **jeffostroff**:

Do a Google search on the escrow's website. Legit escrows have lots of Google results. Fake ones will have one search result, or usually none. Look for complaints other victims have posted online.

If they address you as "Dear Sir", it's probably a scam, because they are using pre-written response templates. Why don't they say something like "Jeff, let's go ahead with the deal"?

When you log into a fake escrow site, it does not say https:// at the start of the URL, and your "SSL secure padlock icon" does not come on at the bottom of your browser. This means the site is not a secure site, so they are lying and you know it's fake.

Go to Register.com and do a "whois" lookup of the escrow company domain name. If the domain name was registered only weeks before, consider them to be fraudulent. The scammers usually reserve several names, rip off a few people, then dump the site.

Verify with the Better Business Bureau at BBB.com if they have a reliability report on your escrow company. It takes 5 seconds. Legitimate escrow services are members of the BBB, and should have a "Satisfactory Record" on the BBB Reliability Report that pops up.

If the escrow company is located outside the U.S., don't use them. Are you nuts? There is no reason to use an offshore escrow company. They are not governed by any U.S. laws.

If you are the seller in an auction and send an expensive product through an escrow, you should always require a signature for delivery.

Always trust your gut feeling. If you get a bad feeling about something, trust your instincts; don't do the deal. Others will come along later.

You get the impression that dealing with escrow companies is fraught with problems? Well, that's definitely the case; fake escrow companies are a large source of eBay-related fraud. Take my previous advice and deal exclusively with Escrow.com, and you'll save yourself a world of headache.

How to Create Happier Customers

How do you create happier buyers—and repeat customers? It's all about customer service, as you'll learn from these tips from the eBay Masters.

Trick #482: **Treat Your Customers the Way You'd Like to Be Treated**

> **kyderbyfan**
> PowerSeller
> Member since 1999, Feedback: Red star

The secret to great customer service is to treat your buyers exactly the way you'd like to be treated. That means good communication, great packaging, and fast shipping—all with a personal touch. As **kyderbyfan** notes:

The secrets to my success are quite simple. I treat my customers as I would like to be treated with the roles reversed. My customers are what keep me in business, so I treat them with the respect and courtesy they deserve—even if it is not always returned. (Most often it is returned, however.) So far this formula has worked quite well.

This also means that you should do what you say you're going to do—you should deliver on your promises and honor your own terms of service. For example, if you state you ship daily, then you should ship daily. Any condition covered in your TOS should be honored. Again, it's how you'd expect to be treated if you were the buyer, right?

Trick #483: **Answer Bidder Questions—Promptly**

> **flyinggirlart**
>
> stores.ebay.com/FlyingGirl-Images
>
> www.flyinggirl.com
>
> Member since 2003, Feedback: Purple star

Many potential buyers have questions before they place a bid. If they don't get their questions answered, they won't bid, plain and simple. That means you need to answer bidder emails promptly and completely—especially in the final hours of the auction, when the snipers come out in force. Make yourself accessible to your bidders; as **flyinggirlart** notes:

> *There is nothing more frustrating than having questions go unanswered as an auction is ending.*

Trick #484: **Communicate!**

> **dr.sminty**
>
> Member since 1999, Feedback: Purple star

It's extremely important to keep your customers informed. Send emails when the auction ends, when you receive payment, and when you ship the item. Answer any and all emails you've received, as promptly as possible. As **dr.sminty** says:

> *Communication should be everyone's primary objective. It is what drives the sale. When someone makes a purchase, they want to be comforted. They want to be assured that they didn't just get ripped off. Lack of communication kills business— especially for potential repeat customers.*

Buyers appreciate it when you keep them in the loop. They don't want to become your email buddy for life, but they do want to know when you've received their payment and when you've shipped their item. Both of these things can be accomplished with simple one-line email messages, and go a long way toward relieving customer anxiety—which makes for more satisfied customers.

How to Sell Specific Types of Items

If there's one thing I've discovered while writing this book, it's that experienced eBay sellers tend to specialize. There's good reason for this—different product categories often operate under completely different sets of rules. What it takes to successfully sell clothing is probably quite different from what it takes to successfully sell collectible coins, or paintings, or whatever. This chapter, then, goes into some detail about the quirks inherent in some specific product categories—as presented by the eBay Masters in each category.

Before we get into the specific tricks, however, here's a piece of general advice. When you want to seriously start selling in a specific category, do your homework. Check out the other auctions in that category, research open and closed listings, and try to identify the strategies used by successful sellers. It's definitely a good idea to get your feet wet before you jump blindly in the pool!

Clothing

We'll start by examining a very popular category—clothing. The clothing category is unique in that it's a mixture of new and used items, and that it's highly dependent on fit and form.

Trick #485: **Find Out Who Manufactured a Specific Item**

bombprices

Member since 2002, Feedback: Turquoise star

Want to know who manufactured a piece of clothing you have for sale? Then check out the FTC's Registration Information Number (RN) database, located at https://rn.ftc.gov/pls/TextileRN/wrnquery$.startup. (The RN database lookup page is shown in Figure 16.1.) The RN is issued by the Federal Trade Commission to U.S. companies that manufacture, import, distribute, or sell textile, wool, or fur products. Enter the company name or other information and you can find out the actual manufacturer behind the store brand.

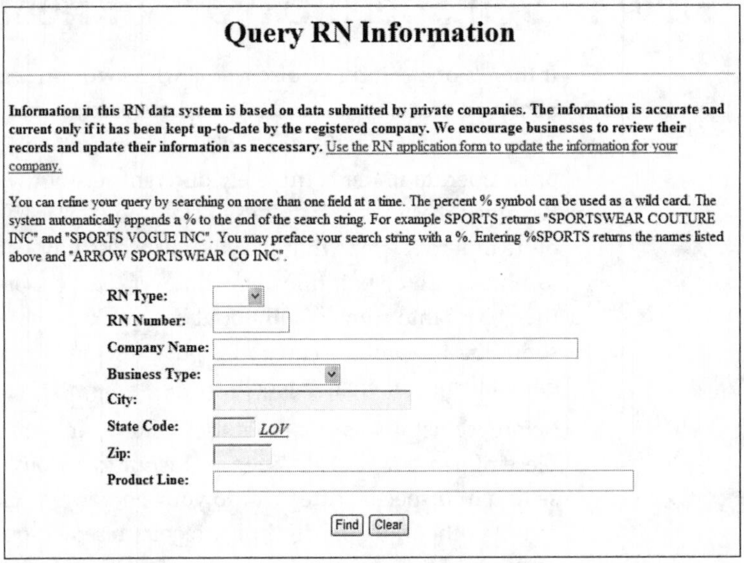

Query RN Information

Information in this RN data system is based on data submitted by private companies. The information is accurate and current only if it has been kept up-to-date by the registered company. We encourage businesses to review their records and update their information as neccessary. Use the RN application form to update the information for your company.

You can refine your query by searching on more than one field at a time. The percent % symbol can be used as a wild card. The system automatically appends a % to the end of the search string. For example SPORTS returns "SPORTSWEAR COUTURE INC" and "SPORTS VOGUE INC". You may preface your search string with a %. Entering %SPORTS returns the names listed above and "ARROW SPORTSWEAR CO INC".

RN Type:
RN Number:
Company Name:
Business Type:
City:
State Code: *LOV*
Zip:
Product Line:

Find   Clear

FIGURE 16.1

Look up manufacturer information in the FTC's RN database.

eBay member **bombprices** relates the following story:

I had bought a dress that was supposed to have come from a major department store, but when I received it, it was a dress from the Dollar General store. There was a big debate if it was made by a major department store and sold to the Dollar General store. Someone posted this site so I could check the RN number and see who made it. Of course it was made by the Dollar General store.

Trick #486: **Include Measurements—Not Just Size**

amrell

stores.ebay.com/The-Hot-Mannequin

Member since 2002, Feedback: Turquoise star

As you well know, a size 10 from one manufacturer fits a little differently from a size 10 from another manufacturer. For that reason, simply listing clothing size doesn't provide enough information to a potential buyer. Go the extra step and provide detailed measurements, especially rise, hips, bust, waist, inseam, neck, circumference of the armhole, and so on.

Seller **betty*blackbent** adds that this is particularly important for vintage items, since sizing has changed several times since the 1940s—and people wear different undergarments now as then, as well.

Trick #487: **Include Fabric Content**

jakki01

Member since 2000, Feedback: Purple star

When creating your item description, don't forget to include the item's fabric content. And if it's a stretchable fabric, include both stretched and unstretched measurements, since the amount of stretch can vary a lot.

Trick #488: **Don't Use Dutch Auctions to Offer Color Choices**

bluemagnoliablossoms

Member since 2003, Feedback: Yellow star

If you have a clothing item available in multiple colors, you might think a Dutch auction is the way to go. After all, you have multiple versions of the same item for sale, right? Well, using a Dutch auction to sell different-colored items is somewhat problematic. What if all the bidders wanted the same color? You'd be in trouble then; you actually don't have multiples of *each color* available.

In fact, eBay discourages this type of "choice" listing; you're not permitted to list a Dutch auction with a choice of colors unless you can fill the entire quantity in any single color listed. The better approach is to create separate listings for each color. You can then refer to those other auctions in your listing description.

Trick #489: **The More Photos, the Better**

amrell

stores.ebay.com/The-Hot-Mannequin

Member since 2002, Feedback: Turquoise star

Let's face it—clothing is sometimes difficult to describe. Yeah, it might be a black dress or a blue shirt, but words seldom do the item justice. Far better to let a picture tell the story. And if one picture's good, two are better. In other words, include lots of photos in your clothing auctions. And, as discussed in Chapter 10, "How to Display Better Product Photos," put your clothing on a mannequin or display dummy to better show how it might look on the buyer.

Trick #490: **Start at 10% of Retail—Relist at 5%**

bombprices

Member since 2002, Feedback: Turquoise star

How you initially price your clothing is important, because this is certainly a category where buyers are looking for real bargains. When you're selling new-with-tag clothing, seller **bombprices** advises you start your auctions at 10% of the original retail price. (Other sellers say you can go up to 30%; it no doubt depends on the item and condition.) If your item doesn't sell first time out, cut the relisting price in half—to 5% of retail.

Trick #491: **Embellish the Clothing for Higher Prices**

milehiauctionaction

Member since 2000, Feedback: Turquoise star

Here's a neat trick, especially when you're reselling used clothing found at thrift stores or yard sales. Take the basic item and embellish it—add painted designs on sleeves or lapels, or sew-on or iron-on transfer designs, or add a bit of lace or crocheting or beading. (This is especially effective on children's clothing and accessories.) A little embellishment like this makes your items appear more special, and will help them sell at "boutique" prices.

Art

Selling original artwork is a unique experience. eBay isn't really an art gallery, which is what makes the process difficult. Still, many experienced artist/sellers make a good living selling their wares via eBay auctions, so read on and see what they advise.

Trick #492: **List Smaller Pieces Along with Featured Pieces**

artchick48

stores.ebay.com/Lee-Smith-Art

www.leesmithart.com

Member since 2001, Feedback: Turquoise star

Larger art sellers can take advantage of a bit of cross-selling by listing alternative pieces to their main pieces. That way, if a buyer doesn't have the room or money for a big piece, you have some alternatives. Here's what **artchick48** does:

Next time you list a big one featured, try to have some smaller, less expensive pieces; maybe open a store when you get a chance. Then you can use the subtitle line to direct buyers to a specific painting or group of paintings in your store.

Trick #493: **Include a Letter of Authenticity**

quiltworks

Member since 1999, Feedback: Turquoise star

Here's something that adds value to the items you sell. When you ship your item, include a letter of authenticity. This tells the buyer that your art will become more valuable over time—which it just might!

Trick #494: **Use Your About Me Page as an Online Art Gallery**

artchick48

stores.ebay.com/Lee-Smith-Art

www.leesmithart.com

Member since 2001, Feedback: Turquoise star

Even if you only sell one piece at a time, you can give potential buyers a feel for style by displaying your other art on your eBay About Me page. Here's what **artchick48** recommends:

You also need to go ahead and set up an eBay About Me page. Add information about yourself and your art; you can even post a few photo examples of your work, put a link to your website, etc.

Trick #495: **You're Only Selling the Artwork—Not Reproduction Rights**

flyinggirlart

stores.ebay.com/FlyingGirl-Images

www.flyinggirl.com

Member since 2003, Feedback: Purple star

Here's something important to remember. When you sell your art, you're only selling that particular piece of work—you still retain copyright and all reproduction rights. That means someone can't buy your painting and then use it to create T-shirts for sale, for example. This is important enough to note in your listing's TOS, as **flyinggirlart** notes:

I post in all of my auctions that buyers are bidding only on the artwork itself, and that all rights to reproduce the image in any form remain with me.

Trick #496: **Supplement Your eBay Sales by Listing with ArtByUs**

tinacampbell56

Member since 2003, Feedback: Turquoise star

Given eBay's low sell-through rates for original artwork, many artists are supplementing their eBay listings by listing with ArtByUs (www.artbyus.com). As you can see in Figure 16.2, ArtByUs is an online marketplace for self-representing artists; it's like an eBay auction that specializes exclusively on original artwork. Here's what **tinacampbell56** found:

> *I personally have sold three paintings on ABU, so there are things selling there. Not a lot, but for a new place it's not too bad, considering it's free to list. I sold a painting there last week and it had more views than my eBay auctions for the entire month. I still think eBay is a pretty good place to list, I just want to spread out a bit.*

FIGURE 16.2

An alternative to eBay just for artists—ArtByUs.

What many artists like is that ArtByUs charges no listing fees and no final value fees. They do charge for listing enhancements, such as Featured and Bold. Obviously, their volume isn't nearly as large as eBay's; on the day I checked, they had just a little more than 1,700 items listed. That's not necessarily a bad thing—with less direct competition, your item stands out more than it does in the crowded eBay marketplace.

Books

You wouldn't think selling books would be that tricky, but you'd be surprised. There are a lot of both casual sellers and professional booksellers selling on eBay, selling everything from the latest *New York Times* bestseller to rare vintage books. With so many books available, it's tough to make your auctions stand out—and to get the proper value for what you're selling.

Trick #497: **Determine the Book's Value Before You Sell**

> **auctioncreations**
>
> stores.ebay.com/Auction-Creations-Gainesville-TA
>
> PowerSeller
>
> Member since 1998, Feedback: Red star

Books are easy items to look up—even when they're old and out of print. There are a couple of good sites on the Web where you can look up a book's value. In particular, check out Alibris (www.alibris.com) and Abebooks (www.abebooks.com). These are both retailers of rare and used books, and their sites can give you a good idea of the current value of just about any title. For more recent titles, use Amazon.com (www.amazon.com) as a guide.

Trick #498: **Start Bidding at Half the Current Value**

> **auctioncreations**
>
> stores.ebay.com/Auction-Creations-Gainesville-TA
>
> PowerSeller
>
> Member since 1998, Feedback: Red star

Once you determine the current value of a book, you can then decide where you want to set the initial bid price—or, in the case of an eBay Store listing, your Buy It Now price. Seller **auctioncreations** likes to set the first bid at half the current value:

> We try to start opening bids at half the asking prices on [Alibris and Abebooks]. If they don't sell, we adjust the price till they are gone.

If you have a particularly rare book, consider setting a higher bid price. If the book is in questionable condition, go lower.

Trick #499: **Sell Old Books in Lots**

> **lady_gotrocks!**
>
> stores.ebay.com/The-Carat-Farm
>
> PowerSeller
>
> Member since 2002, Feedback: Red star

Sometimes old books are just old books. It might take forever to move an assortment of old books one by one. A better idea in this situation is to sell your books in lots. For example, you could sell a lot of 10 westerns, or 10 mysteries, or 10 cookbooks, or whatever. This is a good strategy when the individual titles have little value on their own.

Trick #500: **Sell by the Theme**

> **satnrose**
>
> PowerSeller
>
> Member since 1998, Feedback: Green star

Bookseller **satnrose** recommends posting multiple book auctions using a single theme. Here's the logic:

> *I've become convinced that when you can line up a group of books on a specific theme and list them all in one day, you build up a critical mass of energy, matter, and interest that improves the marketability of every single book in the group.*

If you go this route, just be sure you include mention of and links to your other auctions in each individual item listing.

Trick #501: **You Don't Have to List the Book Title and Author in the Auction Title**

> **satnrose**
>
> PowerSeller
>
> Member since 1998, Feedback: Green star

Believe it or not, you don't *always* have to include the book's title in the listing title. Nor do you have to include the author's name. You'll sometimes get better results by emphasizing the book's subject rather than it's title. That's particularly the case in many nonfiction categories, where the reader is looking for information on a particular topic, and who the author is doesn't matter that much. Here's what **satnrose** found:

> *My number-one mistake is to try to put the author and the title in the item title when that's not strictly necessary. Sometimes emphasizing the subject ("civil war," etc.) will do the trick. Remember that the main objective [of the title] is to get people to actually look at your item description.*

Trick #502: **Include the Illustrator's Name in the Title**

satnrose

PowerSeller

Member since 1998, Feedback: Green star

That said, oftentimes the illustrator of a book—children's books, especially—has as much if not more drawing power than the writer. (This is also the case when selling comic books, where the artist is often the star.) If this is the case, list the illustrator in the item title, either in addition to or instead of the author's name.

Trick #503: **Include All Bibliographical Information in the Listing Description**

aaana

stores.ebay.com/aaanas-Collectibles-and-Books

Member since 2000, Feedback: Red star

When listing a book for auction, there's a standard set of information you always want to include in the item description. This includes:

- Title
- Author
- Illustrator (if any)
- Publisher
- Publication date
- Edition and printing
- Page count
- Hardbound or softbound
- Condition of book and dust jacket (if any)
- Synopsis of the contents

You should also note if it's a book club edition, or if it has any soil, bumps, handwriting, highlighting, library marks, book store stamps, musty odors, and so on. Fortunately, you should be able to get most if not all of this info from the book itself, or from the Alibris or Abebooks sites.

Trick #504: **Describe the Condition Accurately—but Euphemistically**

lludwig

stores.ebay.com/LLudwig-Books

PowerSeller

Member since 1998, Feedback: Green star

When describing a book's condition, be accurate but not necessarily explicitly so. It's okay to do a little "selling" in your description. As experienced bookseller **lludwig** notes:

The real trick in describing a book's condition is to be accurate enough so that the buyer knows what to expect, but to not be so negative that you scare off the potential purchaser.

That means using euphemisms for certain types of damage. For example, you can describe worn or damaged books as "chipped," "short closed tears," "contents age-toned," "very slightly cornerworn," "minimal rubbing," "sunned," and the like.

Fellow seller **satnrose** goes on to advise against using the words "insect" or "cockroach" or "rodent" when describing vermin damage. Suggested euphemisms include: "spotted," "moth-eaten," "stain spots," "wormholes," and "bookworm damage." Just remember this advice:

"Slightly worn and spotted" covers a multitude of evils…

For that matter, why not accentuate the positive? Describe a book in good condition as "clean and tight" or "gift quality," and point out if there is no writing, highlighting, tears, or stains on the pages. What's good about an item is every bit as important as any defects.

Trick #505: **Use Readerware to Catalog Your Inventory**

chain_man

stores.ebay.com/Chain-Man-Books

Member since 2002, Feedback: Red star

When you have a huge inventory of books to sell, you need help in managing that inventory. High-volume seller **chain_man** recommends the use of the Readerware (www.readerware.com) software program, designed especially for booksellers and collectors:

When I first get some new books, I use Readerware to catalog them and hold inventory. I use a scanner to get the ISBN, which Readerware uses to do a lookup to find a multitude of each book's characteristics. Most valuable of these is a description and/or reviews of the book. I can enter the cost (to me) of the book, where I got it, where I'm storing it, the condition, the quantity, the category (which are remarkably similar to my eBay Store categories), and so on into the Readerware form.

By the way, Readerware also offers similar software for cataloging and inventorying CDs, DVDS, and videotapes.

Trick #506: **Skip eBay and Sell on Another Site**

> **rac**
> Member since 1998, Feedback: Yellow star

As good as eBay is, it might not be the best place to sell a large inventory of used books. Many sellers have found better success by signing up to sell their used books on Amazon.com or on eBay's Half.com. Both marketplaces are ideal for selling books, Amazon especially.

You can learn more about Amazon.com and Half.com in Chapter 17, "Turning Your eBay Sales Into a Real Business." Jump ahead if you're interested.

Trick #507: **Trade Titles on PaperBackSwap.com**

> **torreyphilemon**
> PowerSeller
> Member since 1999, Feedback: Red star

Here's another great way to move books that aren't selling on eBay. PaperBackSwap.com (www.paperbackswap.com), shown in Figure 16.3, lets you trade in your old books for other books of your choice. It's better than throwing the slow sellers away!

FIGURE 16.3

Trade in your slow-selling books at PaperBackSwap.com.

Automobiles

We'll end this chapter with a few words of advice for selling items on that most unique part of the eBay site, eBay Motors, courtesy of auto seller **mainedog70**.

Trick #508: **Include Lots of Photos**

> **mainedog70**
>
> PowerSeller
>
> Member since 2001, Feedback: Turquoise star

It's daunting to purchase an expensive car when you're not there in person to kick the tires. Make the process easier for potential buyers by taking and displaying lots and lots of pictures. As **mainedog70** recommends:

eBay lets you use up to 12 photos. Take advantage of that. I usually take shots of the exterior from the side, front, back, and various corners; interior shots of the front and rear seats; a dash shot; an engine shot; and close-ups of any dents or problems. If you are expecting someone to buy a car sight unseen, make sure that they know what it looks like!

Trick #509: **Point Out All Flaws or Problems**

mainedog70

PowerSeller

Member since 2001, Feedback: Turquoise star

It's always good advice to point out any flaws or blemishes on any item you sell, but it's particularly important when selling something as big and expensive as a car. And, as we all know, just about every used car has some sort of imperfection, be it a small ding or a misfiring motor. Again, let's listen to the advice of auto salesman **mainedog70**:

Be positive in your description and photos, but be accurate. A buyer/bidder will find out eventually, and being upfront from the beginning makes the whole process go much easier. You are likely selling a used car, not a new one, and imperfections are expected. If there is a hole in the carpet or if the air conditioning doesn't work, let the bidder know. Being honest about the negatives also makes your positives more believable.

Just think of what you'd like to know before you would buy a car sight unseen from a stranger living half a continent away. Do whatever would make you more comfortable in the same situation!

Turning Your eBay Sales Into a Real Business

Once you've gotten your feet wet selling all those odds and ends from your garage or basement, you might want to take the next step and turn your eBay hobby into a full- or part-time business. People do it all the time; running an eBay business is a great way to supplement your normal income, or (when your business becomes larger) it can become your sole source of revenue.

The difference between selling as a hobby and selling as a business is one of volume and of intent. The volume is self-explanatory; the more merchandise you sell, the greater your income. The intent is quite another thing—it's all about purchasing merchandise with the intention of reselling it online.

Many of the eBay Masters make a good living from running their own eBay businesses. Read on to learn what advice they have for prospective eBay businessmen and -women.

Launching Your eBay Business

Sell enough items and you start generating real money. Hundreds of thousands of eBay members make enough revenue from their eBay sales to quit their day jobs. These folks are running real, honest-to-goodness eBay businesses, from the comfort of their own homes.

Of course, it's a little easier when you walk in the steps of the eBay Masters. Read on to learn some of their eBay business tricks.

Trick #510: **Bone Up on Business Basics**

> **bobbibopstuff**
>
> stores.ebay.com/BobbiBopStuff
>
> www.bobbibopstuff.com
>
> PowerSeller
>
> Member since 1998, Feedback: Red star

If you want to get into serious selling, you have to know what you're doing. Too many would-be eBay sellers are hopelessly naïve about business basics and end up getting in way over their heads when sales pick up. Bottom line, an eBay business is a business, so the more you know about business basics, the better prepared you'll be.

What kinds of stuff am I talking about? Here's what eBay seller **bobbibopstuff** recommends:

> In addition to your research on things to sell and ways to sell them, read up on general business, accounting or bookkeeping, advertising or marketing, office administration, warehousing…that's plenty. Read these not to learn how to do any of this on eBay, but to give yourself a grounding in basic business practices.

The smarter you are about business, the easier it will be to manage your eBay business. Do your homework!

And now's probably as good a time as any to plug my companion book, *Making a Living from Your eBay Business* (Que, 2005). It's a good place to start learning about how to run a real business.

Trick #511: **Write a Business Plan**

> **cubbiegirlauctions**
>
> Member since 2004, Feedback: Red star

Once you've boned up on business basics, the next thing you need to do is write a business plan. Yeah, I know it sounds like a lot of work, but running a (successful) business *is* a lot of work. A solid business plan puts down in writing what you intend to do, how you intend to do it, and how successful you'd like to be. It's like a roadmap to your business' future, complete with projected costs and revenues. Follow the business plan, and you'll know what you're supposed to be doing— and how.

A good business plan consists of six separate sections:

- **Mission**—why you're doing what you're doing
- **Opportunity**—the dynamics of the particular market you're pursuing
- **Strategy**—what you intend to sell, and for how much
- **Organization and operations**—the structure of your operation
- **Strengths and weaknesses**—what you're good at, and what challenges you face
- **Financials**—projected sales and expenses, on a month-by-month basis, for at least the first 12 months

Each section can be as short or as long as necessary. The whole point is to sit down and think everything through before you dive in. The more thought you give it, the better prepared you'll be for whatever happens. Running a business isn't for amateurs!

Oh, and while we're at it, I might as well plug another one of my books that you might find useful. *Teach Yourself Business Plans in 24 Hours* (Alpha Books, 2001) is a guide to creating very detailed business plans for all types of businesses. Check it out.

Trick #512: **Set Definable Goals**

New Trick

kyderbyfan

PowerSeller

Member since 1998, Feedback: Red star

Running a business is a serious thing. As part of developing your business plan, you should set out the goals for your business. These should be definable (and hopefully achievable) financial targets against which you can measure your actual performance.

For example, you might say that within the first 12 months, you want to be generating $10,000 a month in sales, or $5,000 a month in profits, or averaging 100 closed auctions a week, or something similar. Then, when the 12 months are up, you can write yourself a report card and see whether you've achieved those goals you set.

Here's what **kyderbyfan** recommends:

> It is important to set and track goals for your eBay sales. Sellers may have time constraints, financial goals, or other factors that may influence those goals, so each person will have to determine a realistic goal based on their own situation. By setting goals, one can evaluate his or her sales and learn what is working and what is not and make changes accordingly. Try to capitalize on the things that are working well for you, and then try to manage your time more profitably.

Trick #513: **Factor in All Your Costs**

ghsproducts

stores.ebay.com/GHSProducts

Member since 1998, Feedback: Purple star

When you're working on your projected profit and loss statement, make sure you factor in *all* the costs of running your eBay business. That includes the actual cost of merchandise you'll be selling, all your eBay fees (including anticipated PayPal fees), the costs of packaging materials (including tape and labels), shipping costs, and any other unavoidable expenses. Factor in all these costs and then apply an appropriate markup.

And don't complain about those eBay and PayPal costs. I hear a lot of sellers gripe about the five points (or more) they end up paying to the powers that be, but I can't sympathize. eBay is like your landlord, and you have to pay your rent to put up your storefront. (And PayPal costs are comparable to what you'd pay to any bank to open a merchant credit card account.) As seller **ghsproducts** notes, these costs are just part of the deal:

> As for eBay fees, it is a cost of doing business. If you don't see the value then don't sell through that channel.

Accept eBay's fees for what they are, and factor them into your business plan.

Trick #514: **Get the Proper Paperwork**

trapperjohn2000

stores.ebay.com/Molehill-Group-Store

Member since 1998, Feedback: Purple Star

If you're running a legitimate business, you have certain legal obligations. These obligations include registering with the state and federal authorities, paying income tax, collecting sales tax (on in-state sales), and the like.

To find out what you need to do to legally launch a new business, contact your state department of commerce. Most states provide some sort of starter package that shows you what you need, and how to get it. At the very least you'll need a business license and a sales permit or resale certificate (so you can purchase goods wholesale), and maybe (if you've formed a corporation) state and federal tax ID numbers.

For a state-by-state list of where to obtain this information, check out the Where to Obtain Business Licenses page on the Small Business Association website (www.sba.gov/hotlist/license.html).

Trick #515: **Keep Your Expenses Low**

trapperjohn2000

stores.ebay.com/Molehill-Group-Store

Member since 1998, Feedback: Purple Star

When you're first starting your eBay business, you want to keep your expense base as low as possible. The lower your expense base, the less money you have to generate to cover your costs. Don't make any large investments; work with what you have. That means working from home, not renting any additional office or warehouse space, using the materials you have at hand (including your existing computer and printer), and so on.

Trick #516: **Don't Invest a Lot in Inventory—Yet**

trapperjohn2000

stores.ebay.com/Molehill-Group-Store

Member since 1998, Feedback: Purple Star

Along the same lines, it's advisable to work with as little inventory as possible. Until you see how sales shake out, you don't want to invest a lot in inventory. Be cautious about what—and how much—you stock. There's no need to order a six-month supply of merchandise; go with what you think you'll sell through in a week or two. You don't want to get stuck with a lot of unsold inventory if things don't work out, nor do you need to make that kind of investment upfront.

In other words, go slow with the inventory until you get your business up to speed.

Trick #517: **Don't Expect Immediate Success**

| **aacsautographs** |
| stores.ebay.com/AACS-Autographs |
| PowerSeller |
| Member since 1997, Feedback: Yellow shooting star |

Many eager eBay sellers launch their businesses and expect immediate success. I'm sorry, folks, but that's not the way it generally works. Success—in the form of sustained profits—comes only with time and hard work. It's unlikely that your eBay business will be profitable in its first month of operation. It might take several months, or even years, before it starts paying for itself.

Learn from the experience of **aacsautographs**, now a profitable PowerSeller, but in the beginning just another struggling eBayer:

> *In my opinion, the number-one thing you need is patience. We've helped many people start their own eBay businesses and very, very few follow through. Regardless of how much I stress the importance of patience, everyone thinks they'll be different— that is, they think their business will immediately be successful. We took no income from our business for the first couple of years. My wife and I put in very long hours into our business while also working other jobs (I was a high school teacher and basketball coach, and my wife was a secretary). Any money we made on the business went right back into it for the first couple of years.*

With this in mind, make sure you plan accordingly. Work your budget so that your sales start small and then grow over time. As long as you don't plan for immediate profitability, you'll be okay. After all, you're in this for the long haul—right?

Different Types of eBay Businesses

When you're contemplating launching an eBay business, you have one big question to answer: What type of business do you want to run? There are several different types of eBay businesses out there; let's look at each in turn, and what's involved with getting them off the ground.

Trick #518: **Become a Second-Hand Reseller**

| **clact** |
| stores.ebay.com/Once-Upon-A-Bid |
| PowerSeller |
| Member since 2002, Feedback: Red star |

The most common type of eBay business is what I'll call the second-hand reseller. This is, as the name suggests, an eBay seller who buys and sells second-hand merchandise. As a second-hand reseller, you don't sell new merchandise, you don't purchase large lots of closeout items, you don't necessarily specialize in a particular category of collectibles. You sell the kind of stuff that people have lying around the house, cluttering the garage or basement. Some people might call it junk, but to savvy sellers, it's a potential goldmine.

The nice thing about starting a second-hand reseller business is that it's an easy transition from how you're probably currently selling on eBay. Selling old stuff you find lying around the house is how a lot of big-time eBay sellers got started, and it's actually a great way to learn the ropes. Sell a few dozen items like this, and you'll get a good idea of how eBay selling works. You'll gain valuable experience in preparing items for auction, in creating auction listings, in managing the auction process, and in packing and shipping. You might even get the opportunity to deal with a persnickety buyer or two; unpleasant as this may be, it's great training for when you have to provide customer service on a larger scale.

In fact, the only difference between the occasional junk seller and the full-time second-hand reseller is volume. The more stuff you find to sell, the closer you move toward becoming a real eBay business.

Trick #519: **Become a Bulk Reseller**

rosachs

stores.ebay.com/My-Discount-Shoe-Store

PowerSeller

Member since 1997, Feedback: Red star

Reselling lots of onesies and twosies can be profitable, but it's certainly a labor-intensive model. You're always on the search for something new to sell, and you're always reinventing the wheel.

That's why many sellers prefer selling large quantities of a single item to selling small quantities of multiple items. Instead of buying one shirt to resell, you buy 100 or 1,000 shirts—and thus sell 100 or 1,000 units of the same item. In many ways, this is a more efficient business model because you can build your business around a single type of item. You can take one photograph and reuse it in hundreds of item listings, you have to stock only one type of box, and you'll always know what your shipping costs will be. Being a bulk reseller might lack variety, but it makes up for that variety in consistency.

Of course, when you want to sell large quantities of a single item, you have to buy large quantities of a single item. This requires buying in bulk, so you can have enough inventory to last for several weeks' or months' worth of auctions. If you want to become a bulk reseller, you need to check out the closeout and liquidation websites listed in Chapter 6, "How to Find Merchandise to Sell."

Know also that this type of eBay business can be tad risky, because of the large quantities you have to deal with. After all, you're not just buying a dozen jeans, you're taking a dozen dozen (a lot of 144 pairs of jeans), or more. Even if you get the merchandise extra-cheap, that's still a large check you have to write. And, even more challenging, you have to find someplace to store all that merchandise until you sell it—*if* you sell it, of course.

Trick #520: **Sell New Merchandise**

> **bobbibopstuff**
> stores.ebay.com/BobbiBopStuff
> www.bobbibopstuff.com
> PowerSeller
> Member since 1998, Feedback: Red star

eBay has a reputation as a resale marketplace, a great place to buy and sell collectibles and used merchandise. But eBay is also a great place to sell new merchandise, as an officially authorized reseller.

In this business model, you buy merchandise direct from the manufacturer or authorized distributor, just as a traditional bricks-and-mortar retailer does. (In fact, if you're already a bricks-and-mortar reseller looking to branch out online, this model is perfect for you.) You need to establish an official selling relationship with the supplier, which then enables you to sell that supplier's products online. That is, you have to become an authorized dealer, which might mean signing some sort of dealer agreement, agreeing to meet various terms of sale and distribution, and sometimes agreeing to meet specified sales targets. In other cases, becoming an authorized dealer is no more involved than placing an order. How you become a dealer all depends; every supplier does it a little differently.

Where do you find the new merchandise to sell? That's always a challenge, but the wholesaler websites listed in Chapter 6 are good starting points. Once you get set up, it's a simple matter of listing the items you're authorized to sell in your eBay auctions—and in your eBay Store.

Trick #521: **Launch a Collectibles Business**

bushellcollectibles
stores.ebay.com/Bushells-Collectibles
Member since 1999, Feedback: Red star

For many eBay sellers, their businesses began as an offshoot of a hobby. If you're a collector, chances are whatever you collect is actively bought and sold on eBay. And anywhere there's buying and selling, there's a business opportunity!

What kinds of things do people trade on eBay? Just about anything imaginable, from antiques to vintage clothing to comic books to HO trains to political buttons to sports cards to glass milk bottles to Hummel figurines to plastic model kits to pocket watches to Barbie dolls to…well, you get the picture. Just as there are numerous brick-and-mortar stores that specialize in various types of collectibles, there are also many eBay businesses that are collectibles-based.

The step from hobby to business is a matter of setting up yourself to sell the things you collect, and then doing that selling in volume. If you're a serious collector, you're probably already using eBay to purchase items for your collection—it's the world's largest marketplace for collectible items. Well, if you can buy collectibles, you can sell them, too. And there's your business model.

Naturally, running a collecting/trading business is slightly different from simply collecting as a hobby. You need to feed your sales by buying new collectibles on a consistent basis; you need to set up an assembly line to photograph, list, pack, and ship the items you list for sale; and you need to manage your hobby like a business, keeping track of sales and expenses and worrying about taxes and the like. But all that probably won't take much more work than what you're already expending on your hobby. You're just going pro, is all.

Trick #522: **Sell Your Own Crafts and Artwork**

artchick48
stores.ebay.com/Lee-Smith-Art
www.leesmithart.com
Member since 2001, Feedback: Turquoise star

Figuring out what kind of eBay business to run is easy if you're an artist or make your own crafts. Many artists and craftspeople have found eBay to be an essential channel for selling their works. Before eBay, you were limited to local arts and crafts fairs and the occasional gallery showing. With eBay you can sell your work 365 days a year and help generate a more steady and consistent income. Plus, your work gets exposure across the entire country (and around the world, if you like), which dramatically broadens your audience. And the more people who see your work, the better.

Seller **artchick48** offers the following advice to artists looking to sell their works on eBay:

> *Research eBay to see if there's a market for your style of work. Have reasonable expectations according to your circumstances: family obligations, style, medium, and preferred method of working. Some artists may use "formula" or assembly-line methods to produce high volume, or paint 16 hours a day to list 10 to 25 originals per week. Others who have just a few hours a day to create or spend weeks on one work may want to offer prints. As your sales increase, hire out the tedious tasks, the paperwork, accounting, photos, listings, packing, and shipping. The main thing is to be flexible, have patience, and most of all, continue to market your work in other venues.*

Trick #523: **Launch a Trading Assistant Business**

New Trick

> **raeosenbaugh**
>
> stores.ebay.com/OLD-BOOKS-NEW-BOOKS
>
> Member since 2001, Feedback: Red star

One of the easiest types of eBay businesses to launch is a consignment business—that is, becoming an eBay Trading Assistant. The part and parcel of consignment selling is that you're selling someone else's merchandise. The owner contracts with you to manage the entire auction process, which you proceed to do. You take possession of the merchandise, research it, photograph it, write up an item description, and create and launch the auction listing. You manage the auction and collect the buyer's payment when it sells; then you pack it and ship it out to the buyer. You also pay all applicable eBay fees (although you pass them on to the client as part of your fees to him). Your client, the owner of the merchandise, doesn't have to do a thing.

One of the great things about becoming a Trading Assistant is that you probably won't have much in the way of start-up costs. This is because you're already selling on eBay; the items you sell on consignment can piggyback on your existing activity and processes. (It's different if you decide to open a storefront drop-off location, of course; we'll talk about that later in this chapter.)

Here's what seller **raeosenbaugh** says about it:

An eBay consignment business is the perfect add-on business. With your computer, a digital camera, and the knowledge you already have, you will be able to make a little extra over what you already make on eBay. Because you don't need a store, you can set your own hours. You can work at night, or in the afternoon. Work whenever you want. With eBay consignments you can start your business selling other people's stuff. You won't need to risk your own money buying things, hoping to sell them for a profit.

The consignment selling model is becoming so popular that I've devoted an entire chapter of this book to it. Turn to Chapter 19, "How to Make Money as a Trading Assistant," to learn more.

Discovering Other Ways to Sell

Experienced eBay sellers know that eBay isn't the only game in town. If you have merchandise to sell, a simple eBay auction is a good venue, but there might be other ways—and other places—to sell what you have to sell. Read on to learn how the eBay Masters maximize their online sales.

Trick #524: **Open an eBay Store**

smallseeds

stores.ebay.com/Small-Seeds

PowerSeller

Member since 2000, Feedback: Purple star

One way to sell more merchandise is to drive your auction buyers to an eBay Store, where you have even more stuff for sale. We'll talk a lot more about eBay Stores in Chapter 18, "How to Sell More Products in an eBay Store," so turn there if you think this sounds like a good idea.

Trick #525: **Use eBay's Want It Now Feature**

New Trick

trapperjohn2000

stores.ebay.com/Molehill-Group-Store

Member since 1998, Feedback: Purple Star

Another way to bypass the auction process is to go directly to buyers who want to buy what you have for sale. You can do this with eBay's Want It Now feature, where buyers create "wish lists" of specific items. You search the Want It Now listings, and when you find a match, you offer the item for sale to the interested buyer. (eBay still takes their normal cut, of course.)

Start by clicking the Want It Now link on eBay's home page. When the Want It Now page appears, as shown in Figure 17.1, you can browse through the listings by category, or use the Sellers search box to search for specific items that might be listed in the database. Click a particular listing for more detail from the interested buyer, like that shown in Figure 17.2.

To respond to a request, click the Respond button to display the Respond to a Post with a Listing page. If you already have an item listed, enter the item number and click the Respond to a Post button. If you haven't yet listed the item, click the Sell Your Item button, create an item listing, and then return to the Respond to a Post with a Listing page to enter the listing's item number.

The interested buyer is now emailed a message containing a link to your item listing. To place a bid on your item, all the recipient has to do is click a button—and you've just made a sale!

FIGURE 17.1

Looking for prospective buyers with Want It Now.

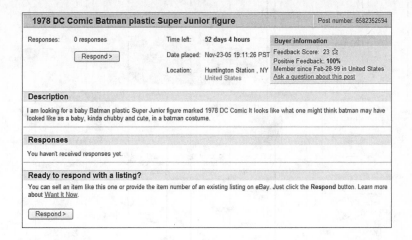

FIGURE 17.2

A hopeful buyer's Want It Now ad.

Trick #526: **Sell on Half.com**

New Trick

photoforyoustore

stores.ebay.com/Photo-For-You

Member since 2000, Feedback: Purple star

If you're tired of the auction grind—and sell items that are more suitable to the fixed-price format—consider selling at a site that specializes in this type of merchandise. eBay runs such a site, called Half.com (half.ebay.com). Half.com is devoted to fixed-price sales of books, CDs, DVDs, and similar products, kind of an eBay Stores without the storefronts. Any user can list merchandise for sale, on a "good til sold" basis. As you can see in Figure 17.3, the Half.com home page looks a little like the Amazon home page, for what it's worth. (We'll also discuss Amazon in the next trick, in case you're interested.)

You list an item for sale on Half.com by using the item's UPC or ISBN code. Half.com then inserts prefilled item information from a massive product database. (It's the same database that feeds eBay's prefilled information in the same categories.) There are no fees for listing an item (yay!), but you do have to pay Half.com a commission when an item sells. You'll pay a 15% commission on items under $50, and lower commissions as the price rises. Instead of a buyer paying you directly, it's Half.com that collects the payment; the site sends you a check for funds due every two weeks.

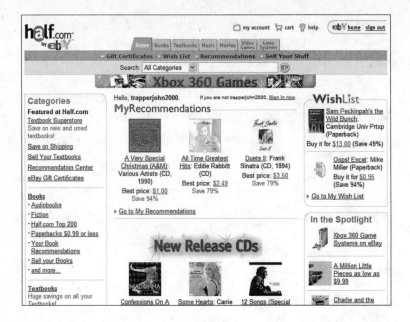

FIGURE 17.3

eBay's Half.com—a fixed-price merchandise.

Many sellers like Half.com for those products that have market demand but won't necessarily sell in the normal seven-day auction period. Here's what **photoforyou-store** does:

> *I often list books, textbooks, CDs, and so on at Half.com because they can remain there until they sell—Half.com doesn't charge their fees until the item sells.*

Trick #527: **Sell in the Amazon Marketplace**

trapperjohn2000

stores.ebay.com/Molehill-Group-Store

Member since 1998, Feedback: Purple star

Another popular fixed-price sales site is one that you're no doubt already familiar with—Amazon.com. That's right, Amazon isn't just a retailer; it also provides a marketplace for fixed-price sales, similar to what Half.com offers.

The Amazon Marketplace lets individuals and small businesses sell all manner of new and used items; it's particularly well-suited to selling used books, CDs, video-tapes, and DVDs (although you're not limited to just these items). Marketplace items are listed as options on Amazon's normal product listing pages, to the right of the main listing, as shown in Figure 17.4. These are the links that pop up when you choose to buy a used item from Amazon; Figure 17.5 shows a typical listing of Marketplace items for sale.

FIGURE 17.4

Another way to sell your stuff, at Amazon.com.

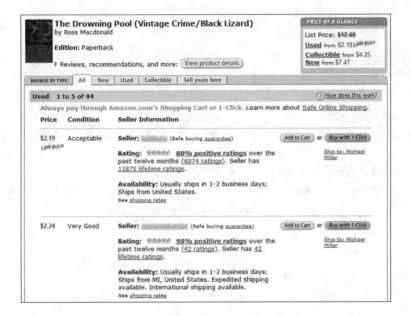

FIGURE 17.5

A list of Marketplace items for sale at Amazon.com.

One nice thing about selling in the Amazon Marketplace is that your customers can integrate their orders and payments with other Amazon merchandise. Customers place their orders with and pay Amazon, then Amazon informs you of the sale and transfers payment (less their fees and plus a reimbursement for shipping costs) to you. You ship the item to the customer.

Cost-wise, it isn't all that different from how eBay works. You pay 99 cents to list an item in the Marketplace (although the fee isn't charged until the item sells), then pay Amazon a percent of the final selling price. (You pay a 6% fee for computers, 8% for electronics and cameras, 10% for items in the Everything Else store, and 15% for all other items.) Each listing lasts for 60 days. To learn more or place a listing, click the Marketplace link on the bottom left side of the Amazon home page (www.amazon.com), in the Make Money section.

Which is the best fixed-price marketplace—Amazon.com or Half.com? Different sellers swear by both. I suggest you experiment with each one to see which works best for you.

Trick #528: **Use Another Online Auction Site**

> **trapperjohn2000**
>
> stores.ebay.com/Molehill-Group-Store
>
> Member since 1998, Feedback: Purple star

As I was writing this chapter, a number of eBay Masters recommended a variety of alternatives to eBay. Since many eBayers tend to grumble about eBay's fees, you'll be interested to note that most of these online auction sites charge lower fees than eBay does; some even let you list for free.

Here are just a few of the most frequently-mentioned sites:

- Amazon.com Auctions (auctions.amazon.com)
- BidVille (www.bidville.com)
- iOffer (www.ioffer.com)
- whaBAM! (www.whabam.com)
- Yahoo! Auctions (auctions.yahoo.com)

For example, Yahoo! Auctions (shown in Figure 17.6), which used to charge lower-than-eBay fees, is now completely free to buyers and sellers. (It still costs to accept PayPal payments, however.) Note, however, that none of these sites are as big as eBay, so traffic levels won't be nearly as great. Which leads us to our next trick…

FIGURE 17.6

A free alternative to eBay—Yahoo! Auctions.

Trick #529: **Open an Alternative Auction Storefront**

trapperjohn2000

stores.ebay.com/Molehill-Group-Store

Member since 1998, Feedback: Purple star

Several of the big third-party auction services sites offer prepackaged web storefronts you can use to sell additional merchandise. Most of these sites insert a link in your eBay listings that leads to a gallery of your listings; the gallery then leads the potential buyer to items for sale on your standalone site. Also, at auction close, the buyer is sent a checkout link that leads the buyer to your standalone site to complete the transaction. This provides another opportunity to sell additional items to the buyer.

The advantage of using a prepackaged storefront over a true freestanding online store is that all the hard work is done for you; all you have to do to put your storefront together is fill out the appropriate forms. You also make more money per item with your own storefront because you don't have eBay taking their cut off the top. In addition, many third-party providers also link to the Amazon Marketplace and Yahoo! Stores and submit your inventory to price-shopping engines such as Shopping.com and BizRate.

The disadvantage of a prepackaged storefront is that, in many cases, it's not really *your* storefront. As with launching an eBay Store, there aren't a lot of customization options, and you often have to settle for a somewhat generic look and feel.

All that said, these are fairly popular alternatives to using the eBay Stores program. Costs are all over the place, running anywhere from $10/month to more than $50/month for a basic storefront, plus some sort of percentage of the final sales price. Features and services vary considerably between sites, as well. With that in mind, here are some of the more popular of these services:

- Ándale Stores (www.andale.com)
- ChannelAdvisor Merchant (www.channeladvisor.com)
- Infopia Marketplace Manager (www.infopia.com)
- Marketworks (www.marketworks.com)
- Vendio Store Manager (www.vendio.com)
- Zoovy (www.zoovy.com)

Trick #530: **Open an eBay ProStores Store**

> **trapperjohn2000**
>
> stores.ebay.com/Molehill-Group-Store
>
> Member since 1998, Feedback: Purple Star

I guess eBay got tired of losing business to third-party storefront services, because they recently launched their own prepackaged storefront service, dubbed eBay ProStores. As you can see in Figure 17.7, eBay ProStores offer pretty much the same types of services you find at the third-party sites, including domain hosting, real-time credit card processing, and an e-commerce shopping cart. Costs run from $29.95/month to $249.95/month, with eBay taking an additional 1% of every sale you make. (Current eBay Stores users get a 30% discount off the monthly fees.) Learn more at www.prostores.com.

Open your own non-eBay storefront with eBay ProStores.

Trick #531: **Open a Full-Fledged Online Store**

> **trapperjohn2000**
>
> stores.ebay.com/Molehill-Group-Store
>
> Member since 1998, Feedback: Purple star

Prepackaged storefronts are fine, but if you want a truly full-featured web store you'll need to build your own website, from scratch. This is a lot of work and will cost a lot of money, so it's not for novice or hesitant sellers. But if you're really serious about making a lot of money on the Internet, building your own e-commerce site is the only way to go.

You'll want to start with registering your own web domain, which you can do at Network Solutions (www.networksolutions.com) or other third-party registration sites. Then you'll need to find a web hosting service, and use Microsoft FrontPage or some other web design tool to build your website.

To power your new storefront, you'll need to incorporate special e-commerce software, complete with inventory management, customer shopping cart, and online checkout. Some of the most popular of these storefront programs include

- AbleCommerce (www.ablecommerce.com)
- AutomatedShops (www.automatedshops.com)

- BazaarBuilder (www.bazaarbuilder.com)
- iNETStore Online (www.inetstore.com)
- Miva Merchant (www.miva.com)

You'll also want to sign up for a merchant credit card program, as discussed back in Chapter 12, "How to Handle Customer Payments," and then start promoting your new site. As I said, it's a lot of work—but it's how real retailers do business!

Should you have your own separate non-eBay online store? It depends on your sales and inventory volume and what you hope to accomplish. The bigger you are (and want to be), the more a separate online store makes sense. But keep in mind that a freestanding online store isn't going to generate sales all by itself; you'll need to promote the store to attract traffic and potential customers. That's where an eBay Store shines; you get all of eBay's traffic without having to spend a penny in advertising. Running your own online store requires an advertising budget, and doing whatever you can to attract as many visitors as possible.

Trick #532: **Buy Online, Sell Offline**

> **berties_house_of_horrors**
>
> stores.ebay.com/Berties-Emporium
>
> PowerSeller
>
> Member since 1999, Feedback: Red star

Most eBay sellers buy their merchandise offline and sell online. But why not do the opposite? It's not impossible to buy things lower priced on eBay than you can locally, which would then enable you to resell those items outside of eBay and make a nice profit. This is especially true if you run a brick-and-mortar store in addition to your eBay business. As **berties_house_of_horrors** suggests:

> *You can buy many items on eBay in wholesale or lot quantities, pay one shipping price, and sell for a profit in your local market, as your buyers are not having to pay a shipping cost.*

Trick #533: **The Grass Isn't Always Greener**

> **mgr1969**
>
> Member since 2001, Feedback: Purple star

As much as you might dislike this or that about eBay (including—and especially—the fees), you have to admit that it works, especially when compared with the alternatives. I've heard from lots of sellers who've left eBay for supposedly greener pastures, only to return when they find that the other grass isn't really green at all. Let's face it. eBay has tens of millions of visitors every day, and no other site out there is nearly as busy. The more visitors, the more people you have looking at your auctions—and the more lookers, the more likely you'll be to sell your item, and at a higher price. Go to a site with less traffic, and you'll probably get a lower selling price—if you sell your item at all.

I like how **mgr1969** approaches the situation:

> *There are free or cheap sites out there and we all like to complain about eBay's fees, but look what we're getting for the money: very high traffic on a site that is now a common-usage word in daily conversation. Weird Al writes songs about it, sitcoms make jokes about it, even people who don't own a computer know what eBay is, even if they've never used it. At least some of them are looking for the things I'm selling (I hope), so I really don't mind the fees that much. I still profit. I'd rather pay a fee and sell something than list it for free and sell nothing.*

I get a lot of requests to do radio and newspaper interviews about buying and selling online. All the interviewers want to talk about eBay, because that's what their readers and listeners are interested in. None of them want to talk about other auction sites. None of them. That tell you something?

Of course, none of this means that you shouldn't check out the other auction sites, or that they can't be included as part of your overall marketing mix. In particular, you might want to use these sites to augment your regular eBay listings. But smart sellers go where the volume is, and eBay definitely has the volume.

Managing Your eBay Business

Part and parcel of running an eBay business is managing that business on a daily basis. That means controlling your costs, tracking your sales and revenues, and calculating your profit (or loss). Read on to learn a little about what's involved.

Trick #534: **Control Your Costs**

New Trick

> **photoforyoustore**
> stores.ebay.com/Photo-For-You
> Member since 2000, Feedback: Purple star

One of the keys to running a profitable business is to know precisely how much money you have coming in, as well as how much money you're paying out. With an eBay business, there are lots of costs to keep track of, most of them in the form of various eBay and PayPal fees. And then there are the fees you pay to your shipping service, the cost of boxes and envelopes and packing peanuts, the cost of labels and printer cartridges, and a whole lot more. It's easy to lose track of some of these costs; but even if you neglect to include them when you're thinking about your eBay auctions, you still have to pay them.

Managing your costs is even more important as the eBay market matures. Experienced sellers will tell you that it's tougher to make a sale today than it was a year or two ago, and that average selling prices are declining. eBay is becoming more of a buyer's market than a seller's one, which means that the key to continued profitability is to manage your costs.

Here's how seller **photoforyoustore** describes the situation:

> Sometimes you might think you are making money, when in fact you are losing money. It is fine to lose money on a few items as long as overall you are making a profit. It is also fine to lose money, or break even, when you are trying to get your feedback numbers built up. However, when you reach a certain point, you want to ensure that you are making money on eBay. I see a lot of sellers that have 50–100 items listed and not one sells; that will cost them about $40–$70 in listing fees. In other words, make sure that what you are selling is profitable.

I can't put it any better. Few eBay sellers *aren't* in it for the money; make sure you track your costs as closely as you track your sales.

Trick #535: **Use Microsoft Money**

> **cubbiegirlauctions**
> Member since 2004, Feedback: Red star

Aside from managing your eBay auctions, you also need to manage your money, which means setting up some sort of accounting system. Probably the easiest way to handle the accounting for your eBay sales is to use a personal finance program. One of the most popular of these is Microsoft Money (www.microsoft.com/money/), which many eBayers swear by. If you've recently purchased a new PC you might have a free version of Money preinstalled on your hard drive; unfortunately, this isn't the version of the program you want to use. For your eBay business use, you probably want to upgrade to Microsoft Money Small Business, which offers a number of basic business accounting functions.

Trick #536: **Use Quicken**

> **bayoupizzazz**
>
> stores.ebay.com/Bayou-Pizzazz
>
> www.bayoupizzazz.com
>
> PowerSeller
>
> Member since 2000, Feedback: Red star

Money's chief competitor in the personal finance software business is Quicken (www.quicken.com). The version you want to check out is Quicken Premier Home & Business, which lets you track your business expenses, record assets and liabilities, generate customer invoices, and create basic financial statements. It's a very versatile program, as eBayer **bayoupizzazz** attests:

> *For handling more transactions and a much more powerful tool, Quicken is awesome. I use it for my recordkeeping. I am able to download all my transactions from PayPal into it, plus my business account data online, which includes my eBay fees and expenses. It almost runs itself!*

Trick #537: **Use Quickbooks**

> **amrell**
>
> stores.ebay.com/The-Hot-Mannequin
>
> Member since 2002, Feedback: Turquoise star

If you do a really high volume of eBay sales, a better option might be Quicken's big brother, QuickBooks (www.quickbooks.com). There are a number of versions of QuickBooks—Basic, Pro, Premier, and Enterprise Solutions; for most eBay businesses, Basic is more than good enough.

You can use QuickBooks not only to do your monthly accounting and generate regular financial statements, but also to manage your inventory, track your sales, and do your year-end taxes. QuickBooks even integrates with PayPal, so you can manage all your PayPal sales from within the QuickBooks program.

Intuit also offers a web-based version of QuickBooks, called QuickBooks Online Edition, which you can access from the main QuickBooks website. This Online Edition keeps all your records online, so you can do your accounting from any computer, using nothing more than your web browser. QuickBooks Online Edition isn't quite as robust as the standalone version, which makes it best for those eBay businesses with simpler needs. You'll pay $19.95 per month for this service.

Trick #538: **Get an Accountant**

> **amrell**
>
> stores.ebay.com/The-Hot-Mannequin
>
> Member since 2002, Feedback: Turquoise star

Even if you use an accounting program such as Money, Quicken, or QuickBooks, you still might want to employ the services of a professional accountant—at least to prepare your year-end taxes. That's because an accountant is likely to be more experienced and qualified than you to manage the tax obligations arising from your eBay sales.

Many eBay sellers use their financial software program to generate their monthly financial statements, but then call in an accountant to prepare their quarterly estimated taxes and year-end tax statements. This is a pretty good combination; you can have your program print out just the right data that your accountant will need to prepare your taxes.

Of course, you can also use an accountant to handle *all* your financial activities. This is a particularly good idea if (1) your eBay business is generating a high volume of sales, and (2) you aren't particularly interested in or good at handling the books. You'll pay for this service, of course, but if your business is big enough, it's probably worth it.

How to Sell More Products in an eBay Store

eBay offers high-volume sellers another way to sell their merchandise. The eBay Stores program provides the facsimile of a retail Storefront within the eBay environment where you can sell Buy It Now (fixed-priced) items outside the normal auction process. In essence, you get to run your own little online Store, with very little in the way of upfront costs or effort. Read on to learn how the eBay Masters use their eBay Stores to supplement their normal auction sales.

Benefits of Opening an eBay Store

Why would you want to open your own eBay Store? Well, it certainly isn't for casual sellers; you do have to set up your own web page and keep the Store filled with merchandise week after week. But if you're a high-volume seller who specializes in a single category (or even a handful of categories), there are benefits to opening your own Store. These include being able to sell additional merchandise (through your Store) than what you have listed in your auctions; being able to display a special eBay Stores icon next to all of your auction lists; making more money per sale than with a standard auction (due to lower Store listing fees), and being able to generate repeat business from future sales to current purchasers. Let's see what the eBay Masters think.

Trick #539: **Use Your Store to Park Unsold Auction Items**

clact

stores.ebay.com/Once-Upon-A-Bid

PowerSeller

Member since 2002, Feedback: Red star

An eBay Store is a great place to "park" items that haven't sold in a normal eBay auction. You can leave them in your Store indefinitely, or just hold them there until you're ready to relist them in auction format again. And the best thing is, while the items are parked, they're still for sale!

Trick #540: **Use Your Store to Sell Fixed-Priced Items**

trapperjohn2000

stores.ebay.com/Molehill-Group-Store

Member since 1998, Feedback: Purple star

Opening an eBay Store is an especially good idea if you have a lot of fixed-priced merchandise to sell. You can put items in your eBay Store before you offer them for auction, and thus have more merchandise for sale than you might otherwise. And, since eBay Store insertion fees are lower than auction listing fees, you'll be decreasing your costs by selling direct rather than through an auction.

Speaking of fees, the eBay Store insertion fee is $0.02 per item for a 30-day listing. To list beyond the 30-day period, you pay an additional $0.02 surcharge for each 30 days. (So to list for 90 days, you pay a total of $0.06.)

Trick #541: **Use Your Store to Sell Lower-Priced Items**

chunkypunkys

stores.ebay.com/chunky-punkys-gifts-and-crafts

Member since 1998, Feedback: Red star

Those lower eBay Store insertion fees make it more attractive to sell lower-priced items in your Store rather than in an auction. You can list an item in your Store for 30 days for just $0.02, no matter what the retail price. That's considerably less than eBay's normal auction insertion fee, and while you still have to pay a final value fee (8% for items under $25), this fee structure makes it easier to turn a profit on low-priced items. As eBay Store seller **chunkypunkys** notes:

> I use [my Store] for my lower-ticket items that I don't want to spend the higher listing fees on.

Trick #542: **Use Your Store to Cross-Sell Related Items to Your Auction Winners**

> **trapperjohn2000**
>
> stores.ebay.com/Molehill-Group-Store
>
> Member since 1998, Feedback: Purple star

Another benefit of selling merchandise in an eBay Store is that eBay will automatically advertise items from your Store at the bottom of your item listing, bid-confirmation, and checkout confirmation pages. These "merchandising placements" help you cross-sell additional merchandise to your auction customers—and add-on sales are highly profitable! For example, if you sell videogame consoles in your auction, cross-sell individual games in your Store. If you sell men's shirts in your auctions, cross-sell ties in your Store. If you sell consumer electronics gadgets in your auctions, cross-sell batteries and other accessories in your Store. You get the idea.

Trick #543: **Use Your Store to Push Multiple Sales**

> **clact**
>
> stores.ebay.com/Once-Upon-A-Bid
>
> PowerSeller
>
> Member since 2002, Feedback: Red star

Unlike your normal auctions, where you're selling one item at a time, it's much easier for buyers to shop for multiple items in your eBay Store. You can make it easier for customers by organizing your Store items into categories; all the buyer has to do is click on the category to see all related merchandise. As eBay Store seller **clact** relates:

I just had one buyer purchase 24 or so items from me over two days. Others pur-chased from 2 to 5 items on a regular basis since the Store opened. Before the Store there were rarely any multiple item purchases, because they would have to scroll through all your listings to find what they want.

Trick #544: **Use Your Store to Sell to Losing Bidders**

clact

stores.ebay.com/Once-Upon-A-Bid

PowerSeller

Member since 2002, Feedback: Red star

Here's one you might not have thought of. For every winning bidder you have in one of your auctions, you probably have at least one losing bidder. Why turn away that person's business? After all, you know he's interested in what you were selling. Well, if you have an eBay Store, you can direct your losing bidders to similar items you have for sale in your Store. As **clact** points out, it's a neat way to have your cake and eat it, too:

Occasionally people will ask you, hey I missed your auction, can you list that item again for me? Or maybe they were outbid and want one also. Instead of relisting through the regular auction process, you can put a Buy It Now item in a Store and sell that item with limited eBay fees. You make money that way.

Trick #545: **Move Items from your eBay Store to Regular Auction Listings**

debijane12000

stores.ebay.com/Debijanes-Music-and-More

Member since 2002, Feedback Red star

Okay, you're sold on the idea of using your eBay Store to sell additional items to your normal auction buyers. But what about going the other direction—using tradi-tional eBay auctions to sell items that haven't sold in your Store?

Sometimes you just need to shake things up; moving an item from one type of sale to another can attract new buyers. Here's what **debijane12000** found:

Here's one way to clean store. I frequently take "dead" items that have been sitting in my eBay Store for ages and put them back to auction. Surprisingly, they'll often sell well there.

Setting Up and Managing Your eBay Store

Running an eBay Store is a little different from managing eBay auctions. For one thing, you don't have to constantly post new listings. You also don't have to worry about all your items ending at the same time. Read on to learn how the eBay Masters do it.

Trick #546: **Sign Up for the Right Store Plan**

> **trapperjohn2000**
>
> stores.ebay.com/Molehill-Group-Store
>
> Member since 1998, Feedback: Purple star

Opening your own eBay Store is as easy as going to stores.ebay.com and clicking through the setup pages. There's nothing overly complex involved; you'll need to create your Store, customize your pages (otherwise known as your virtual Storefront), and list the items you want to sell.

One thing you have to do, however, is choose which type of eBay Store you want. eBay offers three levels of Storefronts, as noted in Table 18.1:

Table 18.1　**eBay Store Levels**

Level	Fee	Features
Basic	$15.95/month	Store listed in every category directory where you have items listed; position based on number of items listed; receive monthly Store reports; free subscription to eBay Selling Manager; the ability to cross-sell products on view item pages; the option of sending 100 email marketing messages a month; and you can create five customizable pages
Featured	$49.95/month	All features of Basic, plus Store rotated through a special featured section on the eBay Stores home page; Store receives priority placement in Related Stores section of search and listings pages; Store featured within the top-level category pages where you have items listed; you receive more detailed monthly reports; you can create 10 customizable pages; free subscription to Selling Manager Pro; the option of sending 1,000 email marketing messages a month; and you receive a $30 credit to spend on the eBay Keyword program

continues

Table 18.1 **Continued**

Level	Fee	Features
Anchor	$499.95/month	All features of Featured, plus premium placement in Related Stores section of search and listings pages; your Store logo will rotate through category directory pages (1 million impressions); the option of sending 4,000 email marketing messages a month; you can create 15 customizable pages; and you get dedicated 24-hour live customer support

My recommendation is to start with the Basic level and see how it goes. Even as your business increases, you might find that the slight additional features of the Featured and Anchor categories aren't worth the additional costs—or maybe they are. Your choice.

Trick #547: **Create a Custom Storefront Page**

chunkypunkys

stores.ebay.com/chunky-punkys-gifts-and-crafts

Member since 1998, Feedback: Red star

A default eBay Store page looks a little bland—kind of like an enhanced list of auction listings. You can, however, choose to customize your Storefront page, adding your own logo, graphics, and so on. And the more you customize your page, the more you establish your Store's brand identity.

For example, Figure 18.1 shows the eBay Storefront of **Chunky Punky's Gifts and Crafts** (stores.ebay.com/chunky-punkys-gifts-and-crafts). Note the use of the distinctive logo/graphic and a cool teal/green color scheme (which you can't see in this black and white book, I know). Contrast this with the **Pins-n-Needle's Sewing Emporium** (stores.ebay.com/Pins-n-Needles-Sewing-Emporium) Storefront, shown in Figure 18.2. They're both eBay Stores, but they're able to establish their own individual identities.

To build your custom Storefront page, click the Seller, Manage Store link at the bottom of your Store page, and then select Store Editing/Store Builder/Custom pages. Once there, you can create a new page based on eBay's templates, or use your own HTML to build a page from scratch.

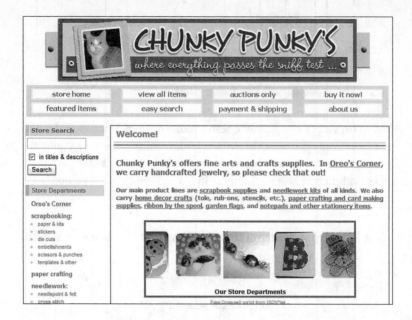

FIGURE 18.1

A typical eBay Store, with custom-designed Storefront page.

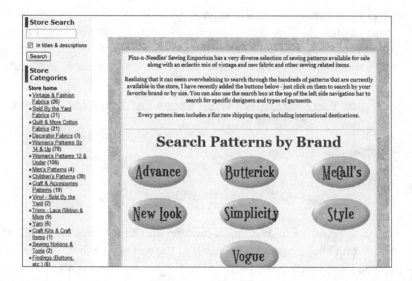

FIGURE 18.2

Another eBay Store, with a different look and feel.

Trick #548: **Make Sure Your Store Is Fully Stocked**

griffin_trader

stores.ebay.com/Naturally-In-New-Orleans-Mardi-Gras

Member since 1999, Feedback: Green star

Having an empty eBay Store doesn't make a lot of sense. To take full advantage of your Storefront, you want to stock it with as many items as you can. The more items for sale, the more you can cross-sell merchandise. It's just like a traditional bricks-and-mortar Store—shoppers like a big selection! If you only have a few items in your Store, you'll miss a lot of sales opportunities.

Trick #549: **Set Multiple Quantities So You Don't Have to Relist When Sold**

pins-n-needles

stores.ebay.com/Pins-n-Needles-Sewing-Emporium

www.ditzyprints.com

Member since 2000, Feedback: Red star

Here's an interesting trick. If you have multiple quantities of the same item, don't create multiple listings within your Store—not only will you have to pay a listing fee for each item, you'll also have to do a relist every time you sell one. Instead, create one listing but with multiple quantities. It's a lot easier, all around.

Trick #550: **Track Your Business with Store Information Reports**

clact

stores.ebay.com/Once-Upon-A-Bid

PowerSeller

Member since 2002, Feedback: Red star

One of the most useful benefits of running an eBay Store is the Store information reports that eBay provides (via email) at the end of each month. These reports will tell you what searches led people to your Store, what items are showing interest, what times of day your Store gets visited, and so on. Seller **clact** waxes enthusiastically about the value of these reports:

When you look at it, you will be able to better post and buy for your eBay selling. For example, one inexpensive item seemed to grab a lot of attention and there were all kinds of searches for it that were driving people to my Store. [Based on that information], I have purchased similar items and have had 100% sell-through.

Smarter sellers are more successful sellers. Use the Store information reports to fine-tune your inventory and increase your sales!

Trick #551: **Don't Forget Your Regular Auctions!**

> **lady_gotrocks!**
>
> stores.ebay.com/The-Carat-Farm
>
> PowerSeller
>
> Member since 2002, Feedback: Red star

Once you open an eBay Store, it's tempting to focus all your attention on the new Storefront. That would be a bad idea. You still need to run and manage your regular eBay auctions, because it's those auctions that drive traffic to your eBay Store. Don't run any auctions, and your Store traffic will dry up! So don't neglect your regular auctions—they're just as important as they've always been.

Promoting Your eBay Store

How do potential buyers find out about your eBay Store? Let's see how the eBay Masters drive business to their Storefronts.

Trick #552: **Cross-Promote in Your Regular Auction Listings**

> **slfcollectibles2**
>
> stores.ebay.com/A-Collectible-Diecast-N-More-Store
>
> stores.ebay.com/A-Gift-for-Her
>
> PowerSeller
>
> Member since 2001, Feedback: Red star

The most common way to draw customers into your eBay Store is via your regular eBay auction listings. That's because eBay will include cross-selling links to your Store listings at the bottom of your auction listings, as shown in Figure 18.3, and on your winning bidders' Bid Confirmation and Checkout Confirmation pages.

FIGURE 18.3

Cross-promoting items from your eBay Store at the bottom of your auction listing pages.

To choose which Store items you want to cross-sell, go to your eBay Store page and click the Seller, Manage Store link. When the Manage Your Store page appears, click the Default Cross-Promotions link. When the next page appears, as shown in Figure 18.4, select which merchandise you want to promote when customers view items in specific product categories. You can then click the Cross-Promotion Preference link to configure *when* eBay displays your cross-promotions, or the Cross-Promotion Display link to configure *how* eBay displays your cross-promotions.

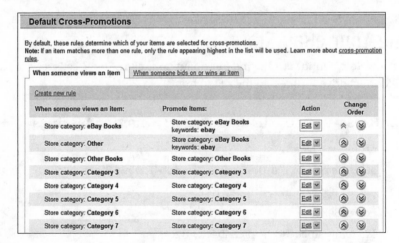

FIGURE 18.4

Configuring your cross-promotion settings.

Trick #553: **Join the eBay Keywords Program**

> **slfcollectibles**
>
> stores.ebay.com/A-Collectible-Diecast-N-More-Store
>
> stores.ebay.com/A-Gift-for-Her
>
> PowerSeller
>
> Member since 2001, Feedback: Red star

Another way to promote your eBay Store is via the eBay Keywords program. This program, administered by adMarketplace, lets you purchase specific eBay keywords; when buyers enter these keywords into eBay's search function, they're greeted with a banner ad that drives them to your eBay Store. This is exactly how keyword advertising works on Google and the big search engine sites, with the exception that eBay Keywords is limited to eBay searches only. You bid on how much you want to pay (per click) for a specific keyword; minimum bid is 10 cents per click. Find out more at the eBay Keywords website (ebay.admarketplace.net), shown in Figure 18.5.

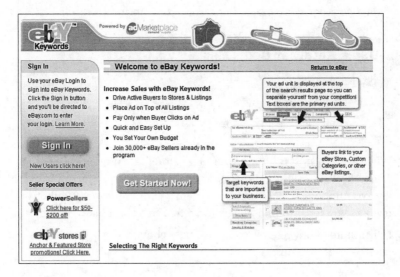

FIGURE 18.5

Advertise your eBay Store via the eBay Keywords program.

Trick #554: **Spread the URL Around**

> **rsgold13**
> Member since 1999, Feedback: Turquoise star

Since you get a dedicated URL with your eBay Store, use it to promote your Store offerings. Here are some ideas from **rsgold13** on how to spread your Store address around:

- Put your Store URL in every email you send to auction buyers, friends, family, and anyone else you communicate with
- Add your Store URL to your customer invoices and packing slips
- Post your Store URL on other online forums, message boards, and news-groups
- Include your Store URL on all your business cards and hardcopy correspondence

As **rsgold13** says:

In other words advertise, advertise, advertise. Any way you can.

Trick #555: **Use a Referrer Code, Get a FVF Credit**

> **ghsproducts**
> stores.ebay.com/ghsproducts
> Member since 1998, Feedback: Purple star

Wherever you post a link to your eBay Store, add a referrer code to the link. When someone clicks on the link + referrer code and ends up buying something, eBay will give you up to a 75% credit on the item's final value fee. In other words, eBay rewards you for bringing buyers to your Store from outside eBay.

Learn more about referrer codes at pages.ebay.com/help/specialtysites/referral-credit-faq.html.

Trick #556: **Redirect to Your Store from a Separate Domain Name**

> **ghsproducts**
> stores.ebay.com/ghsproducts
> Member since 1998, Feedback: Purple star

Of course, the long eBay Store URL can be a tad unwieldy and difficult to remember (and type!). If you want a more professional URL, you'll have to register a separate domain name (from a third-party registrar, as explained in Trick #571) and redirect that domain to your eBay Store URL. Set up the redirect so that anyone entering your domain name is automatically forwarded to your eBay Store. (If you do this, make sure the redirect address includes the eBay referrer code we discussed in the previous trick.) Entering a traditional domain address is certainly a lot easier than entering the complicated eBay Store URL.

Here's what eBay Store seller **ghsproducts** says about it:

> *I did this with my Store and have been very happy with it. It is much easier to have my signature be my name and a simple web address, than use the whole long eBay Store URL plus my referrer code. I think it looks better, too.*

Here's how to see this trick in action. Just type www.ghsproducts.com into your web browser, and you'll be directed to **ghsproducts**' Items for Sale page. Neat!

How to Make Money as a Trading Assistant

Selling your own merchandise is only one way to make money on eBay. One of the newest types of eBay businesses exists to sell other people's merchandise. These so-called eBay resellers or drop-off stores—officially known as eBay Trading Assistants—help non-eBay users sell their goods on eBay, by taking them on consignment and then reselling the items via normal eBay auction. The Trading Assistant handles the entire auction process, from taking photos and listing the item to handling payment and shipping the merchandise. The client doesn't have to bother with the whole eBay process, and the Trading Assistant earns a percentage of the final selling price. Everybody wins!

Setting Up Your Consignment Business

Going into business as a Trading Assistant (TA) can be as simple or as complex as you want to make it. The simple approach is no more difficult than arranging to sell an item for a friend. The more sophisticated approach involves creating a bona fide business, complete with drop-off storefront. Somewhere in-between is the option of joining eBay's official Trading Assistant program. Let's see what the eBay Masters recommend.

Trick #557: Operate Your Trading Assistant Business as Part of Your Normal eBay Activity

judithsconsignments

stores.ebay.com/JUDITHS-CONSIGNMENTS

Member since 2001, Feedback: Turquoise star

When you're setting up your TA business, you can choose to simply add your consignment auctions to your normal eBay auction activity, or to create a separate eBay account to handle your consignment auctions. There are pros and cons for each approach. The advantage of keeping a single account for both TA and non-TA auctions is that it's simpler; you don't have to create a new account or manage two accounts' activities. And, as **judithsconsignments** points out, it's simply a continuation of your present eBay activity:

First, I wouldn't separate my merchandise business from my consignment business. I would keep the identity/brand you have worked so hard to establish, and keep control of that name, identity, and way of doing business.

Trick #558: Keep Your Trading Assistant Activity and Your Regular eBay Activities Separate

trapperjohn2000

stores.ebay.com/Molehill-Group-Store

Member since 1998, Feedback: Purple star

On the other hand, establishing a new eBay account for your consignment auctions helps to keep that business separate from your existing eBay business. That way you can easily track the revenues and profits from your TA sales. (It also keeps any negative feedback you might get from one business from reflecting poorly on your other business.)

Trick #559: **Join eBay's Trading Assistant Program**

trapperjohn2000

stores.ebay.com/Molehill-Group-Store

Member since 1998, Feedback: Purple star

Once you've done all your homework, it's time to join eBay's Trading Assistant program. It doesn't cost you anything, and you get the benefit of being listing in eBay's Trading Assistants Directory—which is how some users find TAs to sell their items for them.

There aren't any really stringent requirements for joining the TA program. Here's all that eBay requires:

- You've sold at least 10 items in the past 90 days
- You have a feedback rating of at least 100
- You have a positive feedback percentage of at least 97%
- Your eBay account is in good standing

That's it. To join up, just go to the Trading Assistants Hub (pages.ebay.com/tahub/), shown in Figure 19.1, and click the Become a Trading Assistant link. Follow the onscreen instructions and you'll be ready to go.

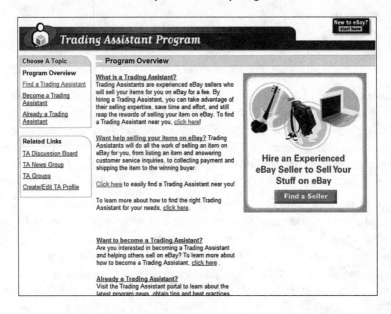

FIGURE 19.1

eBay's Trading Assistant Hub.

Trick #560: **Open a Retail Storefront**

trapperjohn2000
stores.ebay.com/Molehill-Group-Store
Member since 1998, Feedback: Purple star

Many Trading Assistants work out of their home. This requires them to either (1) pick up items from their clients' homes or (2) have their clients drop off items at their home. A more professional (and more expensive) option is to rent your own retail storefront for merchandise drop-offs. Chances are you'll attract more clients with a drop-off location, not only because your signage will provide added visibility, but also because many people will be more comfortable leaving their merchandise at a retail location than at some stranger's house or apartment. You also get lots of added space to store the consigned merchandise and conduct your business.

The downside, of course, is you have additional costs—the rent and utilities for your store, plus signage and the like. And you'll pay those bills every month, no matter how much auction business you do. But you don't need a *big* store, and it doesn't have to be in a high-rent location. Play it smart and you could come out ahead.

Trick #561: **Buy Into a Franchise Operation**

shopofvalues
PowerSeller
Member since 2001, Feedback: Turquoise star

Another option is to not go it alone, but rather buy into one of the several auction drop-off franchise operations that are starting to bloom. With a franchise you get lots of help getting started; the main office will help you choose a retail site and negotiate your lease, plan your store layout, and market your operation. You'll also get training and ongoing operations support, plus the value of the franchise name. For all this, you pay a large upfront fee and a percentage of your monthly revenues.

Is a franchise a good idea? Maybe, especially if you're new to this or want a helping hand getting your business off the ground. Maybe not, if you're an experienced seller, know how to run a business, and prefer to work for yourself (and keep all the profits yourself). If you're interested in doing the franchise thing, definitely check out several different franchises, visit a few of the stores, and talk to some of the franchises. Know what you're getting into before you sign that first check.

Some of the more popular eBay drop-off franchises include

- iSold It (www.i-soldit.com), shown in Figure 19.2
- NuMarkets (www.numarkets.com)
- The Online Outpost (www.theonlineoutpost.com)
- OrbitDrop (www.orbitdrop.com)
- QuikDrop (www.quikdropfranchise.com)

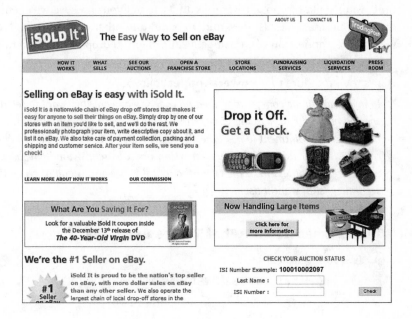

FIGURE 19.2

iSold It, one of the many eBay franchise opportunities available.

Managing Your Consignment Business

Okay, you're convinced—this consignment selling thing is a good deal. But how do you get started? Where do you find clients, how much do you charge, what kind of items do you accept, how do you manage all those auctions… Lots and lots of questions, all answered here by the eBay TA Masters.

Trick #562: **Qualify Your Clients Over the Phone**

powershopper

Member since 1998, Feedback: Purple star

If you have a drop-off location, you can sit behind your counter and wait for your clients to come to you. (Although a little promotion probably wouldn't hurt, which we'll cover later in this chapter.) If you're running your business out of your home, however, how do you handle the merchandise trade-off?

The first step, as recommended by many experienced TAs, is to make your initial contact with clients over the phone. One phone call is all it takes to get a feel for the client, find out what they want to sell, and determine whether it's worth your time. You should also take this opportunity to tell your prospective client about you and your business, discuss fees, and work out any other details. Then, if all goes well on the phone, you can arrange for the client to drop off the merchandise, or for you to pick it up.

Here's the procedure that **powershopper** follows:

> *In my initial phone conversation I get an overview of what they want to sell and ask specific questions to help me identify the items to see if they are promising. I will then set an appointment to meet the client, pick up the items, sign agreements, and collect a $5 per item fee. Later, after doing my research, if the item looks like it might bring a lot less than the client thought it was worth, I call or email them to see if they [still] want it listed.*

Trick #563: **Take Possession of What You're Reselling**

judithsconsignments

stores.ebay.com/JUDITHS-CONSIGNMENTS

Member since 2001, Feedback: Turquoise star

When you agree to sell an item for a client, take that item into your possession. You're in the consignment business, after all. You have to have the item in your possession in order to sell it, and to take photos for the auction listing. Plus, if you don't have it, you don't know for sure that it exists—or that your client hasn't disposed of it elsewhere. Remember, it's your name on the eBay auction; you'll be held responsible if the item isn't actually available for sale.

Trick #564: **Handling In-Home Visits**

internestauctions

stores.ebay.com/Internest-Auctions

Member since 1999, Feedback: Red star

While you can try to get all your clients to drop their items off at your home, chances are you'll have to do some merchandise pickup yourself. Going to a stranger's home can get a little dicey, so you'll want to play it as safe as you can. While one eBay Master recommended taking a 6'2", 300-pound partner, you might not always have that option. Here's what **internestauctions** recommends:

> We go to their houses to pick up their products they want to sell. It has worked out just fine so far, no problems. Just use common sense. If the client is an elderly retired person from a part of town I know as respectable, then I am willing to go. I take a phone and leave a time I will check in or be back. If I'm meeting a younger client, I might agree to a meeting in a restaurant or have them come to me. Be safe, there are weirdoes out there.

Trick #565: **Create a Consignment Contract**

going1nceamc

stores.ebay.com/GOing1nceAMC

www.going1nce.com

PowerSeller

Member since 1999, Feedback: Red star

Always, always, *always* have your client sign a consignment contract for the goods they want you to sell. Your contract can be as long or as short as you want, but it should include the following points:

- The names and contact information for both parties
- The purpose of the contract—that you will offer the items owned by the client for sale on eBay
- The services you, the reseller, will offer (detailing the auction sevices—writing the listing, taking photos, listing the item, managing the auction, handling payment, packing the item, shipping the item, and so on)
- Who takes possession of the merchandise during the transaction (typically you)
- How and when the client can cancel the transaction
- What happens if the item doesn't sell (relist, merchandise returned to the client, whatever)
- Who handles customer complaints and returns
- Fees

For an example of a TA contract, see the sample contract prepared by **going1nceamc** at www.going1nce.com/contract.html. Remember, if you ever have a dispute with a client, referring to the signed contract cements your position—both practically and legally.

Trick #566: **Have a Lawyer Review Your Contract**

New Trick

> **newstartoday**
> PowerSeller
> Member since 2000, Feedback: Red star

Speaking of legalities, simply drawing up a contract isn't quite enough. You need to have that contract reviewed by a lawyer—ideally, one who specializes in small-business matters. TA **newstartoday** tells you why:

> *This will not only help you close any loopholes you did not even know about, but makes you look more professional when dealing with the clients. Yes, it will cost a few dollars now, but in the end it will not only potentially save you money but also give you peace of mind that you are protected.*

Trick #567: **Manage Your Clients' Expectations**

> **judithsconsignments**
> stores.ebay.com/JUDITHS-CONSIGNMENTS
> Member since 2001, Feedback: Turquoise star

As an experienced eBay seller, you're probably going to have a better feel for what an item will sell for than your client will. It's not unusual for a client to have unrealistic expectations of an item's worth. It's your job to manage these expectations so that the client isn't overly disappointed when harsh reality intrudes.

I like the way TA **judithsconsignments** handles it:

> *Unrealistic expectations are common. I address it every time I speak to a prospective client. One technique I use is to let them know upfront that eBay prices are usually lower than what people unfamiliar with eBay may expect. If I know something about the category or item, I tell them a possible sales range; otherwise I tell them that I will let them know what like or similar items have sold for recently, and then I do the research. I do this before I decide whether or not I can (or want to) sell the item. It's always better to tell every prospect (friend or not) what you know than to lead them on to a disappointment.*

Of course, making sure your client signs your contract and gets a copy of it before the auction starts also helps.

Trick #568: **Document All Items for Sale—and Their Condition**

newstartoday
PowerSeller
Member since 2000, Feedback: Red star

It's important that both you and your client are on the same page about what you're selling and what condition those items are in. This way you won't be blamed if an item isn't in pristine condition; you'll have noted it beforehand.

You should have a form made up in advance for this inventory listing, and fill it out at the same time you present the client with your contract. Note the items for sale and their condition, and then make sure the client signs the list and gets a copy of it.

Trick #569: **Valuate the Items Up Front**

rufusduff
PowerSeller
Member since 1999, Feedback: Turquoise star

Along the same lines, you need to establish an accurate valuation of the items you take on consignment. That means doing some homework before you agree to list an item. Use the research tools we discussed in Chapter 6, "How to Find Merchandise to Sell," to get a solid idea of the current selling prices on similar items. After making this valuation, share it with your client—or maybe just show them the lower end of the sales range, so the client won't be disappointed if the item doesn't sell for the absolute maximum value. If the client doesn't like your numbers, they don't have to list with you.

Seller **rufusduff** puts it quite bluntly:

> Clients either have no clue as to the value of their Aunt Tillie's rocking chair (good), or a grossly inflated sense of its potential price (bad). Never let a client get by with telling you what their widget is "worth." In fact, neither of you has a clue just yet— although the market will so inform you. Then you, they, or both can decide whether to proceed.

Trick #570: **Charge a Reasonable Commission—Plus Fees**

newstartoday

PowerSeller

Member since 2000, Feedback: Red star

Now we come to the hard part—determining the fees you charge your clients. My experience is that TA fees are all over the place, from a low of 10% all the way up to 50% of the final selling price. The average fee seems to be in the 25% range. That is, you take 25% of what the item sells for; if you sell an item for $100, your fee is $25.

Of course, you have all the various eBay and PayPal fees to consider. Most TAs charge these fees to the client. So on our $100 item, you'll take out your $25, plus eBay's listing and final value fees, plus the PayPal fees (if any). Some TAs charge an additional fee for packing materials, but as this should be factored into the shipping/handling fee you charge the buyer, this may be double-dipping.

Trick #571: **Charge a Minimum Fee, Even If the Item Doesn't Sell**

newstartoday

PowerSeller

Member since 2000, Feedback: Red star

Some TAs charge a flat $5 or $10 fee for every transaction, typically paid upfront, in addition to your selling commission. This way you get paid something whether the item sells or not. It also helps to weed out the riff-raff if they have to pay a little upfront to get in the game.

Trick #572: **Charge Extra for High-Priced Items**

going1nceamc

stores.ebay.com/GOing1nceAMC

www.going1nce.com

PowerSeller

Member since 1999, Feedback: Red star

If you're asked to sell a particularly pricey item, you might want to charge an additional flat fee (in addition to your normal commission) to handle your additional research and attention. Here's what **going1nceamc** does:

On pricier stuff I've sold for a client, I've charged a $30 set-up fee, which covers extra research on our part and featuring it with its own web page on our site.

Trick #573: **It's Okay to Turn Away Questionable Goods**

judithsconsignments

stores.ebay.com/JUDITHS-CONSIGNMENTS

Member since 2001, Feedback: Turquoise star

Of course, you don't have to accept everything that your clients want you to sell. It's more than okay to turn away goods that you think you'll have a hard time selling, or that you think are worth considerably less than the client does.

You also don't have to accept items that you think were obtained illegally, or that are bogus, counterfeit, or otherwise misrepresented. Here's what **judithsconsignments** advises:

You are under no obligation to sell everything a client asks you to sell. It's better to say no to prospective business you're not comfortable about than to be sorry later; there's more than enough stuff to go around, and there always will be. I often pass on items I don't want to sell for any number of reasons. A simple, "I don't think I can sell that" or "I'll pass on this one" is all it takes.

Trick #574: **Avoid Low-Priced Items**

bluegrassvisions

Member since 2001, Feedback: Red star

Other TAs justifiably try to avoid reselling low-priced items, for the simple reason that there's not enough money in it to make it worth their while. eBay recommends using a TA for items over $50 only; other TAs set their lower limit at $100. Whatever limit you set, you don't want to waste your time selling a lot of $5 and $10 items, when you could be reselling items for $100 or more. Here's what **bluegrassvisions** recommends:

I try to refrain from the sales of items under $100 most times. I simply explain [to the client] that by the time my fees and the eBay fees are extracted, they don't make a great deal.

Trick #575: **Create a Web Page for Your Clients to Track Their Auctions**

> **plane_cents**
>
> www.plane-cents.com
>
> PowerSeller
>
> Member since 2001, Feedback: Turquoise star

Here's a neat little trick that provides some real value to your consignment clients. Once the auction gets started they're probably curious about how the bids are doing, so make it easy for them by creating a link to all the auctions you're running for them.

To do this, you'll need to create a page for this client on your website. You'll then create a button or link on this page that links to an eBay search for that client's auctions. As explained by eBay Master **plane_cents**, here's how to do it.

1. Start by putting some sort of unique identifier in the auction listing description. For example, you can include the text Client ID: XYZ12345, where XYZ are the client's initials, and 12345 is the client's ZIP code.

2. After you've launched the auction, go to eBay's Search page and click the More Search Options link.

3. When the next page appears, enter the client ID number you assigned into the Keyword box and check the Search Title and Description option. Then move to the From Specific Sellers section of the page, select Include, and enter your user ID into the box.

4. Click the Search button to run the search. When the results page appears, copy the URL of this page.

5. Now open the web page for your client in your HTML editor. Create a button or text link, and paste the URL for the search results page into the link properties.

6. Post this page to your website.

When your client goes to this page and clicks his button or link, he's shown the list of his current auctions on the eBay site. To view this trick in action, check out the live links at www.plane-cents.com/auctions.htm.

Trick #576: **Track Your Business with the Plane Cents Spreadsheet**

> **plane_cents**
>
> www.plane-cents.com
>
> PowerSeller
>
> Member since 2001, Feedback: Turquoise star

eBay Master **plane_cents** (AKA Tom Allen) also offers the eBay Trading Assistant Tracker, a predesigned Excel spreadsheet you can use to track all your consignment auctions. It's a fairly elaborate way to track your TA business, as Tom explains:

> *You have the ability to track 50 different clients running 500 auctions each. That's 25,000 total. You can set up a fee structure with 7 different commission rates, depending on the selling price. You can charge the client the fees or pay them yourself. You can automatically calculate eBay final value and PayPal fees. Refunds are automatically calculated into your profits. You can track miscellaneous client fees, TA fees, listing fees, sales tax, estimated shipping, actual shipping, credits, notes, and much more.*

It's a pretty neat setup, as you can see in Figure 19.3. As many TAs attest, it makes running your consignment business that much easier. You can purchase the eBay Trading Assistant Tracker for $24.95 at www.plane-cents.com/trading_assistant_tracker.htm.

Client Name:	Mr. Bigbucks	Plane Cents Trading Assistant Tracker©		
Client ID #:	MBB12345			
Address:	123 Maple Ln.			
City, State, Zip:	Anytown, FL. 12345			
Home Phone:	555-555-5555			
Cell Phone:	555-555-5555	Bid Totals	Shipping	Insurance
E-mail:	bigbucks@cash.com	$4,038.50	$124.80	$3.10

Date	Item ID #	Item Description	eBay listing #	Starting Bid	Ending Bid	Estimated Shipping	Estimated Insurance
1/1/04	MBB12345 A	Sterling Silver Plates	123456789	$9.99	$200.00	$12.00	$0.30
1/2/04	MBB12345 B	Crystal Goblets	123456789	$24.99	$335.00	$22.00	$0.30
1/3/04	MBB12345 C	Indian Head Gold Coin	123456789	$49.99	$340.00	$7.00	$0.30
1/4/04	MBB12345 D	Rolex Watch	123456789	$99.99	$1,200.00	$7.00	$1.20
1/5/04	MBB12345 E	Kodak Digital Camera	123456789	$24.99	$125.00	$8.00	$0.00
1/6/04	MBB12345 F	White China Plates	123456789	$99.99	$445.00	$20.00	$0.30
1/7/04	MBB12345 G	Green China Plates	123456789	$99.99	$0.00	$0.00	$0.00
1/8/04	MBB12345 H	Marvel Comics Spiderman Book	123456789	$9.99	$56.00	$5.45	$0.00
1/9/04	MBB12345 I	Ladies Red Shoes Size 6	123456789	$9.99	$14.50	$5.45	$0.00
1/10/04	MBB12345 J	Mens Christmas Tie	123456789	$0.99	$7.00	$5.45	$0.00
1/11/04	MBB12345 K	Silk Scarf	123456789	$9.99	$78.00	$5.45	$0.00
1/12/04	MBB12345 L	Blue Couch	123456789	$49.99	$90.00	$0.00	$0.00
1/13/04	MBB12345 M	Dog Crate	123456789	$4.99	$15.00	$0.00	$0.00
1/14/04	MBB12345 N	Ruby Ring Size 6	123456789	$99.99	$189.00	$8.00	$0.00
1/15/04	MBB12345 O	Gold Chain	123456789	$24.99	$133.00	$8.00	$0.00
1/16/04	MBB12345 P	Micky Mantle Autographed Baseball	123456789	$99.99	$811.00	$11.00	$0.70

FIGURE 19.3

Just a small part of the many-faceted eBay Trading Assistant Tracker.

Promoting Your Business—and Finding New Clients

The most important part of any eBay consignment business is finding clients! After all, to resell items on eBay you have to have the items to resell. How do you attract clients to your new business? Read on to learn how the eBay Masters do it.

Trick #577: **Add a TA Button or Logo to All Your Auctions**

> **trapperjohn2000**
>
> stores.ebay.com/Molehill-Group-Store
>
> Member since 1998, Feedback: Purple star

You should definitely advertise your TA services in all your eBay auctions—and in any other web pages you might have, as well. You can do this by adding eBay's Trading Assistant button, as shown in Figure 19.4, and link it back to your Trading Assistant page. To do this, you'll need to know your Trading Assistant number (found at the end of the URL for your TA listing), and a little bit of HTML. Here's the code:

<a href="http://contact.ebay.com/ws1/
➡eBayISAPI.dll?ShowMemberToMemberDetails&member=*XXXXX*">
<img src="http://pics.ebaystatic.com/aw/pics/trading_assistant2_88x33.gif"
➡vspace="5" border="0" height="33" width="88"></a>

Replace *xxxxx* with your Trading Assistant number, and the button will be added. Anyone clicking on the button will be taken directly to your eBay TA page.

FIGURE 19.4

Add a button that links to your Trading Assistant page.

Alternately, you can display eBay's Trading Assistant logo (shown in Figure 19.5) instead of a TA button. The URL for the logo is pics.ebay.com/aw/pics/
tradingAssistant/taLogo_100x100.gif; you can insert it on your page (without a link to your TA page) with the following code:

<img src="http://pics.ebay.com/aw/pics/tradingAssistant/taLogo_100x100.gif">

FIGURE 19.5

Add the Trading Assistant logo to all your auction pages.

Trick #578: Include a Link to Your TA Page in All Emails and Correspondence

trapperjohn2000

stores.ebay.com/Molehill-Group-Store

Member since 1998, Feedback: Purple star

This is a simple one. In all your correspondence—online and hardcopy—you should include a mention of your TA business. In emails, this mention should include a link to your TA profile page.

You can use the code in Trick #577 to insert a graphic button or logo, or if you'd rather insert a text link, here's the code:

```
<a href="http://contact.ebay.com/ws1/eBayISAPI.dll?
➥ShowMemberToMemberDetails&member=XXXXX">I'm a Trading Assistant,
let me sell your stuff on eBay for you</a>
```

Obviously, add your own text between the on and off codes, and replace *xxxxx* with your Trading Assistant number.

Trick #579: Build Up Your References

714auctions

Member since 2001, Feedback: Turquoise star

When attracting new clients, it's important to have a good reputation. The best way to do this is to build up a list of references—satisfied customers who would be glad to recommend your services to others.

Your reference list should, of course, be composed of clients who were satisfied with your services. These past clients should also be willing to be contacted by prospective clients, if necessary. So your reference list should contain the client's name, contact info, and a highlight of the services they used or items you sold. As TA **714auctions** notes:

> Many people overlook the value that a few solid references can provide to a prospective client. Once you have established your TA business, you should contact clients about serving as a reference account. Offering reference accounts to client prospects, whether proactively or in response to a request, is one of the best ways to help convince prospects that you provide quality service. A good working number is a list of 3–5 references they can contact to confirm the quality of your TA services.

Trick #580: **Promote, Promote, Promote**

trapperjohn2000

stores.ebay.com/Molehill-Group-Store

Member since 1998, Feedback: Purple star

Promoting your TA business takes some degree of creativity. Here are some fun ideas you might be able to use:

- **Drum up publicity.** This whole eBay thing is still relatively new to the general populace, and the concept of selling other people's stuff on consignment might even be newsworthy. (Especially in a small community, or on a slow news day.) You need to get the word out about what you're doing to all your local media outlets—your local newspaper, radio stations, television stations, you name it. Work up some sample stories, send out a few press releases, make a few phone calls, whatever it takes to get noticed.

- **Pass out business cards—and lots of them**. You're a businessperson, and businesspeople have business cards—and hand them out at the drop of a hat. Make sure everybody you meet gets handed a card, and don't be shy about leaving them behind in restaurants, laundry mats, or other establishments that have local bulletin boards. And make sure every client gets a few to hand out to their friends!

- **Hand out flyers.** If business cards are good, flyers are better. I'm not talking anything fancy here; the kind of simple one-page photocopy you make at Kinko's will do. Print 'em up and hand 'em out, everywhere you can think of—coffeehouses, gyms, school bulletin boards, whatever. Better yet, hire a local kid to stuff them in mailboxes and hang them on doorknobs. The more people see your message, the better!

- **Contact garage sale sellers.** The whole goal in advertising your TA business is to find more stuff to resell. To that end, you might want to think about contacting people who are running garage sales. In particular, you want someone who *ran* a garage sale. You want to contact the seller a few days after their garage sale has ended and offer to help them get rid of the stuff that didn't sell. All that leftover merchandise is great fodder for consignment sales on eBay!

- **Contact local businesses.** One really good source of consignment business is other businesses and small manufacturers in your area. Almost every local manufacturer or business has liquidated, refurbished, or returned product they need to somehow dispose of—and your TA business can help them with this problem. You'd be surprised how eager these companies are to get rid of old merchandise just taking up space in their warehouses.

In other words, be aggressive and be creative—do anything you can to attract people with stuff you can sell!

In this Chapter

- **Advantages of the PowerSeller Program**

- **Tricks of the eBay PowerSellers**

How to Become an eBay PowerSeller

One of the signs of a successful eBay seller is the achievement of PowerSeller status. PowerSellers, quite simply, are those sellers who generate the most revenue, month in and month out. They're the best of the best, in terms of eBay sales. When you become an eBay PowerSeller, you know you've made it.

You can't choose to be a PowerSeller. Instead, eBay chooses you, based on your past sales performance—at least $1,000 average sales per month. If you're chosen, you don't have to pay for the privilege; membership in the PowerSellers program is free.

You can learn more about the PowerSeller program at pages.ebay.com/services/buyandsell/welcome.html. Now let's see what advice eBay's PowerSellers have for you.

Advantages of the PowerSeller Program

eBay rewards its PowerSellers with a variety of perks, but the chief benefit is that to attain PowerSeller status, you've achieved a very high volume of sales. And it's those sales that makes becoming a PowerSeller worthwhile.

That said, you can't ignore the perks—as these eBay PowerSellers will attest.

Trick #581: **PowerSellers Display the PowerSeller Logo in Their Auctions**

New Trick

> **disneyshopper**
>
> stores.ebay.com/Your-Own-Disneyshopper
>
> PowerSeller
>
> Member since 2000, Feedback: Red star

One of the perks of the PowerSellers program is that you get to display the PowerSeller logo (shown in Figure 20.1) in all your auctions. As many buyers—particularly newbies—feel more comfortable buying from experienced sellers, that's a big advantage to becoming a PowerSeller.

FIGURE 20.1

PowerSellers get to display the PowerSeller logo in their auctions.

Trick #582: **PowerSellers Take Advantage of the Perks**

> **lady_gotrocks!**
>
> stores.ebay.com/The-Carat-Farm
>
> PowerSeller
>
> Member since 2002, Feedback: Red star

One of the chief benefits of eBay's PowerSellers program is that PowerSellers qualify for priority customer support. Bronze-level PowerSellers get dedicated 24/7 email support, while higher levels get honest-to-goodness live telephone support—something regular sellers can only dream of. Of course, this support is worthwhile only if you actually need the help, but still it's comforting to know it's available.

In addition, qualified PowerSellers can take advantage of eBay's Healthcare Solutions, a medical insurance plan provided by Marsh Advantage America. There's also a rebate when you use eBay's Direct Pay billing, and access to the PowerSellers Entrepreneur Resource Center, a one-stop site for third-party business services. Not bad for free.

Trick #583: **PowerSellers Join PESA**

 New Trick

> **aacsautographs**
>
> stores.ebay.com/AACS-Autographs
>
> PowerSeller
>
> Member since 1997, Feedback: Yellow shooting star

One of the perks of being a PowerSeller doesn't come from eBay. When you're a PowerSeller, you can join the Professional eBay Sellers Alliance (PESA), which is a nonprofit trade organization for eBay's highest-volume sellers. PESA provides a forum for PowerSellers to network with each other and exchange business ideas. It also provides a collective voice for its members to eBay and to the marketplace at large.

Learn more—and sign up—at PESA's website (www.gopesa.org), shown in Figure 20.2.

FIGURE 20.2

The website of the Professional eBay Sellers Alliance.

Tricks of the eBay PowerSellers

Okay, you're sold. Becoming a PowerSeller is a big deal and something you want to try for. But how do you attain—and maintain—PowerSeller status? There's no one answer to that question, unfortunately, but eBay's PowerSellers do have a fair amount of advise to impart on the subject. So read on to learn how eBay's PowerSellers do that voodoo that they do so well.

Trick #584: **PowerSellers Treat Their eBay Business Like a Real Business**

New Trick

> **bobbibopstuff**
>
> stores.ebay.com/BobbiBopStuff
>
> www.bobbibopstuff.com
>
> PowerSeller
>
> Member since 1998, Feedback: Red star

PowerSellers don't treat their eBay sales lightly. It's not a hobby, it's a business, and they view it as such. That means learning the necessary business skills, doing the necessary business reporting, and running your entire operation like a well-honed business. As PowerSeller **bobbibopstuff** puts it:

> *Be serious about making it a success. If you don't have any business background, check out some books from the library and learn about marketing, customer service, keeping books, and organization. Answer all your mail. Be professional.*

Trick #585: **PowerSellers Do Their Research**

New Trick

> **abc-books**
>
> stores.ebay.com/ABC-Books-by-Ann
>
> www.abcbooksbyann.com
>
> PowerSeller
>
> Member since 1999, Feedback: Red star

You don't get to be a PowerSeller through hard work alone. (Although hard work is necessary, of course.) No, PowerSellers get to that level by being smart about what they buy and sell. That means knowing which categories are hot, what items will sell with the biggest markup, and where they can purchase their merchandise at the lowest possible costs. PowerSellers are also smart about how and when to list their items to maximize sales—the best days of the week to list, the right categories in which to list, and the best starting price to attract the most possible bidders.

Getting smart about all these issues comes with experience, of course, but also requires not a little research. It's the rare PowerSeller that doesn't devote considerable time to researching products and product categories, via a variety of methods—eBay's What's Hot report, eBay's own sales and Stores reports, Ándale Research, Sellathon, and the like. We discussed many of these research tools in Chapter 6, "How to Find Merchandise to Sell," so I won't repeat all that information here. Suffice to say that if you want to attain PowerSeller status, you have to do the same research that PowerSellers do. The good news is that most of these tools are available to any level of seller; the bad news is, you have to spend the time and effort to make these tools pay off.

Trick #586: **PowerSellers Make Their Profit When They Purchase Their Merchandise**

New Trick

berties_house_of_horrors

stores.ebay.com/Berties-Emporium

PowerSeller

Member since 1999, Feedback: Red star

Most PowerSellers know that the real secret to eBay success is that you make your money when you buy, not when you sell. The key is to purchase your merchandise for as low a price as possible. The market will determine the selling price; you have to find merchandise at a low enough cost to make a profit at the market price. The better you are at buying, the more profitable your sales will be. As **berties_house_of_horrors** relates:

> On eBay, name-brand clothing can sell for 25% of MSRP. I make my profit when I buy it at half of this.

When the selling price is determined by the marketplace, the more you pay for your goods, the less money you make. This is why finding the right suppliers and developing strong negotiation skills are so important.

Trick #587: **PowerSellers Turn Their Inventory Fast—to Maximize Their Cash Flow**

New Trick

aacsautographs

stores.ebay.com/AACS-Autographs

PowerSeller

Member since 1997, Feedback: Yellow shooting star

Concurrent with the previous point, you not only have to obtain your inventory cheaply, you also have to move it quickly. You don't make any money on inventory that's sitting in your warehouse or garage. You need to sell what you buy as quickly as possible in order to maximize your cash flow. Some of the largest PowerSellers try to completely turn their inventory within a month of purchase—or even less, as **aacsautographs** notes:

> *If you want to be successful on eBay, it's essential to turn your inventory over fast. That might mean taking a loss on some items, but you need to keep that cash flow. We rarely have more than a week's worth of inventory on hand at any given moment. That keeps us on our toes, but stale inventory and cash-flow blockages are the arch-enemies of a successful eBay business.*

He goes on to provide the following example:

> *I can buy an item for $5 and sell it on eBay for $10 within a week. Or I can sell the same item on another website for $15, but it may take a month to move it. It's better to move it for $10 in a week, because I can then use that $10 and within a week, make $10 more. Therefore, by turning it over quickly and reinvesting it, I can make $15 in two weeks as opposed to making $15 on the initial item (via another sales site) but having it take a month. That's why it's vital on eBay to move inventory fast!*

Trick #588: **PowerSellers Never Run Out of Inventory**

New Trick

> **bobbibopstuff**
>
> stores.ebay.com/BobbiBopStuff
>
> www.bobbibopstuff.com
>
> PowerSeller
>
> Member since 1998, Feedback: Red star

You need to turn your inventory fast—but not so fast that you run out of what you're selling. PowerSellers know that they need a constant flow of merchandise for their eBay auctions, and to keep their eBay Stores well stocked. It's a delicate balancing act to have just enough of your best-selling items in stock, without having too much stock of your slow sellers. As **bobbibopstuff** relates:

> *One of my most embarrassing moments is to tell a buyer that I didn't really have the item in stock that they bought. Don't run out of best-sellers. Don't load up on slow sellers.*

That says it all. You can't sell what you don't have—and if you can't sell, you don't make any money.

Trick #589: **PowerSellers Develop Expertise in a Given Category**

aacsautographs
stores.ebay.com/AACS-Autographs
PowerSeller
Member since 1997, Feedback: Yellow shooting star

It's one thing to sell a variety of odds and ends from around the house. It's quite another to sell the volume of merchandise that's necessary to achieve and maintain PowerSeller status. When we're talking about running 100 or more auctions a week, you have to know more than a little bit about what you're selling. You need to develop expertise about the products you sell—which argues for specializing in a specific category, and becoming expert at it. Here's what PowerSeller **aacsautographs** recommends:

It's extremely difficult, in my experience, to successfully sell something in which you have little or no expertise. Without a deep knowledge of your product, it's hard to know the ins and outs, the trends, the demand, the hot seasons, and so on. It's also difficult to put the blood, sweat, and tears into something that you aren't passionate about. That's why the best businesses often start out as hobbies.

Trick #590: **PowerSellers Sell Higher-Priced Merchandise**

rosachs
stores.ebay.com/My-Discount-Shoe-Store
home.midsouth.rr.com/rosachs/RKS/
PowerSeller
Member since 1997, Feedback: Red star

To become a PowerSeller, you must average $1,000 in sales each month. There are two ways to hit that $1,000 number. You can sell a hundred $10 items, or you can sell ten $100 items. Which approach do you think is easiest?

While there are plenty of PowerSellers selling $10 items, there are many more who hit their targets by selling higher-priced merchandise. When you sell higher-priced items, you not only have to sell fewer items, you also don't have to ramp up all your support services—packing, shipping, inventory, warehouse space, extra staff, and so on. Sell more expensive items, and you might be able to do it all yourself, and in a fraction of the time.

Here's how PowerSeller **rosachs** puts it:

> The best way to become a PowerSeller? Sell expensive stuff. Honest. I sell shoes at an average price of $28 per pair. It takes 108 sales to maintain my Silver PowerSeller status. Someone selling diamond rings at an average price of $300 each needs to sell only 10 rings to do the same. So the "secret" is either mind-boggling volume, or price. It's like every mother has told her daughter at some time or another—"It's just as easy to marry a rich man as a poor one!" It's just as easy to sell $300 rings as it is to sell $30 shoes. Maybe easier.

He goes on to note that Trading Assistants have it a bit easier. Since they don't have to buy what they sell, their upfront costs are lower. And TAs can weed out the low-priced items and specialize in selling higher-priced consignment goods, too. (To learn more about eBay's Trading Assistant program, turn to Chapter 19, "How to Make Money as a Trading Assistant.")

Trick #591: **PowerSellers Are Organized**

New Trick

> **bobbibopstuff**
>
> stores.ebay.com/BobbiBopStuff
>
> www.bobbibopstuff.com
>
> PowerSeller
>
> Member since 1998, Feedback: Red star

When you're running hundreds of auctions a week, you *have* to be organized. Not only is that volume of sales a full-time endeavor, it's one that requires the utmost in organization and efficiency. Trying to keep track of all those listings, digital photos, packages, and shipping invoices is a Herculean task; you can't do it if you're not organized.

PowerSeller **bobbibopstuff** says that it's all about establishing procedures:

> Work out standard processes for your business. Make an auction template and keep it up to date. Decide how many listings you'll do each day, and do them. Make email templates or get an auction management program to help you stay on top of your communications and shipping. Be organized in your approach to getting things done. Make checklists, use tickler files, and pre-print your forms. Have your shipping materials on hand and organized.

Trick #592: **PowerSellers Go Above and Beyond the Call of Duty**

New Trick

> **abc-books**
>
> stores.ebay.com/ABC-Books-by-Ann
>
> www.abcbooksbyann.com
>
> PowerSeller
>
> Member since 1999, Feedback: Red star

Users buy from PowerSellers because they expect superior service. Sometimes this translates into *unusual* service, as in going that extra step beyond the services you quote in your auction listings. After all, offering better customer service than the competition is how you got your feedback rating into the four (or five) digits.

The special services you perform can range from little favors to big challenges. PowerSeller **abc-books** relates this example:

> *I probably do more than I should at times. Like today, when I made a special trip to the UPS Store to ship a package, even though that's not an option in my shipping description. But it paid off for me through my feedback. I have had many buyers comment that they felt comfortable buying from me when they saw my feedback rating.*

Trick #593: **PowerSellers Set Themselves Apart from the Competition**

New Trick

> **aacsautographs**
>
> stores.ebay.com/AACS-Autographs
>
> PowerSeller
>
> Member since 1997, Feedback: Yellow shooting star

The most successful businesses have a unique identity and reputation. "Me too" businesses seldom last, especially among the fierce competition of the eBay marketplace.

To that end, you need to do whatever you can to establish your own business identity. Whether that's a niche product, a huge inventory, ultra-fast shipping, outstanding customer service, or whatever, you need to find something to set your business apart and to keep people coming back to your auctions.

Trick #594: **PowerSellers Cultivate Repeat Customers**

lludwig
stores.ebay.com/LLudwig-Books
PowerSeller
Member since 1998, Feedback: Green star

It costs a lot more money to obtain a new customer than it does to sell an additional item to an existing customer. For that reason, PowerSellers work hard to develop a loyal base of customers, and to keep selling to that base.

How to cultivate repeat customers? Here are five tips from PowerSeller **lludwig**:

1. *Suggest to your buyers that they bookmark your auctions.*

2. *Include a link to your auctions in all emails to your buyers.*

3. *Include the link to your auctions—as well as the suggestion to bookmark your auctions—in the "thanks for payment and your item has been mailed" email.*

4. *If you frequently sell certain types of items, ask your buyers if they would like to be included in your "special customer file" and receive a heads-up when you list those types of items. This especially works well if the buyer has bought several similar items from you. During slow selling times, the minutes spent sending a heads-up often results in a sale.*

5. *Offer reduced shipping when buying more than one item, even if auctions end on different days.*

Trick #595: **PowerSellers Become More Efficient Over Time**

aacsautographs
stores.ebay.com/AACS-Autographs
PowerSeller
Member since 1997, Feedback: Yellow shooting star

Business gets tougher each year, not easier. Every year sees a new influx of competitors, a savvier stream of buyers, increased pressure on prices, and increased costs. An eBay business is no different—and, in fact, may be even more problematic, as **aacsautographs** points out:

eBay raises their fees annually, but average selling prices have been dropping each year for several years. This means that the average eBay seller has to sell more year-to-year to make the same amount of money. However, increasing sales means either

(a) working longer hours, (b) hiring more people, or (c) finding ways to do it faster, better, and more efficiently.

For many sellers, (c) is the only viable alternative. The challenge is to find ways to streamline and automate your business so that you don't just maintain sales (albeit with lower costs), but also grow. Remember, no matter how well things are going for you, there's always a better, more efficient, lower-cost way to do it. Never rest on your laurels.

Trick #596: **PowerSellers Supplement Their Auctions with an eBay Store**

clact

stores.ebay.com/Once-Upon-A-Bid

PowerSeller

Member since 2002, Feedback: Red star

We talked all about eBay Stores in Chapter 18, "How to Sell More Products in an eBay Store," but the advice bears repeating here. You can get only so big from auctions alone; to supplement your auction sales, you need the steady stream of income that an eBay Store can generate. Don't believe me? Look at all the PowerSellers who contributed tricks to this chapter. Every single one of them runs an eBay Store. Coincidence? I don't think so.

And it's not all about additional sales. PowerSeller **clact** points out several advantages for PowerSellers in running an eBay Store, including the low cost of listing items, the detailed sales analysis provided by the Store Information reports, and the fact that you get a store name and web address to market. Plus there's the sales, of course.

Can you reach PowerSeller status without running an eBay Store? Maybe. But adding an eBay Store to your normal auctions certainly helps, in more ways than one.

Trick #597: **PowerSellers Spend Money to Make Money**

aacsautographs

stores.ebay.com/AACS-Autographs

PowerSeller

Member since 1997, Feedback: Yellow shooting star

Becoming more efficient often means investing money in a new software program or monthly service, or even hiring additional employees. However, the increased efficiency that comes with these investments is what enables your business to grow. In other words, you have to spend money to make money. As **aacsautographs** puts it:

It's important to remember that the price of something is not necessarily the real cost. For example, if a particular tool "costs" $100 a month but helps you make an additional $1,000 per month, then the real cost is actually $900—in your favor. I see eBay sellers all the time make the mistake of rejecting a good tool because it "costs too much," without considering how much money it will actually make for them.

Trick #598: **PowerSellers Hire More Help When They Need It**

aacsautographs
stores.ebay.com/AACS-Autographs
PowerSeller
Member since 1997, Feedback: Yellow shooting star

There's no getting around it. When your eBay business gets big enough, you won't be able to manage it all by yourself. That means hiring employees, with all the attendant issues that brings. You may not need to hire full-time employees, however, nor may you need to hire employees year-round. Remember, the summer months are the slowest months, and you may be able to handle your sales by yourself during that period of time. Maybe you only need to hire some part-time employees during the busy holiday season. But however you work it, don't stifle your business' growth by refusing to hire the employees you need.

Trick #599: **PowerSellers Network with Other Sellers**

rosachs
stores.ebay.com/My-Discount-Shoe-Store
home.midsouth.rr.com/rosachs/RKS/
PowerSeller
Member since 1997, Feedback: Red star

PowerSellers know that they have to adapt to changing business conditions. One way to keep on top of the latest trends, as well as to get smarter about what you do, is to network. I'm not talking about computer networking, but good old-fashioned human networking. That means keeping in touch with other eBay buyers and sellers, as well as "offline" businesspeople in your field of expertise. Find clubs or special interest groups or eBay discussion forums related to your eBay business, or just to your personal likes, and keep your ear to the ground about what's going on.

Here's what PowerSeller **rosachs** recommends:

> As a seller, it's easy to get very wrapped up in the day-to-day work of selling on eBay. But you've got to know what's going on outside of eBay, what's hot and what's not, who's having sales, what competition is moving in, what direction various retail prices are headed, and so forth. The easiest way to do all that is networking—find people or groups with common interests, and just share.

Trick #600: **PowerSellers Never Stop Learning**

New Trick

> **berties_house_of_horrors**
>
> stores.ebay.com/Berties-Emporium
>
> PowerSeller
>
> Member since 1999, Feedback: Red star

PowerSellers know that they don't know everything, and that there's always something new to learn. Back in Chapter 1, "How to Get Smarter About Buying and Selling on eBay," we discussed many different ways to increase your eBay knowledge and improve your skills. Well, there's one more way to get smarter about eBay that bears discussion—and you're holding it in your hand.

As I hope you already know, books are great learning tools. There are a slew of eBay-related books on the market (I've written a few of them), and they all contain information that will help you improve your eBay sales. PowerSellers know that spending a few minutes in the local bookstore (or browsing an online bookstore) can pay big dividends down the road.

Modesty forbids me from talking about the usefulness of my own books, but I'm not above quoting PowerSeller **berties_house_of_horrors** on the subject:

> Tricks of the eBay *Masters* is the best $24.99 you will ever spend. As a contributor, I knew a few tricks and then some. But when I got my copy I immediately increased my arsenal of tips ten-fold.

And there you have it. Six hundred tricks from the eBay Masters, guaranteed to help you buy smarter and sell more effectively. So get to it—and put all those tricks to use!

Index